GOODSON MUMBA

Mastering Strategic Management

Tools and Techniques for Success

Copyright © 2024 by Goodson Mumba

All rights reserved. No part of this publication may be reproduced, stored or transmitted in any form or by any means, electronic, mechanical, photocopying, recording, scanning, or otherwise without written permission from the publisher. It is illegal to copy this book, post it to a website, or distribute it by any other means without permission.

First edition

ISBN: 9798333731562

This book was professionally typeset on Reedsy. Find out more at reedsy.com

Contents

Preface		v
Acknowledgement		vii
Dedication		viii
Disclaimer		ix
1	Chapter 1: Introduction to Strategic Management	1
2	Chapter 2: Vision, Mission, and Objectives	19
3	Chapter 3: Environmental Scanning and Industry Analysis	41
4	Chapter 4: Internal Analysis: Assessing Strengths and...	75
5	Chapter 5: Strategic Formulation: Developing Strategies	97
6	Chapter 6: Strategic Implementation: Turning Plans into...	121
7	Chapter 7: Strategic Control and Evaluation	144
8	Chapter 8: Corporate Governance and Ethics in Strategic...	171
9	Chapter 9: Innovation and Strategic Management	198
10	Chapter 10: Digital Transformation and Strategic Management	223
11	Chapter 11: Strategic Management in Small and Medium...	247
12	Chapter 12: Globalization and International Strategies	271

13 Chapter 13: Strategic Leadership	288
14 Chapter 14: Crisis Management and Strategic Resilience	305
15 Chapter 15: Future Trends in Strategic Management	323
About the Author	339

Preface

In the dynamic and ever-evolving world of business, strategic management stands as the cornerstone of organizational success. It is the art and science of formulating, implementing, and evaluating cross-functional decisions that enable an organization to achieve its long-term objectives. As the global business environment becomes increasingly complex and competitive, the need for effective strategic management has never been more critical.

"Mastering Strategic Management: Tools and Techniques for Success" is a comprehensive guide designed to equip managers, entrepreneurs, students, and business leaders with the knowledge and skills necessary to navigate the intricate landscape of strategic management. This book delves deep into the core principles of strategic management, providing practical insights and actionable techniques that can be applied across various industries and organizational contexts.

Each chapter of this book is meticulously crafted to address critical aspects of strategic management, from understanding its fundamental concepts to exploring advanced tools and techniques. We begin with an introduction to the scope and importance of strategic management, tracing its historical development and defining key terminologies. Subsequent chapters delve into vision, mission, and objectives; environmental scanning and industry analysis; internal analysis;

strategy formulation; and implementation.

Throughout the book, we emphasize the importance of adaptability and strategic agility in navigating the uncertainties of the modern business landscape. We explore emerging trends and technologies, the future of work, and the pivotal role of innovation and digital transformation in shaping strategic decisions. Real-world case studies and examples are integrated to provide practical context and demonstrate the application of theoretical concepts.

This book is more than just a guide; it is a strategic companion that will help you unlock new opportunities, overcome challenges, and drive your organization towards sustained success. Whether you are a seasoned strategist or a newcomer to the field, "Mastering Strategic Management" offers valuable insights that will enhance your strategic thinking and decision-making capabilities.

We extend our deepest gratitude to the many professionals, scholars, and practitioners whose contributions and insights have enriched the content of this book. We also thank our readers for their interest and commitment to mastering the art of strategic management.

As you embark on this journey, we hope you find the tools and techniques presented in this book to be both enlightening and empowering. May they serve as a guiding light in your quest for strategic excellence and organizational success.

Sincerely,
Goodson Mumba

Acknowledgement

I would like to eternally and gratefully acknowledge the Almighty God for the infinite intelligence from His universal mind where we draw from all that we come to know and are yet to know. May I also acknowledge and thank everyone that has played a part in my journey of life in terms of spiritual, moral, emotional and material support.

Dedication

I extend my sincerest gratitude to my beloved wife, Edith Mumba, and our children, Angelina, Lubuto, Letticia, Lulumbi, and Butusho, for their unwavering support and understanding throughout the conception, writing, and eventual publication of this book, despite the sacrifices and challenges they endured.

Disclaimer

This book is a work of fiction. Names, characters, businesses, places, events, and incidents are either the products of the author's imagination or used in a fictitious manner. Any resemblance to actual persons, living or dead, or actual events is purely coincidental.

1

Chapter 1: Introduction to Strategic Management

Definition and Scope of Strategic Management

A New Beginning in Lusaka

The year was 2005, and the air in Lusaka buzzed with the energy of a city on the brink of a technological revolution. In a small office nestled in the heart of the capital, Angela Mwewa and Michael Hamalala sat across from each other, the glow of their computer screens illuminating their determined faces.

"Angela, we have the vision. We have the mission," Michael began, his voice steady but infused with excitement. "But to truly succeed, we need a solid strategy. We need strategic management."

Angela nodded thoughtfully. "Strategic management. It's about more than just planning for the next few months. It's about looking ahead, understanding where we want to go, and figuring out the best way to get there."

Michael leaned forward, his eyes shining with conviction. "Exactly. Strategic management involves defining our goals, analyzing our environment, and making decisions that will steer us towards our vision. It's comprehensive, covering everything from resource allocation to leadership."

Angela pulled up a document on her laptop, the draft of their strategic plan. "So, we start by defining strategic management for our team. We need everyone to understand its importance and scope."

She began typing, her fingers flying over the keyboard as she spoke. "Strategic management is the process by which an organization defines its strategy, sets long-term goals, and determines the actions needed to achieve those goals. It involves analyzing both our internal capabilities and the external environment, making informed decisions, and ensuring that we effectively implement our plans."

Michael listened, nodding in agreement. "It's about aligning all aspects of our business with our overall goals. From marketing and finance to human resources and operations, every part of GlobalTech Solutions must work together harmoniously."

Angela paused, looking up from her screen. "And the scope of strategic management? It's wide-reaching. It involves setting our vision and mission, conducting internal and external analyses, formulating strategies, implementing those strategies, and continuously evaluating our performance."

Michael added, "It also means being adaptable. The tech industry is dynamic, and we need to be ready to pivot our strategies in response to market changes or new opportunities."

The room fell silent for a moment as they both contemplated the enormity of the task ahead. But there was no trace of doubt in their eyes—only determination.

Angela broke the silence. "Let's make sure our team understands that strategic management is not just a top-down approach. It requires input and collaboration from everyone. Each member of GlobalTech Solutions has a role to play in our strategic journey."

Michael smiled, a spark of inspiration in his eyes. "We'll hold a workshop. Explain the concepts, the importance, and how each person contributes. We'll use real-world examples and case studies to bring these ideas to life."

Angela nodded. "Agreed. This is the foundation. If we get this right, we set the stage for everything else."

As the day drew to a close, Angela and Michael finalized their plan to introduce strategic management to their team. They knew this was just the beginning of their journey, but with a clear understanding of strategic management's definition and scope, they were ready to lead GlobalTech Solutions towards a future of innovation and success.

And so, in the heart of Lusaka, GlobalTech Solutions took its first step on a path that would not only transform their company but also contribute to the technological advancement of an entire continent.

Importance of Strategic Management in Modern Business

Charting the Course

The following morning, the warm Zambian sun streamed through the windows of the conference room at GlobalTech Solutions. Angela and Michael stood at the front, facing their assembled team. A palpable sense of anticipation filled the air.

Angela began, her voice clear and confident. "Good morning, everyone. Today, we're going to delve into the heart of what will drive our company forward: strategic management. But first, let's talk about why this is so crucial for our success."

She clicked a button on her laptop, projecting a slide onto the screen behind her. It read, "The Importance of Strategic Management in Modern Business."

Michael stepped forward, picking up where Angela left off. "In today's fast-paced business environment, having a clear strategy is not just beneficial—it's essential. The tech industry, in particular, is characterized by rapid changes and intense competition. Without a strategic plan, we risk being reactive instead of proactive, responding to changes rather than leading them."

He paused, letting the weight of his words sink in. "Strategic management helps us define our direction, align our resources, and ensure that every decision we make moves us closer to our long-term goals."

Angela nodded, adding, "It's like navigating a ship. Without a clear course, we could drift aimlessly or end up crashing into obstacles. Strategic management provides us with the tools to chart our course, anticipate challenges, and make informed decisions to stay on track."

One of the team members, a young developer named David,

raised his hand. "How does this impact our day-to-day work?"

Angela smiled. "Great question, David. Strategic management isn't just about high-level planning. It affects every aspect of our operations. When we have a clear strategy, it means that every project you work on, every line of code you write, contributes to a larger goal. Your work becomes part of a cohesive effort, rather than isolated tasks."

Michael added, "It also means better resource allocation. We can identify which projects are most critical to our success and ensure they have the support they need. This reduces wasted effort and increases efficiency."

Angela advanced to the next slide, which displayed a chart showing the correlation between strategic management and business performance. "Studies have shown that companies with strong strategic management practices outperform their peers. They are better at adapting to market changes, capitalizing on new opportunities, and achieving sustainable growth."

Michael pointed to the chart. "This is where we want to be. By embracing strategic management, we position ourselves to not only survive but thrive in the competitive tech landscape. It helps us build a resilient organization that's capable of weathering challenges and seizing opportunities."

The room was silent, the team absorbing the significance of what they were learning. Angela sensed their engagement and pressed on. "Strategic management also fosters a culture of continuous improvement. By regularly evaluating our performance and making necessary adjustments, we ensure that we're always moving forward, always improving."

She looked around the room, making eye contact with each person. "This is why strategic management is so important.

It's the backbone of our success. It's what will allow us to fulfill our mission and realize our vision."

Michael concluded, "We're all in this together. Each one of us has a role to play in executing our strategy. With a shared understanding of its importance, we can work more effectively as a team and achieve great things."

As the session wrapped up, the team members left the room with a renewed sense of purpose and direction. Angela and Michael exchanged a satisfied glance, knowing that they had laid a strong foundation for the journey ahead. GlobalTech Solutions was not just another tech company in Lusaka; it was a company with a clear strategy, poised to make a significant impact in the tech industry across Africa.

And with strategic management guiding their way, Angela and Michael were confident that they could lead their team to new heights of innovation and success.

Historical Development of Strategic Management

Lessons from the Past

Later that afternoon, Angela and Michael reconvened with their team in the conference room, the hum of the city outside a backdrop to the session. The team had already absorbed the definition and importance of strategic management; now it was time to delve into its historical development.

Michael started the session, his tone reflective. "To understand where we're going, it's crucial to understand where we've been. Strategic management, as a formal discipline, has a fascinating history that has shaped its current practices."

He clicked to the next slide, showing a timeline. "The

roots of strategic management can be traced back to military strategy, particularly the work of ancient strategists like Sun Tzu and his seminal work, 'The Art of War.' His principles of strategy, such as knowing the terrain and understanding the enemy, have parallels in business today."

Angela picked up from there. "In the early 20th century, strategic management began to take shape in the business world. Companies like General Motors under Alfred Sloan introduced formalized strategic planning processes. Sloan's approach emphasized decentralized operations, allowing each division to operate semi-independently while aligning with the company's overall strategy."

David, the young developer, leaned forward, intrigued. "So, strategic management evolved from military tactics to business practices?"

Michael nodded. "Exactly. The mid-20th century saw further advancements. The rise of strategic planning frameworks, such as the SWOT analysis developed by Albert Humphrey, provided tools for businesses to systematically analyze their strengths, weaknesses, opportunities, and threats."

Angela advanced the slide to show the rapid changes in the 1980s and 1990s. "During this period, strategic management became more sophisticated. Michael Porter introduced his Five Forces Framework, which helped businesses understand competitive forces and how they impact profitability. His work emphasized the importance of competitive advantage and positioning within an industry."

A hand shot up from the back. It was Linda, the marketing lead. "How did the technological revolution impact strategic management?"

Michael smiled. "Great question, Linda. The late 20th and

early 21st centuries brought the digital revolution, fundamentally changing how businesses operate. With the advent of the internet, companies had to adapt rapidly. Strategic management evolved to include digital strategies, big data analytics, and real-time decision-making processes."

Angela added, "This era also saw the rise of strategic agility. Companies like Amazon and Google exemplified the ability to pivot quickly in response to market changes. Agility and innovation became critical components of strategic management."

The room buzzed with interest as the team absorbed this journey through time. Michael wrapped up the historical overview. "Understanding the historical development of strategic management helps us appreciate the tools and techniques we have today. It shows us that strategic management is not static; it evolves in response to new challenges and opportunities."

Angela nodded in agreement. "And now, we stand at the forefront of this evolution. Here in Lusaka, at GlobalTech Solutions, we are part of this ongoing story. By learning from the past, we can better navigate the future."

The team seemed energized, seeing their work within a larger historical context. The session concluded with Angela and Michael feeling confident that their team was not only informed but inspired by the rich history of strategic management.

As the sun set over Lusaka, casting a golden hue over the city, GlobalTech Solutions stood ready to write the next chapter in the story of strategic management, blending timeless principles with innovative practices to lead the way in Africa's technological revolution.

CHAPTER 1: INTRODUCTION TO STRATEGIC MANAGEMENT

Key Concepts and Terminologies

Building the Strategic Vocabulary

The following day, the team at GlobalTech Solutions gathered once more in the conference room. Angela and Michael were determined to equip their team with a solid understanding of the key concepts and terminologies of strategic management.

Angela started the session with a warm smile. "Good morning, everyone. Today, we're going to dive into the key concepts and terminologies that form the backbone of strategic management. These terms will become part of our everyday language here at GlobalTech Solutions."

She clicked to the first slide, which displayed the word "Vision."

"Let's start with 'Vision.' Your vision statement describes what you want your company to become in the future. It's a long-term aspiration that guides your strategic planning. For us, it's about being the continental leader in technological innovation."

Michael chimed in, "Next is 'Mission.' This is a concise explanation of why our company exists and what it aims to achieve in the present. Our mission at GlobalTech Solutions is to provide cutting-edge technology solutions that empower businesses across Africa."

Angela moved to the next term, "Goals." "Goals are specific, measurable, and time-bound milestones that help us achieve our vision and mission. They provide direction and help us prioritize our efforts."

David raised his hand. "So, goals are like the steps we take to reach our vision and fulfill our mission?"

"Exactly," Angela replied. "And closely related to goals are 'Objectives.' While goals are broad and long-term, objectives are narrow and short-term. They are concrete actions that help us achieve our goals."

Michael advanced the slide to "Strategy." "Strategy is our plan of action designed to achieve our long-term goals and objectives. It outlines how we will compete in the market and what we will do to achieve our vision. It's our roadmap to success."

He then clicked to the next term, "Tactics." "Tactics are the specific actions or steps we take to implement our strategy. While strategies are broad and long-term, tactics are short-term and focused on specific initiatives."

Linda, the marketing lead, interjected, "So, tactics are the day-to-day activities that help us execute our strategy?"

"Precisely," Michael confirmed. "And speaking of executing strategy, let's talk about 'Implementation.' Implementation is the process of putting our strategic plans into action. It involves allocating resources, managing teams, and executing tasks to achieve our objectives."

Angela moved to the final concept, "Evaluation." "Evaluation is the ongoing process of monitoring and assessing our progress towards achieving our goals and objectives. It helps us identify what's working, what isn't, and where we need to make adjustments."

She paused, looking around the room. "These concepts—vision, mission, goals, objectives, strategy, tactics, implementation, and evaluation—are fundamental to strategic management. Understanding and using them correctly will enable us to communicate more effectively and work more cohesively as a team."

Michael added, "It's important that we all speak the same language when it comes to strategy. These terms will help us stay aligned and focused on our shared goals."

Angela then distributed a handout summarizing the key concepts and terminologies. "Keep this with you as a reference. Over time, these terms will become second nature to us, guiding our discussions and decisions."

David glanced at the handout and smiled. "This makes everything so much clearer. It's like we've been given a map to navigate our strategic journey."

Angela nodded. "Exactly, David. With these key concepts and terminologies in hand, we're better equipped to navigate the challenges and opportunities ahead."

The session concluded with a renewed sense of clarity and purpose. The team at GlobalTech Solutions now had a shared vocabulary, a common framework to guide their strategic efforts. As they left the conference room, they were more unified and better prepared to turn their vision into reality.

In the vibrant heart of Lusaka, GlobalTech Solutions continued to build a strong foundation, confident that their understanding of strategic management's key concepts and terminologies would lead them to new heights of innovation and success.

The Strategic Management Process

Crafting the Roadmap

The sun cast a golden glow over Lusaka as the team at GlobalTech Solutions gathered once more in the conference room. The atmosphere was charged with enthusiasm and curiosity, as today, Angela and Michael were set to walk them through the strategic management process.

Angela began, her voice brimming with excitement. "Good morning, everyone. Today, we're going to explore the strategic management process—the step-by-step roadmap that will guide us on our journey to success."

She clicked to the first slide, which displayed a flowchart outlining the process. "The strategic management process consists of five key steps: Goal Setting, Analysis, Strategy Formulation, Strategy Implementation, and Evaluation and Control."

Michael stepped forward to elaborate. "Let's start with the first step: Goal Setting. This is where we define our vision and mission, establish long-term goals, and identify the values that will guide our actions. For us, it's about articulating what we want to achieve and why we exist as a company."

Angela added, "Goal setting provides a clear direction for the entire organization. It ensures that everyone understands our purpose and what we're working towards. Once our goals are set, we move to the next step: Analysis."

She clicked to the next slide, which highlighted internal and external analysis. "In this step, we conduct a thorough analysis of our internal capabilities and the external environment. Tools like SWOT analysis and PESTEL analysis help us identify our strengths, weaknesses, opportunities, and threats. This understanding is crucial for making informed strategic decisions."

Michael nodded, picking up the thread. "With the insights gained from our analysis, we move to Strategy Formulation. Here, we develop strategies that leverage our strengths and opportunities while addressing our weaknesses and threats.

This is where we decide how we will compete in the market and achieve our goals."

The room was silent as the team absorbed the importance of each step. Angela advanced to the next slide, showing a detailed plan. "Next is Strategy Implementation. This is where we put our plans into action. It involves allocating resources, developing detailed action plans, and ensuring that everyone understands their roles and responsibilities."

Michael added, "Implementation is critical because even the best strategies can fail if they are not executed properly. This step requires effective communication, strong leadership, and a commitment to follow-through."

Angela moved to the final step in the process. "The last step is Evaluation and Control. This is an ongoing process where we monitor our progress, measure our performance against our goals, and make necessary adjustments. Regular evaluation helps us stay on track and respond to any changes in the environment."

David, the young developer, raised his hand. "So, it's a continuous cycle?"

"Exactly," Michael replied. "Strategic management is a dynamic process. We continuously loop through these steps, refining our strategies and improving our performance. This iterative approach ensures that we remain agile and responsive to both opportunities and challenges."

Linda, the marketing lead, leaned forward, a thoughtful look on her face. "How do we ensure that everyone is aligned throughout this process?"

Angela smiled. "Great question, Linda. Alignment comes from clear communication and involvement. By engaging everyone in the goal-setting process, sharing our analyses, and involving team members in strategy formulation and implementation, we create a sense of ownership and commitment."

Michael added, "Regular meetings, transparent reporting, and a culture of feedback are also essential. This keeps everyone informed and aligned, ensuring that we move forward as a cohesive unit."

As the session concluded, Angela and Michael could see the confidence growing in their team. The strategic management process was no longer an abstract concept; it was a practical, actionable roadmap they could follow.

The team left the conference room with a clear understanding of the steps involved in the strategic management process. They felt equipped and ready to contribute to the strategic journey of GlobalTech Solutions.

In the heart of Lusaka, as the sun set and the city transitioned into a vibrant evening, GlobalTech Solutions was not just prepared for the future—they were strategically poised to shape it. The process was their roadmap, and with it, they were ready to navigate the challenges and opportunities that lay ahead, steering towards a future of innovation and success.

Benefits and Challenges of Strategic Management

Navigating the Pros and Cons

The day had turned into a warm afternoon as the team at GlobalTech Solutions gathered for the final session on strategic management. The room was filled with a mix of anticipation and curiosity, eager to understand the full spectrum of strategic management—its benefits and challenges.

CHAPTER 1: INTRODUCTION TO STRATEGIC MANAGEMENT

Angela started the session, her tone both encouraging and candid. "Good afternoon, everyone. Today, we'll discuss the benefits and challenges of strategic management. This knowledge will help us appreciate the value of what we're embarking on and prepare us for the hurdles we might face."

She clicked to the first slide, which read, "Benefits of Strategic Management."

Michael stepped forward. "Let's start with the benefits. Strategic management provides a clear direction and a sense of purpose. It aligns our efforts with our long-term goals, ensuring that every action we take contributes to our overarching vision."

Angela added, "Another benefit is improved resource allocation. With a strategic plan, we can allocate our resources more efficiently, focusing on high-impact projects and avoiding waste. This maximizes our productivity and effectiveness."

Linda, the marketing lead, nodded thoughtfully. "That makes sense. Knowing our priorities can help us make better decisions."

Michael smiled. "Exactly, Linda. Strategic management also enhances organizational alignment. When everyone understands our strategy and their role in it, we work more cohesively as a team. This unity boosts morale and fosters a collaborative culture."

Angela continued, "It also helps us anticipate and navigate changes in the market. By regularly analyzing our environment and evaluating our strategies, we stay agile and adaptable. This proactive approach gives us a competitive edge."

David raised his hand. "What about innovation? Does strategic management encourage it?"

"Great question, David," Angela replied. "Yes, it does. A well-defined strategy can create a framework that encourages innovation. By setting clear goals and providing the necessary resources, we can foster a culture where creative ideas are generated and implemented effectively."

The team seemed buoyed by the benefits, but Michael knew it was important to also address the challenges. He clicked to the next slide, "Challenges of Strategic Management."

"While there are many benefits, strategic management also comes with challenges," he began. "One major challenge is the complexity of the process. Developing and implementing a strategic plan requires significant time and effort. It involves detailed analysis, careful planning, and continuous monitoring."

Angela added, "Another challenge is resistance to change. People are naturally resistant to change, especially if it disrupts their routine. Implementing a new strategy often requires a shift in mindset and behavior, which can be difficult."

Linda spoke up, "How can we overcome resistance?"

Michael responded, "Communication and involvement are key. By involving team members in the strategic planning process and clearly communicating the reasons behind the changes, we can build understanding and buy-in. Training and support can also help ease the transition."

Angela continued, "Resource constraints can also pose a challenge. Implementing a strategy often requires significant resources—time, money, and personnel. It's important to ensure we have the necessary resources and manage them effectively."

David asked, "What about external factors? How do we deal

with those?"

Michael nodded. "External factors like economic downturns, competitive actions, and regulatory changes can impact our strategy. To mitigate these risks, we need to remain vigilant and adaptable, continuously monitoring the environment and being prepared to adjust our plans as needed."

Angela concluded, "Lastly, maintaining strategic alignment is an ongoing challenge. As we grow and evolve, it's crucial to regularly review and adjust our strategy to ensure it remains aligned with our vision and goals."

The room fell silent as the team absorbed the dual aspects of strategic management. They understood that while the journey ahead would be filled with benefits, it would also require navigating significant challenges.

Angela wrapped up the session with a note of encouragement. "By being aware of both the benefits and challenges, we can approach strategic management with a balanced perspective. Together, we can leverage its advantages and overcome its obstacles, steering GlobalTech Solutions toward a future of success and innovation."

Michael added, "Remember, we are in this together. With dedication, collaboration, and a clear strategic vision, we can turn challenges into opportunities and achieve great things."

As the team dispersed, there was a shared sense of readiness and resilience. They understood that the road ahead would not be easy, but with strategic management as their guide, they felt prepared to face whatever came their way.

In Lusaka, as the sun set and the city transitioned into a serene evening, GlobalTech Solutions stood united and poised. They were ready to embrace the benefits and tackle the challenges of strategic management, confident in their collective strength and shared vision for the future.

2

Chapter 2: Vision, Mission, and Objectives

Defining Organizational Vision and Mission

Crafting Our Identity

The following week, the atmosphere at GlobalTech Solutions was charged with excitement and anticipation. Angela and Michael had scheduled a special workshop to define the organization's vision and mission. The team gathered in a large conference room, the walls adorned with posters of iconic technological breakthroughs, reminding everyone of the potential impact of their work.

Angela stood at the front of the room, a large whiteboard behind her. "Good morning, everyone. Today, we embark on a crucial journey to define our organizational vision and mission. These statements will serve as our North Star, guiding every decision and action we take."

Michael nodded in agreement. "A clear vision and mission

are essential. They provide direction and inspire us to strive for greatness. Let's start with the vision."

Angela picked up a marker and wrote "Vision" at the top of the whiteboard. "A vision statement is a declaration of what we aspire to become in the future. It should be ambitious and inspiring, painting a picture of our desired long-term impact."

She turned to the team. "Think about where you want to see GlobalTech Solutions in ten, twenty, or even fifty years. What legacy do we want to create?"

Linda, the marketing lead, raised her hand. "I envision us as the leading provider of innovative tech solutions across Africa, driving digital transformation and economic growth."

David, the young developer, chimed in. "I see us pioneering new technologies that not only solve current problems but also anticipate future needs, making technology accessible to everyone."

Angela smiled and began jotting down their ideas. "Great start. Our vision should reflect our ambitions and the positive impact we want to make."

Michael added, "Remember, a vision statement should be concise and easy to remember. It should inspire both our team and our stakeholders."

After a lively discussion and several iterations, the team settled on a vision statement: "To be the leading innovator in technology solutions, driving digital transformation and empowerment across Africa."

Angela wrote it on the whiteboard and underlined it. "This is our vision. It's bold, aspirational, and reflective of our long-term goals."

Michael moved to the next part of the workshop. "Now, let's define our mission. A mission statement explains why we exist as a company and what we aim to achieve in the present. It's more focused and practical than the vision statement."

He wrote "Mission" on the whiteboard below the vision statement. "Our mission should articulate our core purpose and the value we provide to our customers and communities."

Angela turned to the team again. "What do we do every day that sets us apart? How do we create value for our clients and contribute to the broader society?"

Linda spoke up. "We develop cutting-edge tech solutions that help businesses improve efficiency and productivity."

David added, "We also focus on making technology accessible and affordable, ensuring that even small businesses can benefit from our innovations."

Angela captured their inputs on the whiteboard. "Excellent. Our mission should reflect these core activities and the positive impact we aim to make."

After another round of discussions and refinements, the team agreed on a mission statement: "To provide innovative and accessible technology solutions that empower businesses and communities across Africa."

Michael wrote it on the whiteboard and drew a box around it. "This mission statement encapsulates our core purpose and the value we offer. It's specific, actionable, and aligned with our vision."

Angela stepped back, looking at the completed statements. "With our vision and mission clearly defined, we now have a strong foundation for all our strategic planning and decision-making."

The team felt a surge of pride and excitement. They had collaboratively crafted statements that resonated with their collective aspirations and purpose.

Michael concluded the session with a sense of accomplishment. "These statements are not just words on a board. They represent our commitment to our goals and values. They will guide us as we innovate, grow, and make a meaningful impact in the tech industry and beyond."

As the team left the conference room, there was a palpable sense of unity and direction. The vision and mission of GlobalTech Solutions were now clear, guiding their journey towards a future filled with promise and innovation.

In the vibrant heart of Lusaka, GlobalTech Solutions was no longer just a tech company. It was a beacon of innovation and empowerment, ready to transform the digital landscape of Africa with a clear vision and mission lighting their path.

Importance of Clear Vision and Mission Statements

The Power of Clarity

The sun was just beginning to set, casting a warm glow over Lusaka, as the team at GlobalTech Solutions gathered in the conference room once more. The atmosphere was electric with enthusiasm. Having defined their vision and mission, it was now time to understand why these statements were so crucial.

Angela stood at the front of the room, a slide displayed behind her titled, "The Importance of Clear Vision and Mission Statements."

"Good evening, everyone," she began. "Now that we have our vision and mission, it's vital to understand their importance and how they impact our organization."

She clicked to the next slide, which read, "1. Providing

Direction and Purpose."

Michael stepped forward. "A clear vision and mission provide direction and purpose. They act as a compass, guiding our decisions and actions. When faced with tough choices, we can refer back to these statements to ensure we stay aligned with our long-term goals."

He paused, looking around the room. "Imagine navigating without a map or compass. It would be easy to get lost or stray off course. Our vision and mission keep us focused and on track, ensuring that every step we take moves us closer to our desired future."

Angela nodded and clicked to the next point. "2. Unifying the Team."

"A shared vision and mission unify the team," she continued. "They create a sense of belonging and collective purpose. When everyone understands and believes in our vision and mission, we work more cohesively as a team. It fosters collaboration and strengthens our organizational culture."

Linda, the marketing lead, raised her hand. "It's like having a common goal to rally around. It motivates us and keeps us connected."

"Exactly," Angela agreed. "It instills a sense of pride and commitment, making us more resilient and driven."

Michael advanced to the next slide. "3. Enhancing Strategic Planning."

"Clear vision and mission statements are the foundation of effective strategic planning," he explained. "They provide the context for setting goals and developing strategies. Without a clear direction, our planning efforts would lack coherence and focus."

David, the young developer, leaned forward. "So, they help

us make better decisions and prioritize our efforts?"

"Precisely," Michael replied. "They ensure that our strategies are aligned with our long-term aspirations, making our plans more effective and impactful."

Angela moved to the next point. "4. Communicating Our Purpose."

"Our vision and mission also play a critical role in communicating our purpose to external stakeholders," she said. "They convey who we are, what we stand for, and where we're headed. This transparency builds trust and strengthens our relationships with clients, partners, and the community."

Linda nodded thoughtfully. "It's like telling our story to the world."

"Yes," Angela agreed. "It helps us attract and retain customers, investors, and talented employees who resonate with our values and goals."

Michael advanced to the next slide. "5. Driving Performance and Accountability."

"A clear vision and mission drive performance and accountability," he continued. "They set expectations and provide benchmarks for success. When everyone knows what's expected of them and why it matters, they are more likely to be motivated and accountable."

David raised his hand. "It gives us something to measure our progress against, right?"

"Exactly," Michael said. "It creates a culture of performance excellence and continuous improvement."

Angela moved to the final point. "6. Inspiring Innovation and Growth."

"A compelling vision and mission inspire innovation and growth," she said. "They challenge us to think big, push boundaries, and pursue bold ideas. They create an environment where creativity and innovation can thrive."

Linda smiled. "It encourages us to dream and innovate, knowing that our efforts contribute to something bigger."

"Yes," Angela agreed. "It empowers us to take risks, learn from failures, and continuously strive for excellence."

As the session wrapped up, Angela and Michael could see the understanding and appreciation deepening in their team. The importance of their newly defined vision and mission was clear, and the team was ready to leverage them to drive their strategic efforts.

Michael concluded with a note of encouragement. "Our vision and mission are more than just statements. They are powerful tools that provide direction, unify our team, enhance our planning, communicate our purpose, drive performance, and inspire innovation. Together, they form the foundation of our journey towards success."

Angela added, "As we move forward, let's keep our vision and mission at the forefront of everything we do. They are our guiding lights, ensuring that we stay true to our values and achieve our goals."

The team left the conference room with a renewed sense of purpose and determination. They understood that their vision and mission were not just words, but the very essence of their identity and aspirations.

In the heart of Lusaka, as the city transitioned into a calm evening, GlobalTech Solutions stood united and inspired. With their clear vision and mission guiding them, they were ready to embark on their journey of innovation and impact, confident in their collective strength and purpose.

Crafting Effective Mission Statements

The Art of Articulation

A fresh breeze blew through Lusaka as the team at GlobalTech Solutions assembled in their conference room once again. The atmosphere was a blend of focus and anticipation. Angela and Michael were about to guide them through the process of crafting an effective mission statement, ensuring that it truly captured the essence of their organization's purpose and values.

Angela stood at the front, a large flip chart beside her. "Good morning, everyone. Today, we will refine our mission statement, making sure it effectively communicates who we are, what we do, and why we do it."

She wrote the words "Effective Mission Statement" at the top of the flip chart. "An effective mission statement should be clear, concise, and compelling. It should reflect our core values and the unique value we offer to our customers and community."

Michael stepped forward. "Our current mission statement is a great start, but let's delve deeper to ensure it resonates with all our stakeholders. We'll break down the process into key elements."

Angela clicked to the first slide, which read, "1. Clarity and Simplicity."

"First, our mission statement must be clear and simple," she began. "It should be easy to understand and remember, avoiding jargon or complex language."

Linda, the marketing lead, raised her hand. "So, we should aim for straightforward language that everyone can grasp,

CHAPTER 2: VISION, MISSION, AND OBJECTIVES

right?"

"Exactly," Angela replied. "We want everyone, from our employees to our clients, to quickly understand our mission."

Michael advanced to the next slide. "2. Reflecting Core Values."

"Our mission statement should reflect our core values," he explained. "What principles guide our actions and decisions? These values should be evident in our mission."

David, the young developer, chimed in. "Our focus on innovation, accessibility, and community impact should definitely be highlighted."

Angela nodded and wrote "Innovation, Accessibility, Community Impact" on the flip chart. "These are key values we want to emphasize."

Michael clicked to the next point. "3. Defining Our Purpose."

"Next, we need to define our purpose," he continued. "Why do we exist as a company? What difference do we want to make in the world?"

Linda spoke up, "We exist to provide cutting-edge tech solutions that empower businesses and communities."

Angela smiled and wrote it down. "Perfect. This purpose should be at the heart of our mission statement."

Michael moved to the next slide. "4. Identifying Our Unique Value Proposition."

"Our mission statement should also highlight our unique value proposition," he said. "What sets us apart from other tech companies? Why should clients choose us?"

David thought for a moment. "Our commitment to making advanced technology accessible and affordable for even the smallest businesses sets us apart."

Angela jotted this down. "Great point. Our unique value proposition should shine through in our mission."

Michael advanced to the final point. "5. Inspiring and Motivating."

"Finally, our mission statement should be inspiring and motivating," he concluded. "It should ignite passion and commitment, both within our team and among our stakeholders."

Linda nodded enthusiastically. "It should make people feel excited and proud to be part of GlobalTech Solutions."

Angela turned back to the flip chart, where the key elements were now listed. "Let's put it all together. Our mission statement should be clear, reflect our core values, define our purpose, highlight our unique value proposition, and inspire and motivate."

She turned to the team. "Based on these elements, how can we refine our current mission statement?"

The room buzzed with ideas and suggestions. After a collaborative brainstorming session, they arrived at a refined mission statement:

"To innovate and provide accessible, cutting-edge technology solutions that empower businesses and uplift communities across Africa, driven by a commitment to excellence, affordability, and positive impact."

Angela wrote the new mission statement on the flip chart and read it aloud. "This statement captures our essence. It's clear, reflects our values, defines our purpose, highlights our unique value proposition, and is truly inspiring."

Michael looked around the room, seeing the nods of approval and the spark of motivation in everyone's eyes. "This is our mission. It's more than just words—it's a declaration of our identity and aspirations. It will guide us, inspire us, and drive us forward."

Angela added, "Let's carry this mission in everything we do, ensuring it shapes our decisions, actions, and interactions. With this mission, we are ready to make a meaningful impact and achieve great things."

As the session concluded, the team felt a profound sense of clarity and purpose. They had crafted a mission statement that resonated deeply with their collective identity and aspirations.

In Lusaka, as the day progressed and the city buzzed with activity, GlobalTech Solutions stood strong, united by a mission that clearly articulated their purpose and passion. With their new mission statement as their guiding beacon, they were ready to innovate, empower, and transform, driven by a shared vision of a brighter future for Africa.

Setting Strategic Objectives

Turning Vision into Action

The sun was high in the Lusaka sky as the team at GlobalTech Solutions gathered in their bright, open-plan office. Today's session was all about translating their newly minted vision and mission into tangible strategic objectives. Angela and Michael stood ready to guide the team through this crucial step.

Angela began, her voice filled with enthusiasm. "Good afternoon, everyone. Now that we have a clear vision and mission, it's time to set our strategic objectives. These objectives will help us turn our vision into actionable goals."

Michael clicked to the first slide, which read, "Strategic

Objectives: Definition and Importance."

"Strategic objectives are specific, measurable goals that align with our vision and mission," he explained. "They provide a clear roadmap for achieving our long-term aspirations. Without these objectives, our vision remains just a dream."

Linda, the marketing lead, nodded. "So, these objectives are like stepping stones towards our ultimate goals?"

"Exactly," Angela replied. "They break down our vision into manageable, actionable steps. Each objective should be clear, specific, and aligned with our overall strategy."

Michael moved to the next slide, which read, "1. Aligning Objectives with Vision and Mission."

"Our first step is ensuring that our objectives align with our vision and mission," he continued. "For example, if our mission is to provide innovative and accessible tech solutions, our objectives should reflect that by focusing on innovation, accessibility, and customer impact."

David, the young developer, raised his hand. "Can you give us an example?"

Angela nodded. "Sure, David. An example could be: 'Develop and launch three new tech products annually that address the needs of small and medium-sized businesses in Africa.' This objective directly supports our mission."

Michael clicked to the next point. "2. Making Objectives SMART."

"SMART objectives are Specific, Measurable, Achievable, Relevant, and Time-bound," he said. "For our objectives to be effective, they need to meet these criteria."

He wrote "SMART" on the whiteboard and explained each component:

- **Specific**: Clearly defined and focused.
- **Measurable**: Quantifiable, allowing us to track progress.
- **Achievable**: Realistic and attainable.
- **Relevant**: Aligned with our vision and mission.
- **Time-bound**: Set within a specific timeframe.

Linda looked intrigued. "So, if our goal is to expand our market, a SMART objective could be, 'Increase market share by 10% within the next year by targeting new customer segments.'"

"Exactly," Michael affirmed. "It's specific, measurable, achievable, relevant, and time-bound."

Angela moved to the next slide. "3. Prioritizing Objectives."

"With numerous potential objectives, prioritization is key," she said. "We need to focus on the most critical goals that will drive our success. This involves evaluating each objective's impact and feasibility."

David chimed in, "So, we should prioritize objectives that have the highest potential impact on our growth and mission?"

"Precisely," Angela replied. "We must balance ambition with practicality, ensuring our top priorities are both impactful and achievable."

Michael clicked to the next point. "4. Communicating Objectives."

"Once we've set our objectives, clear communication is essential," he said. "Everyone in the organization should understand our strategic objectives and their role in achieving them. This alignment ensures that all efforts are directed towards common goals."

Linda added, "Regular updates and transparency can help

keep everyone on the same page."

"Absolutely," Michael agreed. "Regular communication fosters engagement and accountability."

Angela moved to the final slide. "5. Monitoring and Adjusting Objectives."

"Setting objectives is not a one-time task," she concluded. "We must continuously monitor our progress and adjust our objectives as needed. This agility allows us to respond to changes and stay on course."

Michael nodded. "Regular reviews and performance metrics will help us stay aligned with our strategic goals."

Angela turned to the team. "Now, let's brainstorm some strategic objectives for GlobalTech Solutions. Think about our vision, mission, and the SMART criteria."

The room buzzed with activity as team members shared their ideas. After a productive session, they outlined several strategic objectives, including:

1. **Innovate**: "Launch two groundbreaking tech products annually that cater to underserved markets in Africa."
2. **Expand**: "Increase our presence in five new African countries within the next two years."
3. **Enhance**: "Improve customer satisfaction scores by 15% over the next year through enhanced support and product quality."
4. **Empower**: "Provide technology training to 1,000 small business owners in the next year, fostering digital literacy and business growth."
5. **Sustain**: "Achieve a 20% reduction in operational costs through efficiency improvements and sustainable practices within 18 months."

Michael reviewed the objectives with the team. "These objectives are clear, SMART, and aligned with our vision and mission. They provide a roadmap for our success."

Angela added, "As we work towards these objectives, let's stay focused and committed. Each step we take brings us closer to realizing our vision and fulfilling our mission."

The team felt a renewed sense of direction and purpose. With clear strategic objectives in place, they were ready to take actionable steps towards their ambitious goals.

In the heart of Lusaka, as the day turned into a serene evening, GlobalTech Solutions was not just dreaming of the future—they were actively shaping it. Guided by their vision, mission, and strategic objectives, they were poised to drive innovation, empowerment, and growth across Africa.

Aligning Objectives with Vision and Mission

Ensuring Coherence

As the vibrant city of Lusaka transitioned into the soft glow of the evening, the team at GlobalTech Solutions reconvened in their office. The day's task was critical: ensuring that their strategic objectives were perfectly aligned with their vision and mission.

Angela and Michael were at the helm once again. Angela began, her voice steady and clear. "Good evening, everyone. We've set some great strategic objectives, but our work isn't done. Now, we need to ensure these objectives align seamlessly with our vision and mission. This alignment is crucial for coherence and effectiveness."

Michael stepped forward, clicking to the first slide, which

read, "The Importance of Alignment."

"Alignment between our objectives, vision, and mission ensures that every action we take moves us closer to our long-term goals," he explained. "It creates a unified direction and prevents wasted effort."

David, the young developer, raised his hand. "Can you give an example of what misalignment might look like?"

Angela nodded. "Sure, David. Imagine our mission is to make technology accessible to small businesses, but one of our objectives focuses on developing high-end, expensive tech products that only large corporations can afford. This misalignment would divert our resources and efforts away from our core mission."

Michael moved to the next slide. "Steps to Ensure Alignment."

"Let's walk through the steps to ensure our objectives are aligned with our vision and mission," he said. "First, we'll review our vision and mission statements."

Angela clicked to display the vision and mission on the screen:

Vision: "To be the leading innovator in technology solutions, driving digital transformation and empowerment across Africa."

Mission: "To provide innovative and accessible technology solutions that empower businesses and uplift communities across Africa, driven by a commitment to excellence, affordability, and positive impact."

"With these in mind," Angela continued, "let's examine each strategic objective."

She wrote the first objective on the whiteboard: "Launch two groundbreaking tech products annually that cater to underserved markets in Africa."

"How does this objective align with our vision and mission?" she asked the team.

Linda, the marketing lead, replied, "This directly supports our mission of providing innovative and accessible technology. By focusing on underserved markets, we're also driving empowerment and inclusivity, which ties back to our vision."

Angela smiled. "Exactly. This objective is well-aligned."

Michael wrote the second objective: "Increase our presence in five new African countries within the next two years."

"Thoughts on this one?" he prompted.

David spoke up. "Expanding our presence helps drive digital transformation across Africa, aligning with our vision. It also supports our mission by bringing our solutions to more businesses and communities."

Angela nodded. "Good point. This objective is also well-aligned."

They continued this process for each objective, ensuring that every goal was scrutinized for alignment:

Objective 3: "Improve customer satisfaction scores by 15% over the next year through enhanced support and product quality."

Linda noted, "Enhancing support and product quality ensures our technology solutions are not only innovative but also reliable and accessible, supporting both our mission and vision."

Objective 4: "Provide technology training to 1,000 small business owners in the next year, fostering digital literacy and business growth."

David added, "This objective empowers businesses and uplifts communities, directly supporting our mission. It also drives digital transformation, aligning with our vision."

Objective 5: "Achieve a 20% reduction in operational costs through efficiency improvements and sustainable practices within 18 months."

Michael pointed out, "Reducing costs through efficiency and sustainability ensures we can offer affordable solutions, supporting our mission of accessibility and affordability."

Angela and Michael then facilitated a discussion to refine any objectives that needed better alignment. The team worked collaboratively, ensuring that every strategic goal resonated with their core purpose and aspirations.

Angela concluded the session with a sense of accomplishment. "Alignment ensures that every effort we make is cohesive and directed towards our shared vision and mission. This coherence is what will drive our success."

Michael added, "Let's keep these principles in mind as we move forward. Our vision and mission are our guiding stars, and our objectives are the paths that lead us there."

The team left the office that evening with a clear sense of direction. They had not only set strategic objectives but also ensured these objectives were deeply intertwined with their vision and mission.

In the heart of Lusaka, as the city settled into a tranquil night, GlobalTech Solutions stood unified and focused. With perfectly aligned objectives, they were ready to transform their vision into reality, driving innovation and empowerment across Africa with purpose and passion.

Case Studies of Successful Vision and Mission Statements

Learning from the Best

The conference room at GlobalTech Solutions was buzzing with energy. The team had spent weeks refining their vision and mission statements, aligning their strategic objectives, and now, it was time to draw inspiration from real-world examples. Angela and Michael had prepared a series of case studies to demonstrate how successful companies crafted and implemented their vision and mission statements.

Angela stood at the front of the room, ready to begin. "Good evening, everyone. Today, we'll explore case studies of companies with successful vision and mission statements. These examples will show us how powerful and effective these statements can be when executed well."

Michael clicked to the first slide, which displayed the logo of a well-known global company: Tesla.

Case Study 1: Tesla

Vision: "To create the most compelling car company of the 21st century by driving the world's transition to electric vehicles."

Mission: "To accelerate the world's transition to sustainable energy."

Angela started, "Tesla's vision and mission statements are clear and ambitious. Their vision emphasizes their goal to be a leading car company, while their mission focuses on the broader impact of transitioning to sustainable energy."

Linda, the marketing lead, commented, "Tesla's focus on sustainability and innovation is evident in everything they do, from their products to their marketing."

Michael nodded. "Exactly. Their mission drives their strategic objectives, such as developing affordable electric vehicles and expanding their Supercharger network."

Angela moved to the next slide, which featured another global powerhouse: Google.

Case Study 2: Google

Vision: "To provide access to the world's information in one click."

Mission: "To organize the world's information and make it universally accessible and useful."

David, the young developer, raised his hand. "Google's vision and mission are simple yet powerful. Their focus on accessibility and usefulness is clear."

Michael agreed. "Yes, and this clarity drives their innovation in search algorithms, data storage, and user interface design, ensuring they stay true to their mission."

Angela continued, "Google's strategic objectives, such as enhancing search capabilities and expanding cloud services, directly support their vision and mission."

The next slide displayed the logo of a beloved sports brand: Nike.

Case Study 3: Nike

Vision: "To bring inspiration and innovation to every athlete* in the world." (*If you have a body, you are an athlete.)

Mission: "To do everything possible to expand human potential."

Linda smiled. "Nike's vision and mission are incredibly inclusive and motivating. They emphasize inspiration and innovation for everyone."

Michael added, "Nike's strategic objectives, such as developing cutting-edge athletic gear and promoting fitness initiatives, align perfectly with their mission to expand human potential."

Angela moved to the final slide, which featured a leading social media platform: Facebook (now Meta).

Case Study 4: Meta

Vision: "To give people the power to build community and bring the world closer together."

Mission: "To give people the power to share and make the world more open and connected."

David observed, "Meta's focus on connectivity and community is clear in their vision and mission. Their products, like Facebook and WhatsApp, are designed to connect people."

Michael nodded. "Their strategic objectives, such as enhancing user engagement and expanding global reach, support their mission of making the world more connected."

Angela turned back to the team. "These case studies show us the power of clear, compelling vision and mission statements. They provide direction, inspire innovation, and align strategic objectives with the company's core purpose."

Michael concluded, "As we continue to develop and implement our vision and mission, let's keep these examples in mind. They remind us of the importance of staying true to our values and goals."

Linda added, "Seeing how these successful companies use their vision and mission to drive their actions is really inspiring. It shows us what's possible when we're clear and committed."

Angela wrapped up the session. "Let's take these lessons and apply them to our journey. Our vision and mission are our guiding stars, and with well-aligned objectives, we can achieve great things."

The team left the conference room with a renewed sense of purpose and determination. They had seen firsthand how powerful vision and mission statements could be when effectively executed.

In Lusaka, as the city settled into a calm night, GlobalTech Solutions stood inspired and focused. Armed with the lessons from these case studies, they were ready to drive innovation, empower communities, and transform the technological landscape across Africa. With their vision and mission as their guiding principles, they were poised for success, ready to make a meaningful impact in the world.

3

Chapter 3: Environmental Scanning and Industry Analysis

Navigating the Landscape

The sun peeked through the windows of the GlobalTech Solutions office in Lusaka, casting a warm glow over the team as they gathered for their next strategic session. The topic for today was critical: Environmental Scanning and Industry Analysis. Angela and Michael knew this would be a deep dive into understanding the external factors that could impact their business.

Angela began the session, her tone serious but encouraging. "Good morning, everyone. Today, we'll explore how to scan our environment and analyze our industry. This is crucial for identifying opportunities and threats, and for understanding the competitive landscape."

Michael clicked to the first slide, which displayed the title: "Environmental Scanning."

"Environmental scanning involves systematically examining the external environment to identify factors that could affect our business," he explained. "We look at political, economic, social, technological, environmental, and legal factors—commonly known as PESTEL analysis."

David, the young developer, leaned forward, intrigued. "How do we go about this? It sounds quite comprehensive."

Angela nodded. "It is, David. Let's break it down. We'll start with the political environment."

Political Factors

Michael wrote "Political Factors" on the whiteboard. "These include government policies, trade restrictions, and political stability. For instance, recent government incentives for tech startups in Zambia could be an opportunity for us."

Linda, the marketing lead, chimed in. "But we also need to be aware of potential regulatory changes that could impact our operations."

"Exactly," Angela affirmed. "We need to stay informed and adaptable."

Economic Factors

Next, Angela wrote "Economic Factors" on the board. "These include economic growth, interest rates, and currency exchange rates. Zambia's growing economy and increasing internet penetration present significant opportunities for us."

David added, "But we should also consider inflation rates and economic volatility, which could affect consumer purchasing power."

Social Factors

Michael moved to "Social Factors." "These encompass demographic changes, social attitudes, and cultural trends. The growing youth population in Africa, with their increasing tech-savviness, is a huge market for us."

Linda nodded. "We also need to understand cultural preferences and adapt our products accordingly."

Technological Factors

Angela continued with "Technological Factors." "This includes technological advancements and innovation trends. Staying ahead in technology is vital for us. We need to invest in R&D and keep up with emerging technologies."

David, with a spark of excitement, said, "We should explore AI and machine learning to enhance our product offerings."

Environmental Factors

Next was "Environmental Factors." Michael explained, "These involve ecological and environmental aspects. Sustainable practices are becoming more important. We should aim to minimize our environmental footprint."

Linda agreed. "We could market our products as eco-friendly, which would appeal to environmentally conscious consumers."

Legal Factors

Finally, Angela wrote "Legal Factors." "These include laws and regulations, such as intellectual property rights and consumer protection laws. Compliance is crucial to avoid legal issues."

David added, "We should also consider cybersecurity laws and ensure our products meet all legal requirements."

With the PESTEL analysis covered, Angela moved on to industry analysis.

Industry Analysis

"Next, we'll analyze our industry using Porter's Five Forces model," she said, clicking to the next slide, which showed the five forces: Competitive Rivalry, Threat of New Entrants, Threat of Substitutes, Bargaining Power of Suppliers, and Bargaining Power of Customers.

Competitive Rivalry

Angela started with "Competitive Rivalry." "This looks at the intensity of competition within the industry. In the tech sector, competition is fierce, with many players vying for market share."

Linda noted, "We need to differentiate our products and build strong customer relationships to stand out."

Threat of New Entrants

Michael moved to "Threat of New Entrants." "This examines how easy it is for new competitors to enter the market. Barriers to entry in the tech industry, such as high capital requirements and advanced technical expertise, can be both a challenge and a protection for us."

David commented, "We should leverage our existing infrastructure and expertise to maintain a competitive edge."

Threat of Substitutes

Angela continued with "Threat of Substitutes." "This assesses the likelihood of customers finding alternative solutions. We must innovate continuously to offer superior value that alternatives cannot match."

Linda added, "Understanding customer needs and staying ahead of trends is key to reducing this threat."

Bargaining Power of Suppliers

Michael explained "Bargaining Power of Suppliers." "This force examines how much power suppliers have over us. Diversifying our supplier base can reduce dependency and increase our negotiating power."

David suggested, "We could explore partnerships with local suppliers to enhance reliability and reduce costs."

Bargaining Power of Customers

Finally, Angela discussed "Bargaining Power of Customers." "This looks at how much power our customers have. In the tech industry, informed customers can demand better products and services."

Linda said, "Offering exceptional customer service and unique value propositions can help mitigate this power."

With the PESTEL analysis and Porter's Five Forces model thoroughly explored, Angela wrapped up the session. "Understanding our environment and industry landscape is crucial for making informed strategic decisions. This knowledge will help us navigate challenges and seize opportunities."

Michael concluded, "Let's apply these insights to refine our strategies and ensure our objectives are aligned with external realities."

The team left the room energized and equipped with a deeper understanding of their external environment and industry dynamics. They knew that with this knowledge, they could steer GlobalTech Solutions toward a prosperous future.

As the sun set over Lusaka, casting a golden hue over the city, GlobalTech Solutions stood ready to navigate the complexities of their environment. Armed with the insights from their environmental scanning and industry analysis, they were prepared to adapt, innovate, and thrive in the competitive landscape of the tech industry.

Overview of Environmental Scanning

Scanning the Horizon

As the vibrant city of Lusaka bustled with activity, the GlobalTech Solutions team gathered in their sleek conference room for another crucial meeting. Angela and Michael stood at the front, ready to delve into the first subpoint of their exploration of environmental scanning: an overview of what it entailed and why it was essential.

Angela began with a confident tone, "Good morning, everyone. Today, we'll dive into the basics of environmental scanning. Understanding the external environment is crucial for our strategic planning and long-term success."

Michael clicked to the first slide, which displayed the title: "What is Environmental Scanning?"

"Environmental scanning is the process of systematically surveying and interpreting relevant data to identify external opportunities and threats that could impact our organization," he explained. "It helps us stay informed about changes in the external environment and adapt our strategies accordingly."

David, the young developer, leaned forward, eager to understand more. "So, it's like keeping an eye on everything happening around us that could affect our business?"

"Exactly," Angela replied, smiling. "It's about being proactive rather than reactive. By scanning the environment, we can anticipate changes and prepare for them."

Michael moved to the next slide, which read: "Why Environmental Scanning Matters."

"Let's talk about why this process is so important," he continued. "Firstly, it helps us identify opportunities for growth. By understanding trends and changes in the market, we can capitalize on new opportunities before our competitors do."

Linda, the marketing lead, nodded. "That makes sense. If we can spot a trend early, we can position ourselves to take advantage of it."

Angela added, "Secondly, environmental scanning helps us recognize potential threats. By staying aware of external factors, we can mitigate risks and avoid being blindsided by unexpected challenges."

David asked, "Can you give an example of a threat we might identify through environmental scanning?"

Michael nodded. "Sure, David. For instance, a change in government regulations could affect our operations. If we're aware of these changes in advance, we can adjust our strategies to comply and avoid penalties."

Angela clicked to the next slide: "Components of Environmental Scanning."

"Environmental scanning involves analyzing various external factors," she said. "These include political, economic, social, technological, environmental, and legal factors—often referred to as PESTEL analysis."

She wrote "PESTEL" on the whiteboard and briefly explained each component:

- **Political**: Government policies, political stability, and trade regulations.
- **Economic**: Economic growth, inflation rates, and currency exchange rates.
- **Social**: Demographic trends, social attitudes, and cultural shifts.
- **Technological**: Technological advancements and innovation trends.
- **Environmental**: Ecological factors and sustainability

issues.
- **Legal**: Laws and regulations affecting the industry.

Linda commented, "By examining these factors, we can get a comprehensive view of the external environment."

"Exactly," Michael replied. "And this comprehensive view allows us to make informed decisions and stay ahead of the curve."

Angela moved to the next slide, which read: "Steps in Environmental Scanning."

"Let's go through the steps involved in environmental scanning," she said. "First, we need to identify the key environmental factors that could impact our business."

Michael wrote "Identify Key Factors" on the whiteboard. "This involves brainstorming and discussing potential factors with our team. We need to consider everything from regulatory changes to technological advancements."

David added, "So, it's about gathering as much relevant information as possible?"

"Yes," Angela affirmed. "Next, we need to collect data on these factors."

Michael wrote "Collect Data" on the board. "This can involve researching reports, analyzing market trends, and keeping up with news and developments in our industry."

Linda chimed in, "It's important to use reliable sources and ensure the data is accurate."

"Absolutely," Angela agreed. "After collecting the data, we need to analyze it."

Michael wrote "Analyze Data" on the board. "We look for patterns, trends, and correlations that could impact our business. This analysis helps us make sense of the information we've gathered."

Angela moved to the final step: "Act on Insights."

She wrote "Act on Insights" on the board. "The final step is to use our insights to inform our strategic planning. This involves making decisions and adjustments based on what we've learned from our environmental scan."

Michael concluded, "By following these steps, we can ensure that our strategies are aligned with the external environment, helping us navigate challenges and seize opportunities."

Angela looked around the room, seeing the team's engaged expressions. "Environmental scanning is an ongoing process. The external environment is constantly changing, and we need to stay vigilant and adaptable."

David asked, "How often should we conduct an environmental scan?"

Angela replied, "It's a continuous effort. Regularly monitoring the environment and updating our data is crucial. Depending on the industry dynamics, we might conduct in-depth scans quarterly or biannually, but we should always be on the lookout for significant changes."

Linda added, "This sounds like a lot of work, but it's clear how valuable it is. Staying informed and prepared will give us a competitive edge."

Michael nodded. "Exactly, Linda. It's about building a habit of vigilance and making it part of our organizational culture."

Angela wrapped up the session with a sense of determination. "Let's commit to integrating environmental scanning into our strategic planning process. By doing so, we'll ensure that GlobalTech Solutions remains resilient and forward-thinking in a rapidly changing world."

As the team left the conference room, they felt empowered with a new understanding of the importance of environmental scanning. They were ready to apply this knowledge, keeping a keen eye on the horizon to steer their company toward success.

In the heart of Lusaka, as the city thrived with life, GlobalTech Solutions stood poised and prepared. With their new insights into environmental scanning, they were ready to navigate the complexities of their external environment, turning potential challenges into opportunities for growth and innovation.

PESTEL Analysis - Political, Economic, Social, Technological, Environmental, Legal Factors

Decoding the External Forces

The bustling city of Lusaka hummed with activity as the GlobalTech Solutions team gathered once again in their sunlit conference room. Today, Angela and Michael were ready to guide the team through a comprehensive PESTEL analysis, a key component of their environmental scanning strategy.

Angela began, her voice clear and focused. "Good morning, everyone. We've covered the overview of environmental scanning, and now it's time to dive into PESTEL analysis. This will help us understand the external forces that could impact our business."

Michael clicked to the first slide, which displayed the title: "PESTEL Analysis."

"PESTEL stands for Political, Economic, Social, Technological, Environmental, and Legal factors," he explained. "Each of these elements can significantly influence our strategic decisions. Let's explore each one in detail."

Political Factors

Angela wrote "Political Factors" on the whiteboard. "Political factors include government policies, political stability, tax regulations, and trade restrictions. These can impact how we operate and expand."

Linda, the marketing lead, raised her hand. "Can you give an example of a political factor affecting us?"

"Certainly," Angela replied. "For instance, the Zambian government's recent push for digital transformation includes incentives for tech companies. This presents an opportunity for us to leverage these incentives for growth."

Michael added, "However, political instability or changes in leadership could introduce uncertainties and risks. We need to stay informed about political developments to navigate these challenges effectively."

Economic Factors

Michael wrote "Economic Factors" on the board. "These include economic growth, inflation rates, interest rates, and currency exchange rates. They affect consumer purchasing power and investment opportunities."

David, the young developer, leaned forward. "How does the current economic situation in Zambia impact us?"

Angela responded, "Zambia's growing economy and increasing internet penetration are positive signs. However, we must also consider factors like inflation, which can affect the cost of our operations and the pricing of our products."

Linda noted, "Keeping an eye on these factors helps us adjust our pricing strategies and budget forecasts accordingly."

Social Factors

Angela moved to "Social Factors." "Social factors encompass demographic trends, cultural attitudes, and social norms. Understanding these helps us tailor our products to meet the needs and preferences of our target market."

Michael elaborated, "For example, Zambia has a young and growing population that is becoming increasingly tech-savvy. This trend creates a huge potential market for our products."

Linda added, "But we also need to be sensitive to cultural preferences and ensure our marketing messages resonate with local values and norms."

Technological Factors

Michael wrote "Technological Factors" on the board. "These include technological advancements, innovation trends, and the rate of technological change. Staying ahead in technology is crucial for our competitive edge."

David, with a spark of excitement, said, "We should explore the latest advancements in AI and machine learning to enhance our product offerings."

Angela nodded. "Absolutely. Investing in R&D and keeping up with emerging technologies ensures we remain innovative and relevant."

Environmental Factors

Angela continued with "Environmental Factors." "This includes ecological and environmental aspects, such as climate change, environmental regulations, and sustainability issues."

Michael explained, "Sustainable practices are becoming more important. We should aim to minimize our environmental footprint and consider eco-friendly initiatives."

Linda commented, "Marketing our products as environmentally friendly can also appeal to a growing segment of eco-conscious consumers."

Legal Factors

Finally, Angela wrote "Legal Factors" on the board. "These include laws and regulations, such as intellectual property rights, consumer protection laws, and data privacy regulations. Compliance is crucial to avoid legal issues."

David added, "We should also be aware of cybersecurity laws and ensure our products meet all legal requirements."

Michael summed up, "By understanding these legal factors, we can ensure compliance and build trust with our customers."

Practical Application

Angela moved to the next slide, which displayed a practical application of PESTEL analysis. "Now, let's apply what we've learned to our business. We'll brainstorm key factors for each PESTEL element and discuss their potential impact on GlobalTech Solutions."

She wrote "Political Factors" on the board again and invited the team to contribute.

Linda started, "For political factors, we should monitor government incentives for tech companies and any changes in trade regulations."

David added, "And keep an eye on political stability, as any instability could affect our operations and investment climate."

Angela wrote down their suggestions and moved to "Economic Factors."

Linda said, "We need to track inflation rates and economic growth to adjust our pricing strategies and budget forecasts."

David added, "Also, consider interest rates for any financing or investment opportunities."

The team continued this process for each PESTEL component, contributing insights and discussing their implications:

Social Factors:

- Demographic trends (e.g., growing youth population)
- Cultural attitudes towards technology
- Social media usage patterns

Technological Factors:

- Emerging technologies (e.g., AI, machine learning)
- Technological adoption rates in Zambia
- Investments in R&D

Environmental Factors:

- Climate change impacts
- Sustainability initiatives
- Environmental regulations

Legal Factors:

- Data privacy laws
- Intellectual property rights
- Consumer protection regulations

With the board filled with their collective insights, Angela and Michael concluded the session.

Angela smiled, "Great job, everyone. This comprehensive PESTEL analysis provides a solid foundation for our strategic planning. By understanding these external factors, we can better navigate the complexities of our environment."

Michael added, "Let's use these insights to refine our strategies and ensure we're prepared for any challenges and opportunities that come our way."

As the team left the conference room, they felt empowered with a deeper understanding of the external forces shaping their business environment. They were ready to apply their knowledge and steer GlobalTech Solutions towards success with foresight and strategic clarity.

In the heart of Lusaka, as the city thrived with life, GlobalTech Solutions stood resilient and informed. Armed with their comprehensive PESTEL analysis, they were poised to navigate the external landscape, turning potential challenges into opportunities for innovation and growth.

Porter's Five Forces Model

Navigating Competitive Waters

The early morning sun cast a golden hue over Lusaka, bathing the GlobalTech Solutions office in a warm glow. The team assembled in their modern conference room, ready to tackle the next critical aspect of their strategic planning: Porter's Five Forces Model. Angela and Michael were prepared to guide them through this essential framework for understanding industry competition.

Angela kicked off the session with a confident smile. "Good morning, everyone. Today, we'll delve into Porter's Five Forces Model. This framework will help us understand the competitive dynamics within our industry."

Michael clicked to the first slide, which displayed a diagram of Porter's Five Forces: Competitive Rivalry, Threat of New Entrants, Threat of Substitutes, Bargaining Power of Suppliers, and Bargaining Power of Customers.

"Porter's Five Forces Model is a tool for analyzing the competitive forces that shape every industry," Michael explained. "It helps us identify the strengths and weaknesses in our competitive landscape. Let's break down each force and see how it applies to us."

Competitive Rivalry

Angela wrote "Competitive Rivalry" on the whiteboard. "This force examines the intensity of competition among existing firms in the industry."

Linda, the marketing lead, raised her hand. "What factors

contribute to competitive rivalry?"

"Great question," Angela replied. "Factors include the number of competitors, rate of industry growth, product differentiation, and customer loyalty."

Michael added, "In the tech industry, competition is fierce. Many companies offer similar products, making differentiation and customer loyalty crucial."

David, the young developer, leaned forward. "How can we stand out in such a competitive market?"

Angela nodded. "Innovation and unique value propositions are key. We need to continuously improve our products and services to stay ahead."

Threat of New Entrants

Michael wrote "Threat of New Entrants" on the board. "This force assesses how easy it is for new competitors to enter the market."

Linda asked, "What makes it difficult for new companies to enter our market?"

"Barriers to entry," Michael explained. "These include high capital requirements, advanced technology, strong brand identity, and access to distribution channels."

Angela added, "In our case, developing cutting-edge technology and establishing a strong brand presence can deter new entrants."

David commented, "We should leverage our existing infrastructure and expertise to maintain a competitive edge."

CHAPTER 3: ENVIRONMENTAL SCANNING AND INDUSTRY ANALYSIS

Threat of Substitutes

Angela moved to "Threat of Substitutes." "This force looks at the likelihood of customers finding alternative solutions."

Linda asked, "How do substitutes impact our business?"

"Substitutes can reduce demand for our products," Angela explained. "If customers find a different way to meet their needs, they might switch to those alternatives."

Michael added, "To mitigate this threat, we must offer superior value that alternatives can't match."

David suggested, "Understanding customer needs and continuously enhancing our products will help us stay ahead of substitutes."

Bargaining Power of Suppliers

Michael wrote "Bargaining Power of Suppliers" on the board. "This force examines how much power suppliers have over us."

Linda raised her hand again. "What factors give suppliers more power?"

"Factors include the number of suppliers, uniqueness of their products, and our dependency on them," Michael explained. "If there are few suppliers or if we rely heavily on specific inputs, suppliers have more power."

Angela added, "Diversifying our supplier base and building strong relationships can reduce this power."

David suggested, "We could explore partnerships with local suppliers to enhance reliability and reduce costs."

Bargaining Power of Customers

Angela moved to "Bargaining Power of Customers." "This force looks at how much power our customers have."

Linda asked, "What factors increase customers' bargaining power?"

"Factors include the number of choices available, the importance of each customer to our business, and the cost of switching to a competitor," Angela explained.

Michael added, "In the tech industry, informed customers can demand better products and services. Offering exceptional customer service and unique value propositions can help mitigate this power."

Practical Application

Angela moved to the next slide, which showed a practical application of Porter's Five Forces Model. "Now, let's apply these concepts to GlobalTech Solutions. We'll brainstorm key factors for each force and discuss their potential impact on our business."

She wrote "Competitive Rivalry" on the board again and invited the team to contribute.

Linda started, "For competitive rivalry, we need to analyze our main competitors and understand their strengths and weaknesses. We should also look at industry growth rates and how we can differentiate our products."

David added, "We could focus on developing unique features and providing excellent customer support to build loyalty."

Angela wrote down their suggestions and moved to "Threat

of New Entrants."

Linda said, "We should monitor the entry of new companies into the market and assess the barriers they face. Strengthening our brand and leveraging our technological expertise will help us stay competitive."

David added, "Investing in advanced technology and R&D will keep us ahead of potential new entrants."

The team continued this process for each of the five forces, contributing insights and discussing their implications:

Threat of Substitutes:

- Identifying potential substitutes
- Enhancing product features
- Understanding customer needs and preferences

Bargaining Power of Suppliers:

- Diversifying supplier base
- Building strong supplier relationships
- Exploring local partnerships

Bargaining Power of Customers:

- Offering exceptional customer service
- Providing unique value propositions
- Building strong customer relationships

With the board filled with their collective insights, Angela and Michael concluded the session.

Angela smiled, "Great job, everyone. Porter's Five Forces

Model provides a robust framework for understanding our competitive environment. By analyzing these forces, we can develop strategies to navigate and succeed in our industry."

Michael added, "Let's use these insights to refine our strategic plans and ensure we're prepared for any challenges and opportunities that come our way."

As the team left the conference room, they felt empowered with a deeper understanding of the competitive forces shaping their industry. They were ready to apply their knowledge and steer GlobalTech Solutions toward success with strategic clarity and foresight.

In the heart of Lusaka, as the city thrived with life, GlobalTech Solutions stood resilient and informed. Armed with their comprehensive analysis of Porter's Five Forces, they were poised to navigate the competitive waters of the tech industry, turning potential challenges into opportunities for innovation and growth.

Analyzing Industry Life Cycles

Navigating the Waves of Change

In the heart of Lusaka, the GlobalTech Solutions team gathered once more in their sleek conference room, ready to embark on the next leg of their journey through industry analysis. Today's focus: analyzing industry life cycles. Angela and Michael stood at the front, prepared to guide their team through the complexities of industry evolution.

Angela began with a calm yet determined voice, "Good morning, everyone. Today, we're diving into the analysis of industry life cycles. Understanding where our industry stands in its life cycle will help us anticipate changes and adapt our strategies accordingly."

Michael clicked to the first slide, displaying the title: "Analyzing Industry Life Cycles."

"Every industry goes through a series of stages," he explained. "From inception to decline, these stages shape the competitive landscape and influence our strategic decisions."

Introduction to Industry Life Cycles

Angela wrote "Introduction to Industry Life Cycles" on the whiteboard. "An industry life cycle consists of four main stages: introduction, growth, maturity, and decline."

David, the young developer, raised his hand. "What happens in each stage?"

"In the introduction stage, new products or services are introduced to the market," Angela explained. "Growth follows as demand increases, and competition intensifies. Maturity is characterized by stable growth and fierce competition among established players. Finally, the decline stage sees a decrease in demand and industry consolidation."

Assessing Industry Life Cycle

Michael moved to "Assessing Industry Life Cycle." "To assess where our industry stands, we need to consider factors such as market growth, technological innovation, and competitive intensity."

Linda, the marketing lead, nodded. "How do we know if our industry is in the growth or maturity stage?"

"Good question," Michael replied. "In the growth stage,

we'll see rapid market expansion, increasing demand, and high levels of innovation. Conversely, the maturity stage is marked by slower growth rates, market saturation, and intensified competition."

Angela added, "By analyzing these factors, we can gauge the stage of our industry life cycle and adjust our strategies accordingly."

Strategic Implications

Angela moved to "Strategic Implications." "Each stage of the industry life cycle presents unique challenges and opportunities. Understanding these implications helps us make informed strategic decisions."

Michael elaborated, "In the introduction stage, we focus on product development and market penetration. As the industry enters the growth stage, we invest in expansion and innovation to capture market share."

Linda commented, "In the maturity stage, we need to differentiate our products and services to maintain our competitive edge. And in the decline stage, we may need to consider diversification or exiting the market altogether."

Practical Application

Angela clicked to the next slide, which displayed a practical application of analyzing industry life cycles. "Now, let's apply what we've learned to GlobalTech Solutions. We'll discuss the characteristics of each stage and identify where our industry might currently stand."

She wrote "Introduction Stage" on the board again and

invited the team to contribute.

David started, "For the introduction stage, we should focus on developing innovative products and gaining market acceptance. We need to invest in R&D and marketing to create awareness and drive adoption."

Linda added, "We should also be prepared for high initial costs and slow revenue growth as we establish ourselves in the market."

The team continued this process for each stage of the industry life cycle, contributing insights and discussing their implications:

Growth Stage:

- Rapid market expansion
- Increasing demand
- High levels of innovation

Maturity Stage:

- Slower growth rates
- Market saturation
- Intensified competition

Decline Stage:

- Decrease in demand
- Industry consolidation
- Consideration of diversification or exit strategies

With the board filled with their collective insights, Angela and Michael concluded the session.

Angela smiled, "Great job, everyone. Analyzing industry life cycles provides valuable insights into the dynamics of our industry. By understanding these stages, we can adapt our strategies to navigate the waves of change."

Michael added, "Let's use these insights to refine our strategic plans and ensure we're positioned for success, no matter where our industry stands in its life cycle."

As the team left the conference room, they felt empowered with a deeper understanding of the evolution of their industry. They were ready to apply their knowledge and steer Global-Tech Solutions toward success with strategic foresight and agility.

In the heart of Lusaka, as the city thrived with life, Global-Tech Solutions stood resilient and forward-thinking. Armed with their analysis of industry life cycles, they were poised to navigate the changing tides of their industry, turning challenges into opportunities for growth and innovation.

Identifying Key Success Factors in Industry

Unveiling the Path to Success

In the vibrant city of Lusaka, the GlobalTech Solutions team gathered once again in their modern conference room, eager to explore the next phase of their industry analysis journey. Today's focus: identifying the key success factors in their industry. Angela and Michael stood at the front, ready to lead their team through this critical aspect of strategic planning.

Angela began with a confident tone, "Good morning, everyone. Today, we'll dive into identifying the key success factors in our industry. Understanding these factors is essential for developing strategies that will lead to our success."

Michael clicked to the first slide, which displayed the title: "Identifying Key Success Factors."

"Key success factors are those elements that are critical for achieving success in our industry," he explained. "By identifying and focusing on these factors, we can strengthen our competitive position and drive growth."

Introduction to Key Success Factors

Angela wrote "Introduction to Key Success Factors" on the whiteboard. "Key success factors can vary depending on the industry. They encompass a wide range of elements, including market demand, technological innovation, operational efficiency, and customer satisfaction."

David, the young developer, raised his hand. "How do we identify these factors?"

"Good question," Angela replied. "We can identify key success factors through market research, competitor analysis, and insights from industry experts. It's about understanding what drives success in our industry and aligning our strategies accordingly."

Analyzing Key Success Factors

Michael moved to "Analyzing Key Success Factors." "Let's explore some common key success factors and discuss their relevance to our industry."

Linda, the marketing lead, nodded. "Can you give us an example?"

"Of course," Michael said. "In the tech industry, innovation is often a key success factor. Companies that innovate and stay ahead of technological trends are better positioned to succeed."

Angela added, "Another key success factor is customer satisfaction. Satisfied customers are more likely to be loyal and recommend our products to others, driving growth and profitability."

Strategic Implications

Angela moved to "Strategic Implications." "Once we've identified key success factors, we need to incorporate them into our strategic planning process. This involves aligning our resources and efforts to capitalize on these factors."

Michael elaborated, "For example, if innovation is a key success factor, we should invest in research and development to develop cutting-edge products. If customer satisfaction is critical, we should focus on delivering exceptional customer service and building strong relationships."

Linda commented, "By prioritizing these key success factors, we can differentiate ourselves from competitors and create sustainable competitive advantage."

Practical Application

Angela clicked to the next slide, which displayed a practical application of identifying key success factors. "Now, let's apply what we've learned to GlobalTech Solutions. We'll brainstorm key success factors for our industry and discuss how we can leverage them to achieve success."

She wrote "Innovation" on the board again and invited the team to contribute.

David started, "For innovation, we should focus on staying ahead of technological trends and developing unique features that set us apart from competitors."

Linda added, "We should also foster a culture of innovation within our organization, encouraging creativity and experimentation."

The team continued this process for each key success factor, contributing insights and discussing their implications:

Customer Satisfaction:

- Providing exceptional customer service
- Building strong customer relationships
- Implementing feedback mechanisms

Operational Efficiency:

- Streamlining processes and workflows
- Optimizing resource allocation
- Investing in technology for automation

Market Demand:

- Identifying emerging trends and customer needs
- Developing products that meet market demand
- Expanding into new markets or market segments

With the board filled with their collective insights, Angela and Michael concluded the session.

Angela smiled, "Great job, everyone. Identifying key success factors provides us with a roadmap to success. By focusing on these factors, we can drive growth and achieve our strategic objectives."

Michael added, "Let's use these insights to refine our strategic plans and ensure we're leveraging our strengths to their fullest potential."

As the team left the conference room, they felt empowered with a deeper understanding of the factors driving success in their industry. They were ready to apply their knowledge and steer GlobalTech Solutions toward success with strategic clarity and purpose.

In the heart of Lusaka, as the city thrived with life, GlobalTech Solutions stood resilient and determined. Armed with their identification of key success factors, they were poised to navigate the competitive landscape of the tech industry, turning challenges into opportunities for innovation and growth.

Practical Tools for Environmental Analysis

Equipping Ourselves for Insightful Analysis

In the heart of Lusaka, the GlobalTech Solutions team gathered once more in their bright conference room, ready to explore the practical tools that would enhance their environmental analysis capabilities. Angela and Michael stood at the front, prepared to guide their team through this crucial aspect of strategic planning.

Angela began with enthusiasm, "Good morning, everyone. Today, we'll be diving into practical tools for environmental analysis. These tools will help us gather valuable insights and make informed decisions to drive our business forward."

Michael clicked to the first slide, which displayed the title: "Practical Tools for Environmental Analysis."

"Environmental analysis requires systematic approaches and tools to gather, analyze, and interpret data effectively," he explained. "Let's explore some practical tools that we can use for this purpose."

Introduction to Practical Tools

Angela wrote "Introduction to Practical Tools" on the whiteboard. "There are various tools available to help us conduct environmental analysis. These tools range from simple frameworks to sophisticated software solutions."

Linda, the marketing lead, raised her hand. "Can you give us examples of these tools?"

"Certainly," Angela replied. "Some common tools include SWOT analysis, PESTEL analysis, Porter's Five Forces Model, and scenario planning. Each tool offers a unique perspective on the external environment and helps us identify opportunities and threats."

SWOT Analysis

Michael moved to "SWOT Analysis." "SWOT analysis is a simple yet powerful tool for assessing the strengths, weaknesses, opportunities, and threats facing our organization."

David, the young developer, leaned forward. "How do we conduct a SWOT analysis?"

"We identify our strengths and weaknesses by assessing

internal factors such as resources, capabilities, and processes," Michael explained. "Then, we analyze external factors such as market trends, competitor actions, and regulatory changes to identify opportunities and threats."

PESTEL Analysis

Angela continued with "PESTEL Analysis." "PESTEL analysis helps us understand the external factors that impact our business. It examines political, economic, social, technological, environmental, and legal factors."

Linda asked, "How do we conduct a PESTEL analysis?"

"We systematically evaluate each factor and its implications for our business," Angela replied. "For example, we assess how political stability, economic growth, and technological advancements affect our operations and strategies."

Porter's Five Forces Model

Michael moved to "Porter's Five Forces Model." "Porter's Five Forces Model helps us analyze the competitive forces within our industry. It assesses the threat of new entrants, bargaining power of buyers and suppliers, threat of substitutes, and competitive rivalry."

David commented, "That sounds comprehensive. How do we apply Porter's Five Forces Model?"

"We examine each force to understand its impact on our industry and competitive position," Michael explained. "For instance, we assess the barriers to entry, power dynamics between buyers and suppliers, and the availability of substitutes."

Scenario Planning

Angela concluded with "Scenario Planning." "Scenario planning involves developing multiple scenarios of possible future outcomes and assessing their implications for our business."

Linda raised her eyebrows. "How do we create scenarios?"

"We identify key uncertainties and drivers of change in our environment," Angela replied. "Then, we develop plausible scenarios based on different combinations of these factors and assess their potential impact on our business."

Practical Application

Michael clicked to the next slide, which displayed a practical application of using these tools for environmental analysis. "Now, let's apply what we've learned to GlobalTech Solutions. We'll use these tools to conduct a comprehensive analysis of our external environment and identify strategic insights."

He wrote "SWOT Analysis" on the board again and invited the team to contribute.

David started, "For strengths, our cutting-edge technology and strong brand reputation give us a competitive advantage."

Linda added, "Our weaknesses include reliance on a single supplier for key components and limited presence in emerging markets."

The team continued this process for each aspect of the SWOT analysis and other tools, contributing insights and discussing their implications:

- Identifying political, economic, social, technological, environmental, and legal factors affecting the business

(PESTEL Analysis)
- Analyzing the competitive forces within the industry (Porter's Five Forces Model)
- Developing scenarios of possible future outcomes and their implications (Scenario Planning)

With the board filled with their collective insights, Angela and Michael concluded the session.

Angela smiled, "Great job, everyone. These practical tools provide us with valuable frameworks for environmental analysis. By leveraging these tools effectively, we can make informed decisions and navigate the complexities of our external environment."

Michael added, "Let's use these insights to refine our strategic plans and ensure we're prepared for any challenges and opportunities that come our way."

As the team left the conference room, they felt equipped with a deeper understanding of the tools that would enhance their environmental analysis capabilities. They were ready to apply their knowledge and steer GlobalTech Solutions toward success with strategic clarity and foresight.

In the heart of Lusaka, as the city thrived with life, GlobalTech Solutions stood resilient and empowered. Armed with their practical tools for environmental analysis, they were poised to navigate the ever-changing business landscape, turning challenges into opportunities for growth and innovation.

4

Chapter 4: Internal Analysis: Assessing Strengths and Weaknesses

Unveiling the Core of GlobalTech Solutions

In the heart of Lusaka, within the sleek confines of the GlobalTech Solutions headquarters, the team gathered with anticipation for their next strategic exploration. Today, their focus shifted inward as they embarked on a journey of self-assessment: an internal analysis to uncover the strengths and weaknesses that defined their organization. Angela and Michael, the stalwart leaders of GlobalTech Solutions, stood at the forefront, ready to guide their team through this critical examination.

Angela's voice echoed with purpose, "Good morning, everyone. Today, we delve deep into our organization's core to assess our strengths and weaknesses. Understanding these internal factors is crucial for identifying areas of competitive advantage and areas needing improvement."

Michael, with a reassuring nod, added, "Indeed. Our

strengths amplify our capabilities, while our weaknesses highlight areas for growth and development. Let's embark on this journey of introspection together."

Unveiling Strengths

Angela began by illuminating the concept of strengths, "Strengths are the pillars upon which our organization stands tall. They encompass our unique assets, capabilities, and advantages that set us apart from competitors."

Linda, the perceptive marketing lead, chimed in, "What are some examples of strengths?"

Angela smiled, "Our talented team of developers, our robust technology infrastructure, and our strong brand reputation are among our notable strengths. These elements form the foundation of our competitive advantage."

Confronting Weaknesses

Michael shifted the focus to weaknesses, "Conversely, weaknesses are the areas where we fall short or face challenges. They represent opportunities for improvement and growth."

David, the ambitious young developer, inquired, "How do we identify weaknesses?"

"By examining our internal processes, resources, and performance metrics," Michael responded. "For example, inefficient workflows, outdated technology, or skill gaps within our team could be considered weaknesses."

Strategic Implications

Angela emphasized the strategic implications of this analysis, "Understanding our strengths allows us to capitalize on opportunities and defend against threats. Conversely, addressing our weaknesses positions us for growth and resilience."

Michael added, "By aligning our strategies with our internal capabilities, we can maximize our potential for success."

Practical Application

Angela guided the team through a practical application of internal analysis, "Now, let's apply what we've learned to GlobalTech Solutions. We'll conduct a SWOT analysis to assess our strengths and weaknesses, along with opportunities and threats in our external environment."

Michael echoed her sentiment, "Through this process, we'll gain valuable insights that will inform our strategic decisions and shape the future of our organization."

As the team delved into their internal assessment, the room buzzed with energy and determination. They scrutinized every aspect of their organization, from their technological prowess to their operational efficiencies, laying bare both their triumphs and their challenges.

Conclusion

As the session drew to a close, Angela and Michael addressed the team, their voices filled with pride and optimism. "Well done, everyone. Through this internal analysis, we've gained a clearer understanding of our organization's strengths and weaknesses. Armed with this knowledge, we're better equipped to chart a course for success."

Michael's gaze swept across the room, "Let's harness our strengths to seize opportunities and address our weaknesses with determination and innovation. Together, we will propel GlobalTech Solutions to new heights of excellence."

With renewed determination and a deeper understanding of their organization's core, the team dispersed, eager to apply their insights and drive GlobalTech Solutions towards a future filled with success and achievement.

In the heart of Lusaka, amidst the bustling energy of the city, GlobalTech Solutions stood poised and resolute. With their strengths amplified and their weaknesses confronted, they were ready to conquer new horizons and realize their vision of technological innovation and excellence.

Overview of Internal Analysis

Peering into the Heart of GlobalTech Solutions

In the heart of Lusaka, within the modern confines of the GlobalTech Solutions headquarters, the team convened once more, their focus honed on dissecting the internal workings of their organization. Today marked the commencement of their internal analysis journey, a quest to unravel the intricacies of their strengths and weaknesses. Angela and Michael, the seasoned captains of GlobalTech Solutions, stood ready to lead their crew through this introspective voyage.

Angela's voice resonated with authority as she addressed the team, "Good morning, everyone. Today, we embark on a journey of self-discovery, delving deep into the core of GlobalTech Solutions to assess our strengths and weaknesses. This internal analysis will lay the groundwork for our strategic roadmap ahead."

Michael, with a reassuring nod, added, "Indeed. Understanding our internal landscape is paramount as we navigate the ever-evolving seas of the tech industry. Let us begin this voyage with purpose and determination."

Setting the Stage

Angela set the stage for the internal analysis, "At its essence, internal analysis involves a comprehensive examination of our organization's inner workings. It's about uncovering the capabilities, resources, and dynamics that drive our operations."

Linda, the insightful marketing lead, sought clarification, "What aspects of our organization will we be examining?"

Angela responded, "We'll be scrutinizing every facet of our organization, from our human capital and technological infrastructure to our operational processes and cultural ethos. No stone will be left unturned in our quest for self-understanding."

Navigating Strengths

Michael navigated the discussion towards strengths, "Strengths are the bedrock upon which our organization stands tall. They embody our unique assets, competencies, and advantages that give us a competitive edge in the market."

David, the eager young developer, interjected, "How do we

identify our strengths?"

"Through introspection and analysis," Michael elucidated, "We'll examine our core competencies, market positioning, and brand reputation to uncover the elements that propel us forward."

Confronting Weaknesses

Angela steered the conversation towards weaknesses, "Conversely, weaknesses are the areas where we falter or face challenges. They represent opportunities for improvement and growth."

David leaned forward, "How do we confront our weaknesses?"

"By acknowledging them candidly," Angela affirmed, "We'll assess our internal processes, resource limitations, and performance gaps to identify areas ripe for enhancement."

Strategic Implications

Michael underscored the strategic implications of the internal analysis, "Understanding our internal landscape enables us to capitalize on our strengths and mitigate our weaknesses. It lays the groundwork for informed decision-making and strategic alignment."

Angela echoed his sentiment, "By aligning our strategies with our internal capabilities, we can chart a course for sustainable growth and competitive advantage."

Embarking on the Journey

With the stage set and the objectives clear, the team braced themselves for the journey ahead. Armed with determination and resolve, they ventured forth into the depths of their organization, ready to unearth the treasures of their strengths and confront the shadows of their weaknesses.

As they delved deeper into the intricacies of GlobalTech Solutions, the air crackled with anticipation and energy. With each revelation, they gained a clearer understanding of their organization's essence, laying the foundation for a future brimming with promise and possibility.

In the heart of Lusaka, amidst the hum of innovation and the pulse of progress, GlobalTech Solutions embarked on a voyage of self-discovery. With their strengths illuminated and their weaknesses confronted, they stood poised on the precipice of greatness, ready to carve their path to success in the ever-changing landscape of the tech industry.

Resource-Based View (RBV) of the Firm

Unveiling the Wealth Within

In the heart of Lusaka, within the dynamic confines of the GlobalTech Solutions headquarters, the team delved deeper into their internal analysis, seeking to uncover the wealth of resources that fueled their organization's engine. Today, their focus shifted to the Resource-Based View (RBV) of the firm, a lens through which they could discern the unique assets and capabilities that set them apart in the competitive landscape. Angela and Michael, the visionary leaders of GlobalTech

Solutions, stood poised to guide their team through this enlightening exploration.

Angela's voice rang out with conviction as she addressed the team, "Good morning, everyone. Today, we illuminate the Resource-Based View of the firm, a strategic framework that emphasizes the internal resources and capabilities that drive our competitive advantage. Let us uncover the wealth within GlobalTech Solutions."

Michael, with a nod of agreement, added, "Indeed. The RBV offers us a lens through which we can discern the treasures that lie within our organization. Let us embark on this journey of discovery with open minds and eager hearts."

Understanding the RBV

Angela elucidated the concept of the RBV, "At its core, the Resource-Based View posits that competitive advantage arises from the unique bundle of resources and capabilities possessed by an organization. These resources can include tangible assets such as technology and infrastructure, as well as intangible assets such as knowledge and brand reputation."

Linda, the astute marketing lead, sought clarification, "How do we identify these resources?"

Angela responded, "Through a systematic assessment of our organization's assets, competencies, and strategic capabilities. It's about recognizing the wealth of resources that underpin our competitive advantage."

Unearthing Core Competencies

Michael directed the team's attention towards core competencies, "Core competencies are the unique capabilities and skills that distinguish us from competitors. They are the secret sauce that propels us forward in the market."

David, the eager young developer, interjected, "How do we determine our core competencies?"

"We identify them through a process of introspection and analysis," Michael explained, "By evaluating our organization's skills, knowledge, and expertise, we can pinpoint the capabilities that drive our success."

Strategic Implications

Angela emphasized the strategic implications of the RBV, "Understanding our internal resources and capabilities enables us to leverage them strategically for competitive advantage. It allows us to allocate resources effectively, invest in areas of strength, and develop capabilities that drive long-term success."

Michael echoed her sentiment, "By aligning our strategies with our core competencies, we can chart a course for sustainable growth and resilience in the face of market challenges."

Embarking on the Journey

With the RBV as their guiding light, the team embarked on a journey of introspection and discovery. They delved deep into the recesses of GlobalTech Solutions, uncovering a treasure trove of resources and capabilities that lay hidden beneath the surface.

As they unearthed the wealth within their organization, the air crackled with excitement and anticipation. With each revelation, they gained a deeper understanding of their competitive advantage and a renewed sense of purpose in their quest for excellence.

In the heart of Lusaka, amidst the pulse of innovation and the hum of progress, GlobalTech Solutions embraced the Resource-Based View of the firm. Armed with newfound insights and a clearer vision of their internal landscape, they stood poised on the brink of greatness, ready to harness the wealth within and propel themselves to new heights of success in the competitive arena of the tech industry.

VRIO Framework: Value, Rarity, Imitability, Organization

Unraveling the Blueprint of Success

In the heart of Lusaka, within the innovative hub of GlobalTech Solutions, the team embarked on the next leg of their internal analysis journey, guided by the illuminating principles of the VRIO framework. Today, their focus sharpened on unraveling the blueprint of success, dissecting their internal resources and capabilities through the lens of value, rarity, imitability, and organization. Angela and Michael, the strategic architects of GlobalTech Solutions, stood ready to lead their team through this insightful exploration.

Angela's voice resonated with purpose as she addressed the team, "Good morning, everyone. Today, we delve deep into the VRIO framework, a powerful tool for assessing the strategic importance of our internal resources and capabilities. Let us unravel the blueprint of our success and unlock the keys to our competitive advantage."

Michael, with a nod of agreement, added, "Indeed. The VRIO framework offers us a systematic approach to evaluating the value, rarity, imitability, and organizational support of our resources. Let us embark on this journey of discovery with vigor and determination."

Unveiling Value

Angela elucidated the concept of value within the VRIO framework, "Value refers to the capability of our resources and capabilities to create value and contribute to our competitive advantage. It's about discerning the tangible and intangible benefits they bring to our organization."

Linda, the insightful marketing lead, sought clarification, "How do we determine the value of our resources?"

Angela responded, "Through a careful analysis of their contribution to our products, services, and overall performance. It's about identifying the ways in which they enhance our competitive position and drive customer value."

Assessing Rarity

Michael directed the team's attention towards rarity, "Rarity pertains to the uniqueness and scarcity of our resources and capabilities relative to competitors. It's about identifying the rare gems that set us apart in the market."

David, the eager young developer, interjected, "How do we

assess the rarity of our resources?"

"We evaluate their scarcity and uniqueness," Michael explained, "By considering factors such as exclusivity, proprietary technology, and specialized expertise, we can discern the rarity of our resources and their potential for competitive advantage."

Evaluating Imitability

Angela steered the conversation towards imitability, "Imitability examines the extent to which our resources and capabilities can be replicated or imitated by competitors. It's about safeguarding our competitive advantage against mimicry and emulation."

David leaned forward, "How do we safeguard against imitation?"

"Through barriers to imitation," Angela affirmed, "These may include patents, trademarks, trade secrets, and unique organizational practices that make it difficult for competitors to replicate our advantages."

Ensuring Organizational Support

Michael underscored the importance of organizational support within the VRIO framework, "Organization assesses the extent to which our resources are effectively utilized, integrated, and aligned with our strategic objectives. It's about ensuring that our organization is structured to leverage our resources for maximum impact."

Angela echoed his sentiment, "By aligning our resources with our strategic goals and fostering a culture of innovation and collaboration, we can ensure that our organization is primed to extract maximum value from our resources."

Embarking on the Journey

With the pillars of the VRIO framework as their guide, the team embarked on a journey of assessment and discovery. They delved deep into the inner workings of GlobalTech Solutions, scrutinizing every resource and capability with a discerning eye.

As they assessed the value, rarity, imitability, and organizational support of their internal assets, the air crackled with anticipation and excitement. With each revelation, they gained a clearer understanding of their competitive advantage and a renewed sense of purpose in their pursuit of excellence.

In the heart of Lusaka, amidst the buzz of innovation and the pulse of progress, GlobalTech Solutions embraced the VRIO framework as a blueprint for success. Armed with newfound insights and a strategic roadmap for the future, they stood poised on the brink of greatness, ready to leverage their internal resources and capabilities to drive success in the competitive arena of the tech industry.

Core Competencies and Competitive Advantage

Forging the Edge of Excellence

In the heart of Lusaka, within the pulsating nucleus of GlobalTech Solutions, the team delved deeper into their internal analysis, navigating the intricate web of core competencies and competitive advantage. Today, their focus sharpened on forging the edge of excellence, as they sought to uncover the essence of their competitive prowess. Angela and Michael, the strategic architects of GlobalTech Solutions, stood ready to guide their team through this enlightening exploration.

Angela's voice resonated with clarity as she addressed the team, "Good morning, everyone. Today, we illuminate the nexus between core competencies and competitive advantage, unveiling the strategic assets that propel us to the forefront of the industry. Let us forge the edge of excellence and harness our strengths to dominate the market."

Michael, with a nod of agreement, added, "Indeed. Our core competencies are the bedrock of our competitive advantage, the secret sauce that sets us apart from competitors. Let us embark on this journey of discovery with determination and purpose."

Defining Core Competencies

Angela elucidated the concept of core competencies, "Core competencies are the unique capabilities and skills that distinguish us from competitors. They represent the collective knowledge, expertise, and talents that underpin our competitive advantage."

Linda, the perceptive marketing lead, sought clarification, "How do we identify our core competencies?"

Angela responded, "Through introspection and analysis. It's about recognizing the capabilities that drive our success and contribute to our value proposition. These competencies are not easily replicable by competitors and form the cornerstone of our competitive advantage."

Leveraging Competitive Advantage

Michael directed the team's attention towards competitive advantage, "Competitive advantage stems from our ability to leverage our core competencies to outperform competitors. It's about creating superior value for customers and capturing a larger share of the market."

David, the eager young developer, interjected, "How do we leverage our competitive advantage?"

"We capitalize on our strengths," Michael affirmed, "By aligning our core competencies with market opportunities and customer needs, we can differentiate ourselves from competitors and establish a dominant position in the industry."

Strategic Implications

Angela underscored the strategic implications of core competencies and competitive advantage, "Understanding our core competencies enables us to focus our resources and efforts on areas where we have a distinct advantage. It allows us to develop strategies that amplify our strengths and mitigate our weaknesses, driving sustainable growth and profitability."

Michael echoed her sentiment, "By leveraging our core competencies effectively, we can create barriers to entry, fend off competitive threats, and position ourselves as leaders in the market."

Embarking on the Journey

With the nexus between core competencies and competitive advantage illuminated, the team embarked on a journey of strategic alignment and execution. They delved deep into the fabric of GlobalTech Solutions, identifying the core competencies that formed the backbone of their success.

As they leveraged their strengths to forge a competitive edge, the air crackled with anticipation and excitement. With each revelation, they gained a deeper understanding of their strategic position and a renewed sense of purpose in their pursuit of excellence.

In the heart of Lusaka, amidst the whirlwind of innovation and the symphony of progress, GlobalTech Solutions forged ahead, armed with the knowledge of their core competencies and the determination to dominate the market. With their edge of excellence honed to perfection, they stood poised on the brink of greatness, ready to conquer new frontiers and redefine the future of the tech industry.

Conducting a SWOT Analysis

Unveiling the Strategic Landscape

In the heart of Lusaka, within the dynamic quarters of GlobalTech Solutions, the team converged once more to unravel the strategic landscape through the lens of a SWOT analysis. Today, their focus sharpened on dissecting their internal strengths and weaknesses, while also scrutinizing the external opportunities and threats that shaped their path forward. Angela and Michael, the stalwart leaders of GlobalTech Solutions, stood poised to guide their team through this pivotal examination.

Angela's voice reverberated with purpose as she addressed the team, "Good morning, everyone. Today, we embark on a journey of strategic introspection, as we conduct a SWOT analysis to assess our internal strengths and weaknesses, along with the external opportunities and threats that confront us. Let us unveil the strategic landscape and chart a course for success."

Michael, with a nod of agreement, added, "Indeed. The SWOT analysis offers us a comprehensive framework for understanding our position in the market and identifying areas of strategic focus. Let us embark on this journey with clarity and determination."

Uncovering Internal Strengths

Angela began by illuminating the internal strengths of GlobalTech Solutions, "Our strengths are the pillars of our organization, the capabilities and assets that propel us forward in the market. They encompass our technological expertise, our talented workforce, and our strong brand reputation."

Linda, the astute marketing lead, sought clarification, "How do we identify our internal strengths?"

Angela responded, "Through a systematic examination of our resources, capabilities, and performance metrics. It's about recognizing the areas where we excel and leveraging these strengths to our advantage."

Confronting Internal Weaknesses

Michael directed the team's attention towards internal weaknesses, "Conversely, our weaknesses are the vulnerabilities that pose challenges to our success. They may include outdated technology, skill gaps within our team, or inefficient processes."

David, the eager young developer, interjected, "How do we address our internal weaknesses?"

"We confront them head-on," Michael affirmed, "By identifying areas for improvement and implementing strategies to mitigate our weaknesses. It's about turning our vulnerabilities into opportunities for growth and development."

Identifying External Opportunities

Angela steered the conversation towards external opportunities, "Opportunities are the avenues for growth and expansion that exist in the external environment. They may include emerging market trends, technological advancements, or shifts in consumer preferences."

David leaned forward, "How do we identify external opportunities?"

"We scan the external landscape," Angela explained, "By analyzing market trends, monitoring competitor actions, and staying attuned to changes in the regulatory environment. It's about seizing opportunities as they arise and capitalizing on them to drive our business forward."

Mitigating External Threats

Michael underscored the importance of external threats, "External threats are the challenges and risks that pose obstacles to our success. They may include intense competition, economic downturns, or changes in industry regulations."

Angela echoed his sentiment, "We mitigate these threats through proactive planning and risk management. It's about anticipating potential challenges and developing strategies to safeguard our organization against them."

Strategic Implications

With the strategic landscape unveiled, Angela and Michael emphasized the implications of the SWOT analysis, "Understanding our internal strengths and weaknesses, along with the external opportunities and threats, enables us to develop strategies that leverage our strengths, address our weaknesses, capitalize on opportunities, and mitigate threats. It lays the groundwork for informed decision-making and strategic alignment."

Embarking on the Journey

With the strategic landscape laid bare, the team embarked on a journey of strategic planning and execution. They harnessed the insights gleaned from the SWOT analysis to chart a course for success, leveraging their strengths to seize opportunities and fortifying their weaknesses against threats.

As they navigated the strategic landscape with purpose and determination, the air crackled with anticipation and excitement. With each strategic decision, they propelled GlobalTech Solutions forward, towards a future brimming with promise and possibility.

In the heart of Lusaka, amidst the whirlwind of innovation and the symphony of progress, GlobalTech Solutions stood poised on the brink of greatness. Armed with the insights of the SWOT analysis, they were ready to conquer new frontiers and redefine the future of the tech industry.

Leveraging Strengths and Mitigating Weaknesses

Harnessing Potential, Overcoming Challenges

In the heart of Lusaka, within the bustling confines of GlobalTech Solutions, the team gathered once more, their focus honed on leveraging strengths and mitigating weaknesses uncovered through their rigorous internal analysis. Today, they stood at the precipice of strategic action, poised to harness their potential and overcome challenges with strategic precision. Angela and Michael, the steadfast leaders of GlobalTech Solutions, stood ready to guide their team through this transformative endeavor.

Angela's voice rang out with determination as she addressed the team, "Good morning, everyone. Today, we stand on the threshold of strategic action, as we leverage our internal strengths to capitalize on opportunities and mitigate our weaknesses to overcome challenges. Let us harness our potential and forge a path to success."

Michael, with a nod of agreement, added, "Indeed. Our strengths are the fuel that propels us forward, while our weaknesses are the obstacles we must overcome. Let us embark on this journey with courage and resolve."

Leveraging Internal Strengths

Angela began by highlighting the importance of leveraging internal strengths, "Our strengths are the foundation of our competitive advantage, the assets and capabilities that set us apart in the market. It's imperative that we leverage these strengths to seize opportunities and drive our business forward."

Linda, the perceptive marketing lead, sought clarification, "How do we leverage our internal strengths?"

Angela responded, "By aligning them with our strategic objectives and capitalizing on them to create value for our customers and stakeholders. It's about maximizing our strengths to achieve our organizational goals and maintain our competitive edge."

Mitigating Internal Weaknesses

Michael directed the team's attention towards mitigating internal weaknesses, "Conversely, our weaknesses are the vulnerabilities that pose challenges to our success. It's essential that we address these weaknesses proactively to prevent them from undermining our efforts."

David, the eager young developer, interjected, "How do we mitigate our internal weaknesses?"

"We confront them head-on," Michael affirmed, "By implementing strategies to improve our processes, develop our capabilities, and close skill gaps within our team. It's about turning our weaknesses into opportunities for growth and improvement."

Strategic Implications

Angela underscored the strategic implications of leveraging strengths and mitigating weaknesses, "By harnessing our internal strengths and mitigating our weaknesses, we position ourselves for sustainable growth and success. It enables us to capitalize on opportunities, defend against threats, and achieve our strategic objectives with confidence."

Michael echoed her sentiment, "It's about leveraging our strengths to overcome obstacles and propel our organization forward on the path to greatness."

Embarking on the Journey

With the roadmap to success illuminated, the team embarked on a journey of strategic action and execution. They harnessed their internal strengths to seize opportunities and fortified their weaknesses against threats with determination and resolve.

As they navigated the strategic landscape with purpose and vision, the air crackled with anticipation and excitement. With each strategic decision, they propelled GlobalTech Solutions forward, towards a future brimming with promise and possibility.

In the heart of Lusaka, amidst the whirlwind of innovation and the symphony of progress, GlobalTech Solutions stood poised on the brink of greatness. Armed with the insights of their internal analysis, they were ready to conquer new frontiers and redefine the future of the tech industry.

5

Chapter 5: Strategic Formulation: Developing Strategies

Forging the Path Ahead

In the vibrant heart of Lusaka, within the visionary halls of GlobalTech Solutions, a pivotal moment unfolded as the team gathered to embark on the next phase of their journey: strategic formulation. Today marked the dawn of a new era, as they set out to craft the blueprint that would shape the future of their organization. Angela and Michael, the stalwart captains of GlobalTech Solutions, stood at the helm, ready to lead their team through the intricacies of strategic development.

Angela's voice resonated with purpose as she addressed the team, "Good morning, everyone. Today, we stand on the threshold of strategic formulation, as we chart the course that will define the future of GlobalTech Solutions. Let us forge the path ahead with clarity, creativity, and conviction."

Michael, with a nod of agreement, added, "Indeed. Strategic

formulation is the art of turning vision into action, of translating our aspirations into tangible strategies that propel us towards our goals. Let us embark on this journey with determination and foresight."

Defining Strategic Direction

Angela began by emphasizing the importance of strategic direction, "At the heart of strategic formulation lies the need to define our organizational direction and set clear objectives for the future. It's about articulating our vision, mission, and goals in a way that inspires and guides our actions."

Linda, the insightful marketing lead, sought clarification, "How do we define our strategic direction?"

Angela responded, "Through a process of reflection, analysis, and consultation. It's about understanding our strengths, weaknesses, opportunities, and threats, and aligning them with our long-term aspirations. Our strategic direction serves as the compass that guides our journey and informs our decision-making."

Crafting Strategic Alternatives

Michael directed the team's attention towards crafting strategic alternatives, "With our strategic direction in mind, we must now explore various paths and possibilities for achieving our objectives. It's about generating creative ideas and innovative approaches that leverage our strengths and address our challenges."

David, the eager young developer, interjected, "How do we craft strategic alternatives?"

"We brainstorm," Michael affirmed, "By engaging in collaborative discussions, conducting market research, and leveraging our collective expertise, we can generate a range of strategic options. It's about thinking outside the box and exploring new horizons."

Evaluating Strategic Options

Angela steered the conversation towards evaluating strategic options, "Once we've generated a range of alternatives, we must assess their feasibility, viability, and potential impact. It's about conducting thorough analysis and weighing the risks and rewards of each option."

David leaned forward, "How do we evaluate strategic options?"

"We employ strategic frameworks and decision-making tools," Angela explained, "such as cost-benefit analysis, scenario planning, and risk assessment. It's about making informed choices that align with our strategic objectives and maximize our chances of success."

Selecting Optimal Strategies

Michael underscored the importance of selecting optimal strategies, "Ultimately, we must choose the strategies that best position us to achieve our goals and fulfill our vision. It's about prioritizing options, making tough decisions, and committing to the path that offers the greatest potential for success."

Angela echoed his sentiment, "By selecting optimal strategies, we set ourselves on a trajectory towards growth, innovation, and excellence. It's about charting a course that leads us towards our desired future."

Embracing Strategic Implementation

With the strategic blueprint in hand, the team embraced the challenge of strategic implementation. They committed themselves to turning vision into action, to executing their chosen strategies with precision and dedication.

As they embarked on this transformative journey, the air crackled with anticipation and excitement. With each strategic decision, they propelled GlobalTech Solutions forward, towards a future brimming with promise and possibility.

In the heart of Lusaka, amidst the whirlwind of innovation and the symphony of progress, GlobalTech Solutions stood poised on the brink of greatness. Armed with a clear strategic direction and a commitment to action, they were ready to conquer new frontiers and redefine the future of the tech industry.

Levels of Strategy: Corporate, Business, Functional

Scaling the Summit: Unveiling Strategic Hierarchies

In the bustling corridors of GlobalTech Solutions, a pivotal discourse unfolded as the team delved deeper into the realm of strategic formulation, unraveling the intricate hierarchies that governed their path to success. Today, their focus sharpened on scaling the summit of strategic hierarchies, as they navigated the levels of corporate, business, and functional strategy with precision and purpose. Angela and

Michael, the steadfast navigators of GlobalTech Solutions, stood ready to guide their team through this enlightening exploration.

Angela's voice resonated with clarity as she addressed the team, "Good morning, everyone. Today, we ascend the strategic summit, unveiling the hierarchical layers of corporate, business, and functional strategy that shape our organizational trajectory. Let us scale these heights with insight, intention, and ingenuity."

Michael, with a nod of agreement, added, "Indeed. Strategic hierarchies provide the framework through which we translate our vision into action, aligning our objectives at every level of the organization. Let us embark on this journey of exploration with determination and strategic acumen."

Understanding Corporate Strategy

Angela began by elucidating the concept of corporate strategy, "At the apex of our strategic hierarchy lies corporate strategy, which defines the overarching direction and scope of our organization. It's about making choices regarding the industries we operate in, the markets we serve, and the portfolio of businesses we manage."

Linda, the perceptive marketing lead, sought clarification, "How does corporate strategy influence our organization?"

Angela responded, "Corporate strategy guides decisions related to diversification, mergers and acquisitions, and portfolio management. It's about ensuring that our various businesses and units are aligned with our overall vision and contribute to our long-term success."

Navigating Business Strategy

Michael directed the team's attention towards business strategy, "Beneath corporate strategy lies business strategy, which focuses on how we compete within specific markets or industries. It's about defining our competitive positioning, target markets, and value proposition."

David, the eager young developer, interjected, "How do we develop our business strategy?"

"We analyze our competitive landscape," Michael explained, "Identifying market opportunities, assessing competitor strengths and weaknesses, and crafting strategies that enable us to differentiate ourselves and capture value in the market."

Executing Functional Strategy

Angela steered the conversation towards functional strategy, "At the operational level of our organization, we have functional strategy, which outlines the specific actions and initiatives undertaken by individual departments or functions. It's about aligning our resources and capabilities to support our business-level objectives."

David leaned forward, "How do we implement functional strategy?"

"We optimize our processes and capabilities," Angela affirmed, "Streamlining operations, developing talent, and leveraging technology to enhance efficiency and effectiveness. It's about ensuring that every function contributes to our overall strategic goals."

Strategic Integration

With the layers of strategic hierarchy unveiled, Angela and Michael emphasized the importance of strategic integration, "By aligning our corporate, business, and functional strategies, we ensure coherence and consistency across all levels of the organization. It's about fostering synergy and collaboration to drive our collective success."

Embarking on the Journey

Armed with a clear understanding of strategic hierarchies, the team embarked on a journey of strategic alignment and integration. They harnessed the power of corporate, business, and functional strategies to chart a unified course towards their organizational vision.

As they ascended the strategic summit with purpose and determination, the air crackled with anticipation and excitement. With each strategic decision, they propelled GlobalTech Solutions forward, towards a future brimming with promise and possibility.

In the heart of Lusaka, amidst the whirlwind of innovation and the symphony of progress, GlobalTech Solutions stood poised on the brink of greatness. Armed with a comprehensive understanding of strategic hierarchies, they were ready to conquer new frontiers and redefine the future of the tech industry.

Generic Competitive Strategies: Cost Leadership, Differentiation, Focus

Carving the Niche: Crafting Competitive Excellence

In the bustling corridors of GlobalTech Solutions, the air was charged with anticipation as the team delved deeper into the realm of strategic formulation, exploring the bedrock principles of competitive strategy. Today, their focus sharpened on carving the niche of competitive excellence, as they navigated the terrain of generic competitive strategies with determination and insight. Angela and Michael, the seasoned architects of GlobalTech Solutions, stood ready to guide their team through this illuminating exploration.

Angela's voice resonated with clarity as she addressed the team, "Good morning, everyone. Today, we immerse ourselves in the crucible of competitive strategy, unveiling the time-tested principles of cost leadership, differentiation, and focus. Let us carve the niche of competitive excellence and propel GlobalTech Solutions to new heights of success."

Michael, with a nod of agreement, added, "Indeed. Competitive strategy is the cornerstone of our success, guiding us in our quest to outperform rivals and capture value in the market. Let us embark on this journey with strategic acumen and unwavering resolve."

Pursuing Cost Leadership

Angela began by illuminating the concept of cost leadership, "At the heart of cost leadership lies the pursuit of operational excellence and efficiency. It's about becoming the low-cost producer in our industry, offering products or services at a price that competitors cannot match."

Linda, the perceptive marketing lead, sought clarification, "How do we achieve cost leadership?"

Angela responded, "We optimize our production processes, streamline supply chains, and leverage economies of scale to drive down costs. It's about relentlessly pursuing efficiency and cost-saving measures to maintain a competitive edge."

Embracing Differentiation

Michael directed the team's attention towards differentiation, "Conversely, differentiation is about offering unique and distinct products or services that set us apart from competitors. It's about creating value for customers through innovation, quality, or unique features."

David, the eager young developer, interjected, "How do we differentiate ourselves?"

"We innovate," Michael affirmed, "By investing in research and development, cultivating a culture of creativity, and continually pushing the boundaries of what is possible. It's about offering customers something truly unique and compelling."

Focusing on Niche Markets

Angela steered the conversation towards focus strategy, "In addition to cost leadership and differentiation, focus strategy involves targeting a specific segment or niche within the market. It's about tailoring our products or services to meet the unique needs of a particular group of customers."

David leaned forward, "How do we focus our efforts?"

"We specialize," Angela explained, "By concentrating our resources and efforts on serving a narrow market segment exceptionally well. It's about understanding the needs and preferences of our target customers and delivering value in a way that competitors cannot match."

Strategic Integration

With the principles of generic competitive strategies unveiled, Angela and Michael emphasized the importance of strategic integration, "By combining elements of cost leadership, differentiation, and focus, we can create a sustainable competitive advantage that positions us for success in the market. It's about crafting a strategy that leverages our strengths and exploits opportunities to outperform rivals."

Embarking on the Journey

Armed with a deep understanding of competitive strategy, the team embarked on a journey of strategic differentiation and focus. They harnessed the power of cost leadership, differentiation, and focus to carve out a niche of competitive excellence in the market.

As they forged ahead with purpose and determination, the air crackled with anticipation and excitement. With each strategic decision, they propelled GlobalTech Solutions forward, towards a future brimming with promise and possibility.

In the heart of Lusaka, amidst the whirlwind of innovation and the symphony of progress, GlobalTech Solutions stood poised on the brink of greatness. Armed with a comprehensive understanding of generic competitive strategies, they were ready to conquer new frontiers and redefine the future of the tech industry.

Growth Strategies: Expansion, Diversification, Mergers, Acquisitions

Sowing the Seeds of Growth: Navigating Strategic Expansion

In the bustling hive of GlobalTech Solutions, the atmosphere buzzed with excitement as the team delved deeper into the realm of strategic formulation, exploring the fertile ground of growth strategies. Today, their focus honed on sowing the seeds of growth, as they navigated the terrain of expansion, diversification, mergers, and acquisitions with keen anticipation. Angela and Michael, the seasoned visionaries of GlobalTech Solutions, stood poised to guide their team through this enlightening exploration.

Angela's voice rang out with clarity as she addressed the team, "Good morning, everyone. Today, we set our sights on the horizon of growth, unveiling the strategic avenues of expansion, diversification, mergers, and acquisitions. Let us sow the seeds of growth and cultivate a future ripe with opportunity."

Michael, with a nod of agreement, added, "Indeed. Growth is the lifeblood of our organization, fueling our aspirations and propelling us towards our vision of success. Let us embark on this journey with foresight and determination."

Embracing Expansion Strategies

Angela began by illuminating the concept of expansion strategies, "At the heart of expansion lies the pursuit of growth through increased market share, geographic reach, or product/service offerings. It's about seizing opportunities to expand our presence and extend our influence in the market."

Linda, the perceptive marketing lead, sought clarification, "How do we pursue expansion?"

Angela responded, "We explore new markets, territories, or customer segments, leveraging our existing capabilities and resources to fuel growth. It's about identifying untapped opportunities and capitalizing on them to drive our business forward."

Exploring Diversification

Michael directed the team's attention towards diversification, "Diversification involves expanding our business into new markets or industries that are unrelated to our current offerings. It's about spreading risk and seizing new opportunities for growth."

David, the eager young developer, interjected, "Why is diversification important?"

"We mitigate risk," Michael affirmed, "By diversifying our portfolio, we insulate ourselves from the volatility of individual markets or industries. It's about creating a balanced portfolio of businesses that collectively contribute to our long-term success."

Pursuing Mergers and Acquisitions

Angela steered the conversation towards mergers and acquisitions, "In addition to organic growth, we can pursue growth through mergers and acquisitions, acquiring other companies to expand our capabilities, enter new markets, or achieve synergies."

David leaned forward, "How do we approach mergers and acquisitions?"

"We identify strategic targets," Angela explained, "Companies that complement our strengths, fill gaps in our portfolio, or offer opportunities for synergy. It's about conducting thorough due diligence and negotiating deals that create value for our organization and our stakeholders."

Strategic Integration

With the spectrum of growth strategies unveiled, Angela and Michael emphasized the importance of strategic integration, "By combining elements of expansion, diversification, mergers, and acquisitions, we can create a comprehensive growth strategy that positions us for success in the market. It's about seizing opportunities, mitigating risks, and maximizing value for our organization."

Embarking on the Journey

Armed with a deep understanding of growth strategies, the team embarked on a journey of strategic expansion and diversification. They harnessed the power of organic growth, mergers, and acquisitions to sow the seeds of growth and cultivate a future ripe with opportunity.

As they forged ahead with determination and foresight, the air crackled with anticipation and excitement. With each strategic decision, they propelled GlobalTech Solutions forward, towards a future brimming with promise and possibility.

In the heart of Lusaka, amidst the whirlwind of innovation and the symphony of progress, GlobalTech Solutions stood poised on the brink of greatness. Armed with a comprehensive growth strategy, they were ready to conquer new frontiers and redefine the future of the tech industry.

Stability and Retrenchment Strategies

Navigating the Winds of Change: Ensuring Organizational Resilience

In the bustling corridors of GlobalTech Solutions, a sobering discourse unfolded as the team delved deeper into the realm of strategic formulation, exploring the delicate balance between stability and retrenchment strategies. Today, their focus shifted towards navigating the winds of change, as they grappled with the complexities of ensuring organizational resilience in the face of adversity. Angela and Michael, the steadfast guardians of GlobalTech Solutions, stood ready to guide their team through this somber yet crucial exploration.

Angela's voice, tinged with gravity, resonated as she addressed the team, "Good morning, everyone. Today, we confront the reality that amidst growth and expansion, there may come times when stability and retrenchment strategies are necessary to ensure the resilience and longevity of our organization. Let us navigate these winds of change with wisdom, compassion, and strategic foresight."

Michael, with a solemn nod, added, "Indeed. While stability is the bedrock upon which we build our success, retrenchment is a measure reserved for dire circumstances, to be implemented with caution and consideration for our most valuable resource—our human capital. Let us proceed with the understanding that our people are our greatest asset, deserving of our utmost care and respect."

Embracing Stability Strategies

Angela began by shedding light on stability strategies, "Stability strategies are designed to maintain the status quo and ensure organizational equilibrium during times of relative calm. It's about consolidating our gains, optimizing our operations, and reinforcing our competitive position in the market."

Linda, the perceptive marketing lead, sought clarification, "How do we embrace stability strategies?"

Angela responded, "We focus on efficiency and optimization, streamlining our processes, and fine-tuning our operations to enhance productivity and profitability. It's about fostering a culture of stability and resilience that enables us to weather the inevitable storms of the business landscape."

Considering Retrenchment as a Last Resort

Michael directed the team's attention towards retrenchment strategies, "Conversely, retrenchment strategies are implemented in times of crisis or decline, when drastic measures are necessary to ensure the survival of the organization. It's a measure of last resort, to be considered only when all other options have been exhausted."

David, the eager young developer, interjected, "When is retrenchment warranted?"

"We exercise caution," Michael affirmed, "Retrenchment should only be considered in cases of incompetence or extreme financial distress, and even then, it must be approached with sensitivity and empathy towards our employees. Human resource is our most valuable asset, and we must prioritize their well-being above all else."

Strategic Integration

With the gravity of stability and retrenchment strategies weighing heavy on their minds, Angela and Michael emphasized the importance of strategic integration, "By maintaining a delicate balance between stability and retrenchment, we ensure the resilience and longevity of our organization. It's about navigating the winds of change with wisdom and compassion, always prioritizing the well-being of our people."

Embarking on the Journey

Armed with a deep understanding of stability and retrenchment strategies, the team embarked on a journey of organizational resilience and adaptability. They vowed to navigate the tumultuous seas of the business landscape with wisdom and compassion, always prioritizing the well-being of their most valuable asset—their people.

As they forged ahead with determination and empathy,

the air crackled with a sense of solemn purpose. With each strategic decision, they reaffirmed their commitment to ensuring the resilience and longevity of GlobalTech Solutions, come what may.

In the heart of Lusaka, amidst the whirlwind of innovation and the symphony of progress, GlobalTech Solutions stood poised on the brink of greatness. Armed with a comprehensive understanding of stability and retrenchment strategies, they were ready to navigate the winds of change and redefine the future of the tech industry.

International and Global Strategies

Unveiling Global Horizons: Navigating the World Stage

In the vibrant corridors of GlobalTech Solutions, an air of anticipation filled the room as the team delved deeper into the realm of strategic formulation, exploring the expansive vistas of international and global strategies. Today, their focus shifted towards unveiling global horizons, as they prepared to navigate the complexities of the world stage with insight and innovation. Angela and Michael, the visionary leaders of GlobalTech Solutions, stood ready to guide their team through this exhilarating exploration.

Angela's voice, tinged with excitement, resonated as she addressed the team, "Good morning, everyone. Today, we embark on a journey beyond borders, unveiling the strategic opportunities and challenges of international and global strategies. Let us embrace the diversity and dynamism of the global marketplace with courage, curiosity, and strategic acumen."

Michael, with a nod of agreement, added, "Indeed. As we expand our horizons and venture into new territories, let us do so with humility and respect for the cultures and customs of the diverse communities we encounter. Let us forge partnerships and alliances that transcend geographical boundaries and propel GlobalTech Solutions to new heights of success."

Embracing International Expansion

Angela began by shedding light on international expansion, "International expansion involves entering new markets outside of our domestic borders, seizing opportunities for growth and diversification on a global scale. It's about adapting our products, services, and strategies to meet the unique needs and preferences of customers in different countries and regions."

Linda, the perceptive marketing lead, sought clarification, "How do we embrace international expansion?"

Angela responded, "We conduct thorough market research, analyze cultural nuances, and tailor our offerings to resonate with local audiences. It's about building relationships and establishing a presence in foreign markets, one step at a time."

Pursuing Global Integration

Michael directed the team's attention towards global integration, "Conversely, global integration involves leveraging our resources, capabilities, and networks to create a unified and cohesive global strategy. It's about standardizing processes, sharing best practices, and fostering collaboration across borders to achieve economies of scale and scope."

David, the eager young developer, interjected, "How do we pursue global integration?"

"We embrace diversity," Michael affirmed, "By recognizing the unique strengths and perspectives of each region, while also fostering a sense of unity and shared purpose that transcends geographical boundaries. It's about harnessing the collective power of our global team to drive innovation and excellence."

Navigating Cross-Cultural Challenges

Angela steered the conversation towards the challenges of cross-cultural management, "As we expand into new markets and engage with diverse communities, we must navigate the complexities of cross-cultural communication and collaboration. It's about fostering cultural intelligence and empathy, and adapting our approach to suit the cultural context of each region."

David leaned forward, "How do we navigate cross-cultural challenges?"

"We listen," Angela explained, "We listen with an open mind and a willingness to learn from others. We seek to understand the values, norms, and traditions that shape the perspectives of our global counterparts, and we adapt our behavior and communication style accordingly."

Strategic Integration

With the vast expanse of international and global strategies laid before them, Angela and Michael emphasized the importance of strategic integration, "By embracing international expansion and global integration, we position GlobalTech Solutions as a truly global player, capable of competing and thriving in the diverse and dynamic marketplace of the 21st century. It's about seizing the opportunities of globalization while also navigating its complexities with wisdom and humility."

Embarking on the Journey

Armed with a deep understanding of international and global strategies, the team embarked on a journey of global exploration and expansion. They embraced the diversity and dynamism of the global marketplace with courage and curiosity, forging partnerships and alliances that transcended geographical boundaries.

As they navigated the world stage with insight and innovation, the air crackled with anticipation and excitement. With each strategic decision, they propelled GlobalTech Solutions forward, towards a future brimming with promise and possibility.

In the heart of Lusaka, amidst the whirlwind of innovation and the symphony of progress, GlobalTech Solutions stood poised on the brink of global greatness. Armed with a comprehensive understanding of international and global strategies, they were ready to conquer new frontiers and redefine the future of the tech industry on a global scale.

Aligning Strategy with Organizational Goals

The Symphony of Alignment: Orchestrating Success

In the dynamic corridors of GlobalTech Solutions, a sense of purpose permeated the air as the team delved deeper into the realm of strategic formulation, unraveling the intricate dance of aligning strategy with organizational goals. Today, their focus sharpened on orchestrating success, as they navigated the symphony of alignment with precision and harmony. Angela and Michael, the master conductors of GlobalTech Solutions, stood poised to lead their team through this enlightening orchestration.

Angela's voice, resonating with clarity, filled the room as she addressed the team, "Good morning, everyone. Today, we delve into the art of alignment, weaving together the threads of strategy and organizational goals to create a tapestry of success. Let us orchestrate our actions with intention, ensuring that every note we play contributes to the harmonious melody of our organizational vision."

Michael, with a nod of agreement, added, "Indeed. Alignment is the linchpin of strategic success, ensuring that our actions are directed towards the achievement of our overarching goals. Let us proceed with unity of purpose and clarity of vision."

Defining Organizational Goals

Angela began by emphasizing the importance of defining organizational goals, "At the heart of alignment lies the need to clearly articulate our organizational goals and objectives.

It's about setting a clear direction for our organization, outlining the milestones we aim to achieve and the metrics by which we will measure our success."

Linda, the perceptive marketing lead, sought clarification, "How do we define our organizational goals?"

Angela responded, "We engage in strategic planning, involving key stakeholders in the process of setting goals that reflect our collective aspirations and priorities. It's about ensuring that our goals are ambitious yet achievable, inspiring our team to strive for excellence."

Crafting Strategic Initiatives

Michael directed the team's attention towards crafting strategic initiatives, "Once we have defined our organizational goals, we must identify the strategic initiatives required to achieve them. It's about translating our goals into actionable plans and projects that drive our organization forward."

David, the eager young developer, interjected, "How do we craft strategic initiatives?"

"We prioritize," Michael affirmed, "Identifying the initiatives that align most closely with our goals and have the greatest potential to create value for our organization. It's about focusing our resources and efforts on the initiatives that will have the greatest impact on our long-term success."

Aligning Resources and Capabilities

Angela steered the conversation towards aligning resources and capabilities, "With our strategic initiatives in place, we must ensure that our resources and capabilities are aligned to support their execution. It's about optimizing our human, financial, and technological resources to maximize our effectiveness and efficiency."

David leaned forward, "How do we align our resources and capabilities?"

"We invest strategically," Angela explained, "Allocating resources to areas that are critical to the success of our strategic initiatives and divesting from those that no longer align with our goals. It's about ensuring that we have the right people, with the right skills, in the right roles to drive our strategy forward."

Monitoring and Adjusting

With alignment as their guiding principle, Angela and Michael emphasized the importance of continuous monitoring and adjustment, "By regularly assessing our progress against our goals, we can identify any misalignments or obstacles and make adjustments as needed. It's about remaining agile and responsive to changes in the external environment and the evolving needs of our organization."

Embarking on the Journey

Armed with a deep understanding of alignment, the team embarked on a journey of strategic orchestration and harmonization. They aligned their actions with their organizational goals, ensuring that every decision and initiative contributed to the realization of their overarching vision.

As they navigated the symphony of alignment with precision and harmony, the air crackled with anticipation and excitement. With each strategic decision, they propelled GlobalTech Solutions forward, towards a future brimming with promise and possibility.

In the heart of Lusaka, amidst the whirlwind of innovation and the symphony of progress, GlobalTech Solutions stood poised on the brink of greatness. Armed with a comprehensive understanding of alignment, they were ready to orchestrate their success and redefine the future of the tech industry with clarity, purpose, and unity of vision.

6

Chapter 6: Strategic Implementation: Turning Plans into Action

Importance of Strategic Implementation

From Vision to Reality: Breathing Life into Strategy

In the pulsating heart of GlobalTech Solutions, a fervent energy filled the room as the team gathered to embark on a new chapter in their strategic journey: implementation. Today, their focus honed on the pivotal role of turning plans into action, as they prepared to breathe life into their strategic vision with determination and resolve. Angela and Michael, the stalwart captains of GlobalTech Solutions, stood ready to lead their team through this transformative voyage.

Angela's voice, infused with conviction, resonated as she addressed the team, "Good morning, everyone. Today, we stand at the precipice of transformation, poised to bridge the gap between vision and reality through strategic implementation. Let us embark on this journey with unwavering commitment and a shared sense of purpose."

Michael, with a nod of agreement, added, "Indeed. Strategic implementation is the crucible where plans are forged into action, where dreams take flight and aspirations become achievements. Let us proceed with diligence and determination, knowing that every step we take brings us closer to our ultimate destination."

Unveiling the Importance of Implementation

Angela began by illuminating the importance of strategic implementation, "At the heart of our strategic journey lies the crucial task of turning our plans into action. Strategic implementation is the engine that drives organizational progress, transforming abstract concepts into tangible results."

Linda, the perceptive marketing lead, sought clarification, "Why is strategic implementation so important?"

Angela responded, "Strategic implementation is the linchpin of success. It's about translating our strategic vision into concrete initiatives and activities that propel our organization forward. Without effective implementation, even the most well-crafted strategies remain mere aspirations, unrealized and unfulfilled."

Executing with Precision

Michael directed the team's attention towards execution, "Execution is the cornerstone of strategic implementation. It's about aligning resources, mobilizing teams, and executing plans with precision and agility. It's about turning intentions into actions and actions into outcomes."

David, the eager young developer, interjected, "How do we ensure effective execution?"

"We focus on accountability," Michael affirmed, "Assigning clear roles and responsibilities, setting measurable targets, and holding ourselves and each other accountable for results. It's about fostering a culture of ownership and accountability that drives performance and delivers results."

Overcoming Implementation Challenges

Angela steered the conversation towards overcoming implementation challenges, "While strategic implementation is essential, it is not without its challenges. From resistance to change to resource constraints, we may encounter obstacles along the way. It's about identifying these challenges and proactively addressing them to ensure smooth execution."

David leaned forward, "How do we overcome implementation challenges?"

"We collaborate," Angela explained, "We leverage the collective expertise and insights of our team, seeking input and feedback to overcome obstacles and find innovative solutions. It's about harnessing the power of collaboration to surmount challenges and drive progress."

Celebrating Milestones

With the importance of implementation unveiled, Angela and Michael emphasized the importance of celebrating milestones, "As we embark on this journey of strategic implementation, let us not forget to celebrate our achievements along the way. Each milestone reached is a testament to our collective effort and commitment, a stepping stone on the path to our ultimate success."

Embarking on the Journey

Armed with a deep understanding of the importance of implementation, the team embarked on a transformative journey of turning plans into action. They approached strategic implementation with diligence and determination, knowing that each step they took brought them closer to their strategic vision.

As they navigated the path from vision to reality with unwavering resolve, the air crackled with anticipation and excitement. With each milestone achieved, they drew closer to their ultimate destination, propelled by the power of strategic implementation.

In the heart of Lusaka, amidst the whirlwind of innovation and the symphony of progress, GlobalTech Solutions stood poised on the brink of greatness. Armed with a comprehensive understanding of strategic implementation, they were ready to turn their aspirations into achievements and redefine the future of the tech industry with determination, resilience, and unwavering commitment.

Resource Allocation and Budgeting

Harnessing Resources: The Engine of Execution

In the bustling corridors of GlobalTech Solutions, a sense of purpose permeated the air as the team delved deeper into the realm of strategic implementation, unraveling the intricacies of resource allocation and budgeting. Today, their focus shifted towards harnessing the engine of execution, as they prepared to allocate resources and budget effectively to bring their strategic vision to life. Angela and Michael, the seasoned architects of GlobalTech Solutions, stood ready to guide their team through this vital phase of implementation.

Angela's voice, infused with determination, resonated as she addressed the team, "Good morning, everyone. Today, we embark on a journey of resource allocation and budgeting, where every decision we make has the power to shape the course of our strategic implementation. Let us wield our resources wisely and strategically, ensuring that we allocate them in a manner that maximizes our impact and accelerates our progress."

Michael, with a nod of agreement, added, "Indeed. Resource allocation and budgeting are the bedrock of effective execution, enabling us to translate our strategic vision into tangible actions and outcomes. Let us proceed with clarity of purpose and a keen understanding of the value of every resource at our disposal."

Optimizing Resource Allocation

Angela began by shedding light on the importance of resource allocation, "At the heart of strategic implementation lies the task of allocating resources in a manner that aligns with our strategic priorities and maximizes our organizational effectiveness. It's about ensuring that we have the right people, with the right skills, in the right roles, and that we allocate financial, technological, and other resources in a manner that supports our strategic initiatives."

Linda, the perceptive marketing lead, sought clarification, "How do we optimize resource allocation?"

Angela responded, "We prioritize ruthlessly, identifying the initiatives and projects that align most closely with our strategic goals and allocating resources accordingly. It's about making strategic trade-offs and focusing our resources where they will have the greatest impact."

Budgeting for Success

Michael directed the team's attention towards budgeting, "Conversely, budgeting is the process of allocating financial resources to support our strategic initiatives and activities. It's about setting realistic financial targets, allocating funds to different departments and projects, and ensuring that we have the necessary resources to execute our plans effectively."

David, the eager young developer, interjected, "How do we budget for success?"

"We budget strategically," Michael affirmed, "Setting aside funds for strategic priorities and investments that drive long-term growth and sustainability. It's about balancing short-term needs with long-term objectives and ensuring that we allocate resources in a manner that supports our strategic vision."

Monitoring and Adjusting

Angela steered the conversation towards monitoring and adjusting, "Once we have allocated resources and set budgets, we must monitor our progress closely and make adjustments as needed. It's about staying agile and responsive to changes in the external environment and the evolving needs of our organization, reallocating resources as priorities shift and new opportunities emerge."

David leaned forward, "How do we monitor and adjust?"

"We track performance," Angela explained, "Regularly assessing our progress against our strategic goals and financial targets, and making adjustments as needed to stay on course. It's about fostering a culture of continuous improvement and adaptability that enables us to navigate the complexities of strategic implementation with agility and resilience."

Strategic Integration

With the importance of resource allocation and budgeting unveiled, Angela and Michael emphasized the importance of strategic integration, "By aligning our resource allocation and budgeting processes with our strategic priorities, we ensure that every resource we allocate contributes to the realization of our strategic vision. It's about weaving together the threads of strategy and execution to create a tapestry of success."

Embarking on the Journey

Armed with a deep understanding of resource allocation and budgeting, the team embarked on a journey of effective execution and organizational effectiveness. They approached resource allocation and budgeting with diligence and foresight, knowing that every decision they made would impact the success of their strategic initiatives.

As they navigated the complexities of implementation with precision and agility, the air crackled with anticipation and excitement. With each resource allocated and budget set, they drew closer to their strategic goals, propelled by the power of effective resource management and strategic alignment.

In the heart of Lusaka, amidst the whirlwind of innovation and the symphony of progress, GlobalTech Solutions stood poised on the brink of greatness. Armed with a comprehensive understanding of resource allocation and budgeting, they were ready to harness the engine of execution and redefine the future of the tech industry with clarity, purpose, and unwavering commitment.

Organizational Structure and Design

Building the Foundation: The Architecture of Execution

In the vibrant hub of GlobalTech Solutions, a palpable sense of anticipation filled the room as the team delved deeper into the realm of strategic implementation, exploring the nuances of organizational structure and design. Today, their focus shifted towards building the foundation of execution, as they prepared to sculpt the organizational architecture that would bring their strategic vision to life. Angela and Michael, the visionary architects of GlobalTech Solutions, stood ready to guide their team through this transformative journey.

Angela's voice, infused with determination, resonated as she addressed the team, "Good morning, everyone. Today, we embark on a journey of organizational structure and design, where every decision we make has the power to shape the landscape of our strategic implementation. Let us build our organizational architecture with intention and foresight, ensuring that it supports and enables the execution of our strategic vision."

Michael, with a nod of agreement, added, "Indeed. Organizational structure and design are the scaffolding upon which execution is built, providing the framework that enables our team to work together effectively towards our common goals. Let us proceed with clarity of purpose and a commitment to designing an organization that fosters collaboration, innovation, and excellence."

Crafting the Organizational Structure

Angela began by shedding light on the importance of organizational structure, "At the heart of strategic implementation lies the task of crafting an organizational structure that aligns with our strategic priorities and facilitates effective execution. It's about defining roles, responsibilities, and reporting relationships in a manner that supports our strategic initiatives and enables seamless coordination and communication across the organization."

Linda, the perceptive marketing lead, sought clarification, "How do we craft the organizational structure?"

Angela responded, "We start with our strategic goals and initiatives, identifying the key functions and departments that are critical to their success. We then design a structure that allocates resources and responsibilities in a manner that optimizes collaboration, innovation, and efficiency."

Designing for Agility and Adaptability

Michael directed the team's attention towards organizational design, "Conversely, organizational design is the process of aligning our structure with our strategic goals and adapting it to the changing needs of our organization and the external environment. It's about designing an organization that is agile, adaptable, and responsive to changes in the market and the industry."

David, the eager young developer, interjected, "How do we design for agility and adaptability?"

"We foster flexibility," Michael affirmed, "Designing our organization in a manner that enables us to quickly respond to changes in customer preferences, technological advancements, and competitive pressures. It's about breaking down silos, empowering teams to make decisions autonomously, and fostering a culture of experimentation and innovation."

Cultivating a Culture of Collaboration

Angela steered the conversation towards fostering collaboration, "While organizational structure and design provide the framework for execution, it is our culture that ultimately determines our ability to work together effectively towards our common goals. It's about cultivating a culture of collaboration, communication, and teamwork that enables us to leverage the diverse talents and perspectives of our team to drive innovation and excellence."

David leaned forward, "How do we cultivate a culture of collaboration?"

"We lead by example," Angela explained, "Modeling the behaviors and values that we want to see reflected in our organization. We encourage open communication, celebrate diversity, and empower our team members to contribute their unique talents and insights towards our shared goals. It's about creating an environment where every voice is heard, and every contribution is valued."

Strategic Integration

With the importance of organizational structure and design unveiled, Angela and Michael emphasized the importance of strategic integration, "By crafting an organizational structure and design that aligns with our strategic priorities and fosters a culture of collaboration and innovation, we create the foundation for effective execution. It's about building an organization that is agile, adaptable, and resilient, capable of navigating the complexities of the business landscape with confidence and creativity."

Embarking on the Journey

Armed with a deep understanding of organizational structure and design, the team embarked on a journey of building the foundation of execution. They approached organizational structure and design with intention and foresight, knowing that the decisions they made would shape the landscape of their strategic implementation.

As they sculpted the organizational architecture with clarity and purpose, the air crackled with anticipation and excitement. With each decision they made, they drew closer to their strategic goals, propelled by the power of effective organizational design and strategic alignment.

In the heart of Lusaka, amidst the whirlwind of innovation and the symphony of progress, GlobalTech Solutions stood poised on the brink of greatness. Armed with a comprehensive understanding of organizational structure and design, they were ready to build an organization that fostered collaboration, innovation, and excellence, and redefine the future of the tech industry with determination, resilience, and unwavering commitment.

Leadership and Strategic Change Management

Guiding the Journey: Navigating Change with Purpose

In the dynamic corridors of GlobalTech Solutions, a sense of anticipation filled the air as the team delved deeper into the realm of strategic implementation, exploring the crucial role of leadership and strategic change management. Today, their focus shifted towards guiding the journey, as they prepared to navigate the winds of change with purpose and resilience. Angela and Michael, the steadfast leaders of GlobalTech Solutions, stood ready to steer their team through this transformative voyage.

Angela's voice, infused with determination, resonated as she addressed the team, "Good morning, everyone. Today, we embark on a journey of leadership and strategic change management, where our ability to navigate change with purpose and resilience will determine our success. Let us lead with courage and conviction, inspiring our team to embrace change as an opportunity for growth and innovation."

Michael, with a nod of agreement, added, "Indeed. Leadership and strategic change management are the cornerstones of effective implementation, enabling us to overcome obstacles, inspire confidence, and mobilize our team towards our common goals. Let us proceed with clarity of vision and a commitment to leading by example."

Inspiring Visionary Leadership

Angela began by shedding light on the importance of visionary leadership, "At the heart of strategic implementation lies the need for visionary leadership, leaders who can inspire and motivate their team to embrace change and pursue excellence. It's about painting a compelling vision of the future, one that ignites passion and commitment among our team members and rallies them towards a common purpose."

Linda, the perceptive marketing lead, sought clarification, "How do we inspire visionary leadership?"

Angela responded, "We lead with authenticity and integrity, demonstrating a clear commitment to our vision and values through our words and actions. We empower our team members to contribute their unique talents and perspectives towards our shared goals, fostering a culture of innovation, collaboration, and accountability."

Managing Strategic Change

Michael directed the team's attention towards strategic change management, "Conversely, strategic change management is the process of planning, implementing, and managing change within our organization to achieve our strategic objectives. It's about anticipating resistance, mitigating risks, and ensuring that our team members are equipped with the tools and resources they need to navigate change effectively."

David, the eager young developer, interjected, "How do we manage strategic change?"

"We communicate," Michael affirmed, "We communicate openly and transparently with our team members, keeping them informed about the reasons for change, the expected impact, and their role in the process. We provide them with the support and resources they need to adapt to change, and we celebrate their successes along the way."

Fostering a Culture of Innovation

Angela steered the conversation towards fostering a culture of innovation, "While leadership and strategic change management provide the foundation for effective implementation, it is our culture that ultimately determines our ability to adapt and thrive in the face of change. It's about fostering a culture of innovation, agility, and continuous improvement that empowers our team members to challenge the status quo and embrace new ideas and opportunities."

David leaned forward, "How do we foster a culture of innovation?"

"We encourage experimentation," Angela explained, "We create an environment where our team members feel empowered to take risks, experiment with new ideas, and learn from failure. We celebrate creativity and innovation, recognizing and rewarding those who dare to think differently and push the boundaries of what is possible."

Strategic Integration

With the importance of leadership and strategic change management unveiled, Angela and Michael emphasized the importance of strategic integration, "By inspiring visionary leadership, managing strategic change effectively, and fostering a culture of innovation, we create the conditions for successful implementation. It's about leading with courage and conviction, navigating change with purpose and resilience, and empowering our team to achieve greatness."

Embarking on the Journey

Armed with a deep understanding of leadership and strategic change management, the team embarked on a journey of transformation and growth. They approached leadership with courage and conviction, embracing change as an opportunity for innovation and progress.

As they navigated the winds of change with purpose and resilience, the air crackled with anticipation and excitement. With each decision they made, they drew closer to their strategic goals, propelled by the power of visionary leadership and strategic change management.

In the heart of Lusaka, amidst the whirlwind of innovation and the symphony of progress, GlobalTech Solutions stood poised on the brink of greatness. Armed with a comprehensive understanding of leadership and strategic change management, they were ready to guide their team through the transformative journey ahead, leading with courage, conviction, and unwavering commitment.

Communication and Stakeholder Engagement

Building Bridges: The Power of Connection

In the bustling corridors of GlobalTech Solutions, a sense of anticipation filled the air as the team delved deeper into the realm of strategic implementation, exploring the critical role of communication and stakeholder engagement. Today, their focus shifted towards building bridges, as they prepared to harness the power of connection to drive their strategic initiatives forward. Angela and Michael, the steadfast leaders of GlobalTech Solutions, stood ready to guide their team through this transformative phase of implementation.

Angela's voice, infused with determination, resonated as she addressed the team, "Good morning, everyone. Today, we embark on a journey of communication and stakeholder engagement, where our ability to connect with others and build meaningful relationships will determine our success. Let us communicate with clarity and empathy, forging partnerships and alliances that propel our strategic initiatives forward."

Michael, with a nod of agreement, added, "Indeed. Communication and stakeholder engagement are the lifeblood of effective implementation, enabling us to build trust, foster collaboration, and mobilize support for our strategic goals. Let us proceed with openness and transparency, recognizing the power of connection to drive positive change."

Fostering Open Communication

Angela began by shedding light on the importance of open communication, "At the heart of strategic implementation lies the need for open and transparent communication, both internally within our organization and externally with our stakeholders. It's about sharing information, ideas, and feedback openly and honestly, creating a culture of trust and collaboration that enables us to work together towards our common goals."

Linda, the perceptive marketing lead, sought clarification,

"How do we foster open communication?"

Angela responded, "We lead by example, communicating with our team members in a manner that is clear, respectful, and empathetic. We create channels and platforms for communication that enable our team members to share their thoughts, ideas, and concerns freely, and we actively listen to their feedback and incorporate it into our decision-making process."

Engaging Stakeholders

Michael directed the team's attention towards stakeholder engagement, "Conversely, stakeholder engagement is the process of building relationships and partnerships with individuals and groups who have a vested interest in our organization and its success. It's about understanding their needs, concerns, and expectations, and working collaboratively with them to achieve mutually beneficial outcomes."

David, the eager young developer, interjected, "How do we engage stakeholders?"

"We involve them," Michael affirmed, "We involve our stakeholders in the strategic planning and decision-making process, seeking their input and feedback on matters that affect them. We keep them informed about our progress and achievements, and we seek opportunities to collaborate with them on initiatives that align with their interests and objectives."

Building Trust and Credibility

Angela steered the conversation towards building trust and credibility, "While communication and stakeholder engagement provide the foundation for effective implementation, it is trust and credibility that ultimately determine the success of our efforts. It's about building trust with our stakeholders through our actions and decisions, demonstrating integrity, reliability, and a genuine commitment to their interests and concerns."

David leaned forward, "How do we build trust and credibility?"

"We deliver results," Angela explained, "We deliver on our promises and commitments, consistently striving for excellence and exceeding the expectations of our stakeholders. We demonstrate integrity and transparency in our actions, admitting mistakes when necessary and taking responsibility for our decisions. It's about building a reputation for reliability and accountability that inspires confidence and trust."

Strategic Integration

With the importance of communication and stakeholder engagement unveiled, Angela and Michael emphasized the importance of strategic integration, "By fostering open communication, engaging stakeholders effectively, and building trust and credibility, we create the conditions for successful implementation. It's about building bridges, forging connections, and mobilizing support for our strategic initiatives."

Embarking on the Journey

Armed with a deep understanding of communication and stakeholder engagement, the team embarked on a journey of connection and collaboration. They approached communication with clarity and empathy, recognizing the power of open dialogue to build trust and foster collaboration.

As they engaged stakeholders with openness and transparency, the air crackled with anticipation and excitement. With each connection they forged, they drew closer to their strategic goals, propelled by the power of connection and collaboration.

In the heart of Lusaka, amidst the whirlwind of innovation and the symphony of progress, GlobalTech Solutions stood poised on the brink of greatness. Armed with a comprehensive understanding of communication and stakeholder engagement, they were ready to build bridges, forge connections, and redefine the future of the tech industry with determination, resilience, and unwavering commitment.

Monitoring and Adjusting Implementation Plans

Navigating the Course: Charting a Path to Success

In the bustling headquarters of GlobalTech Solutions, a sense of purpose filled the room as the team delved deeper into the realm of strategic implementation, exploring the vital role of monitoring and adjusting implementation plans. Today, their focus shifted towards navigating the course, as they prepared to chart a path to success through vigilant monitoring and agile adjustment. Angela and Michael, the stalwart captains of GlobalTech Solutions, stood ready to guide their team through this pivotal phase of implementation.

Angela's voice, infused with determination, resonated as she addressed the team, "Good morning, everyone. Today, we embark on a journey of monitoring and adjusting implementation plans, where our ability to navigate the course with vigilance and adaptability will determine our success. Let us chart a path to success through rigorous monitoring, insightful analysis, and agile adjustment."

Michael, with a nod of agreement, added, "Indeed. Monitoring and adjusting implementation plans are the compass and rudder of effective execution, enabling us to stay on course and navigate the complexities of implementation with confidence and agility. Let us proceed with clarity of vision and a commitment to continuous improvement."

Vigilant Monitoring

Angela began by shedding light on the importance of vigilant monitoring, "At the heart of strategic implementation lies the need for vigilant monitoring, the continuous tracking of our progress against our strategic goals and milestones. It's about collecting data, analyzing performance metrics, and identifying areas where we are excelling and where we need to improve."

Linda, the perceptive marketing lead, sought clarification, "How do we monitor implementation plans?"

Angela responded, "We establish key performance indicators (KPIs) that align with our strategic goals and initiatives, allowing us to measure our progress objectively. We leverage technology and analytics to track our performance in real-time, enabling us to identify trends and patterns and make data-driven decisions."

Agile Adjustment

Michael directed the team's attention towards agile adjustment, "Conversely, agile adjustment is the process of making timely and informed changes to our implementation plans based on our monitoring and analysis. It's about being responsive to changes in the external environment and the evolving needs of our organization, and adapting our plans accordingly to stay on course."

David, the eager young developer, interjected, "How do we adjust implementation plans?"

"We iterate," Michael affirmed, "We iterate on our plans based on the insights we gather from our monitoring and analysis, making incremental changes and improvements to optimize our performance. We remain flexible and open-minded, willing to pivot our strategies and tactics as needed to achieve our strategic goals."

Continuous Improvement

Angela steered the conversation towards continuous improvement, "While monitoring and adjusting implementation plans provide the framework for effective execution, it is our commitment to continuous improvement that ultimately determines our success. It's about fostering a culture of learning, innovation, and adaptability that enables us to stay ahead of the curve and drive sustainable growth."

David leaned forward, "How do we foster continuous

improvement?"

"We reflect," Angela explained, "We reflect on our successes and failures, extracting lessons learned and best practices that we can apply to future initiatives. We seek feedback from our team members and stakeholders, soliciting their input on ways we can improve our processes and practices. It's about embracing a growth mindset and a relentless pursuit of excellence."

Strategic Integration

With the importance of monitoring and adjusting implementation plans unveiled, Angela and Michael emphasized the importance of strategic integration, "By vigilantly monitoring our progress and agilely adjusting our plans, we create the conditions for successful implementation. It's about navigating the course with vigilance and adaptability, and continuously improving our performance to achieve our strategic goals."

Embarking on the Journey

Armed with a deep understanding of monitoring and adjusting implementation plans, the team embarked on a journey of continuous improvement and growth. They approached monitoring with diligence and analysis, recognizing the power of data-driven decision-making to drive success.

As they adjusted their plans with agility and flexibility, the air crackled with anticipation and excitement. With each adjustment they made, they drew closer to their strategic goals, propelled by the power of continuous improvement and strategic alignment.

In the heart of Lusaka, amidst the whirlwind of innovation and the symphony of progress, GlobalTech Solutions stood poised on the brink of greatness. Armed with a comprehensive understanding of monitoring and adjusting implementation plans, they were ready to chart a path to success with determination, resilience, and unwavering commitment.

7

Chapter 7: Strategic Control and Evaluation

The Role of Strategic Control

Steering the Ship: Navigating Towards Success

In the heart of GlobalTech Solutions, a solemn air hung as the team delved into the realm of strategic control and evaluation, exploring the vital role it played in steering their ship towards success. Today, their focus was on understanding the role of strategic control, the compass that would guide them through the turbulent waters of implementation. Angela and Michael, the seasoned captains of GlobalTech Solutions, stood ready to chart their course through this crucial chapter.

Angela's voice, laced with determination, resonated as she addressed the team, "Good morning, everyone. Today, we embark on a journey into the realm of strategic control and evaluation, where our ability to steer the ship with precision and foresight will determine our success. Let us navigate with clarity of purpose and a commitment to achieving our strategic goals."

Michael, with a nod of agreement, added, "Indeed. Strategic control is the compass that guides our journey, enabling us to monitor our progress, identify deviations from our course, and make timely adjustments to stay on track. Let us proceed with vigilance and determination, knowing that our success depends on our ability to navigate the complexities of implementation with skill and insight."

Understanding Strategic Control

Angela began by shedding light on the role of strategic control, "At the heart of strategic management lies the need for strategic control, the process of monitoring our progress against our strategic goals and taking corrective action when necessary. It's about ensuring that we stay on course and achieve the outcomes we set out to accomplish."

Linda, the perceptive marketing lead, sought clarification, "How does strategic control work?"

Angela responded, "Strategic control works by establishing standards and benchmarks against which we can measure our performance. We collect data, analyze trends, and compare our actual performance to our desired outcomes. If we identify deviations from our course, we take corrective action to realign our efforts and stay on track."

Maintaining Alignment

Michael directed the team's attention towards maintaining alignment, "Conversely, strategic control is also about ensuring that our actions remain aligned with our strategic goals and objectives. It's about evaluating the effectiveness of our strategies and initiatives and adjusting them as needed to achieve our desired outcomes."

David, the eager young developer, interjected, "How do we maintain alignment?"

"We communicate," Michael affirmed, "We communicate our strategic goals and objectives clearly and consistently throughout the organization, ensuring that every team member understands their role in achieving them. We provide feedback and guidance to ensure that our actions remain aligned with our strategic priorities, and we celebrate our successes along the way."

Adapting to Change

Angela steered the conversation towards adapting to change, "While strategic control provides the framework for monitoring our progress, it's also about being agile and adaptable in the face of change. It's about recognizing when circumstances evolve and being willing to adjust our strategies and plans accordingly to stay ahead of the curve."

David leaned forward, "How do we adapt to change?"

"We remain flexible," Angela explained, "We remain open-minded and receptive to new ideas and opportunities, willing to pivot our strategies and tactics as needed to respond to changes in the market and the industry. We leverage our insights and expertise to anticipate trends and capitalize on emerging opportunities, staying one step ahead of the competition."

Strategic Integration

With the importance of strategic control unveiled, Angela and Michael emphasized the importance of strategic integration, "By understanding the role of strategic control, we create the conditions for successful implementation. It's about steering the ship with precision and foresight, navigating the complexities of implementation with skill and insight."

Embarking on the Journey

Armed with a deep understanding of strategic control, the team embarked on a journey of achievement and excellence. They approached strategic control with vigilance and determination, knowing that their success depended on their ability to navigate the complexities of implementation with skill and insight.

As they charted their course towards success, the air crackled with anticipation and excitement. With each decision they made, they drew closer to their strategic goals, propelled by the power of strategic control and strategic alignment.

In the heart of Lusaka, amidst the whirlwind of innovation and the symphony of progress, GlobalTech Solutions stood poised on the brink of greatness. Armed with a comprehensive understanding of strategic control, they were ready to steer the ship towards success with determination, resilience, and unwavering commitment.

Types of Strategic Control: Premise, Implementation, Strategic Surveillance, Special Alert

Navigating the Instruments: Guiding the Ship through the Storm

In the command center of GlobalTech Solutions, a solemn atmosphere prevailed as the team delved deeper into the realm of strategic control and evaluation, exploring the various instruments that would guide their ship through the storm of implementation. Today, their focus was on understanding the different types of strategic control, the navigational tools that would help them steer their course with precision and agility. Angela and Michael, the seasoned navigators of GlobalTech Solutions, stood ready to lead their crew through this critical phase of their journey.

Angela's voice, brimming with determination, resonated as she addressed the team, "Good morning, everyone. Today, we continue our exploration into the realm of strategic control and evaluation, delving into the various types of strategic control that will guide our journey. Let us familiarize ourselves with these instruments, equipping ourselves with the knowledge we need to navigate the complexities of implementation with confidence and resilience."

Michael, with a nod of agreement, added, "Indeed. Understanding the different types of strategic control is essential for effective navigation, as each type serves a specific purpose in monitoring our progress and ensuring that we stay on course. Let us proceed with clarity of purpose and a commitment to leveraging these instruments to achieve our strategic goals."

Premise Control: Setting the Foundation

Angela began by shedding light on premise control, "At the heart of strategic control lies premise control, the process of monitoring the underlying assumptions and conditions upon which our strategic plans are based. It's about ensuring that our plans remain grounded in reality and that our assumptions about the future are accurate and reliable."

Linda, the perceptive marketing lead, sought clarification, "How does premise control work?"

Angela responded, "Premise control works by evaluating the validity of our assumptions and testing them against the reality of the market and the industry. It's about collecting data, conducting market research, and analyzing trends to ensure that our strategic plans are based on sound principles and informed insights."

Implementation Control: Monitoring Progress

Michael directed the team's attention towards implementation control, "Conversely, implementation control is the process of monitoring our progress in executing our strategic plans and initiatives. It's about tracking our performance against our predetermined goals and milestones and identifying deviations from our course."

David, the eager young developer, interjected, "How do we monitor implementation?"

"We track," Michael affirmed, "We track our progress using key performance indicators (KPIs) and other metrics that align with our strategic objectives. We compare our actual performance to our planned targets and take corrective action when necessary to ensure that we stay on track."

Strategic Surveillance: Anticipating Changes

Angela steered the conversation towards strategic surveillance, "While implementation control focuses on monitoring our progress, strategic surveillance is about scanning the external environment for changes and trends that could impact our strategic plans. It's about being proactive and anticipating shifts in the market and the industry before they occur."

David leaned forward, "How do we conduct strategic surveillance?"

"We scan," Angela explained, "We scan the horizon for emerging trends, technologies, and competitors that could affect our business. We gather intelligence from various sources, such as market research, industry reports, and competitor analysis, and use this information to inform our strategic decisions and plans."

Special Alert Control: Responding to Crises

Michael concluded with special alert control, "Finally, special alert control is the process of responding to crises and unexpected events that threaten to derail our strategic plans. It's about being prepared to act swiftly and decisively in the face of adversity, minimizing the impact of disruptions and restoring normalcy as quickly as possible."

Strategic Integration

With the understanding of the different types of strategic control unveiled, Angela and Michael emphasized the importance of strategic integration, "By leveraging premise control, implementation control, strategic surveillance, and special alert control, we create a comprehensive framework for monitoring our progress and ensuring that we stay on course. Let us navigate the complexities of implementation with skill and foresight, leveraging these instruments to guide our ship through the storm."

Embarking on the Journey

Armed with a deep understanding of the various types of strategic control, the team embarked on a journey of vigilance and agility. They approached strategic control with clarity and determination, knowing that their success depended on their ability to navigate the complexities of implementation with skill and foresight.

As they leveraged premise control, implementation control, strategic surveillance, and special alert control to guide their journey, the air crackled with anticipation and determination. With each instrument they wielded, they drew closer to their strategic goals, propelled by the power of strategic control and strategic alignment.

In the heart of Lusaka, amidst the tumultuous seas of innovation and competition, GlobalTech Solutions stood poised on the brink of greatness. Armed with a comprehensive understanding of strategic control, they were ready to navigate their ship through the storm of implementation with confidence, resilience, and unwavering determination.

Performance Measurement Systems

Gauging the Wind: Measuring Performance for Success

In the strategic command center of GlobalTech Solutions, the air was filled with the hum of focused determination as the team delved deeper into the realm of strategic control and evaluation. Their journey now led them to understand the crucial role of performance measurement systems, the instruments that would allow them to gauge the wind and adjust their sails for success. Angela and Michael, the seasoned navigators at the helm, prepared to guide their team through this critical phase.

Angela's voice, infused with determination, resonated as she addressed the team, "Good morning, everyone. Today, we continue our journey into the realm of strategic control and evaluation, focusing on the vital role of performance measurement systems. These systems will serve as our barometers, providing us with the data and insights we need to measure our progress and make informed decisions."

Michael, with a nod of agreement, added, "Indeed. Performance measurement systems are essential tools in our strategic toolkit, enabling us to track our performance, identify areas for improvement, and ensure that we remain aligned with our strategic goals. Let us proceed with precision and clarity, leveraging these systems to navigate our course effectively."

Establishing Performance Metrics

Angela began by shedding light on the importance of establishing performance metrics, "At the heart of performance measurement lies the need to establish clear and relevant metrics that align with our strategic goals and objectives. These metrics will serve as our benchmarks, allowing us to measure our progress and evaluate our performance."

Linda, the perceptive marketing lead, sought clarification, "How do we establish effective performance metrics?"

Angela responded, "We start by identifying the key drivers of our success and the outcomes we want to achieve. We then translate these drivers and outcomes into specific, measurable, achievable, relevant, and time-bound (SMART) metrics that provide a clear and objective basis for evaluating our performance."

Collecting and Analyzing Data

Michael directed the team's attention towards the process of collecting and analyzing data, "Conversely, once we have established our performance metrics, we need to collect and analyze the data that will inform our evaluation. This involves gathering data from various sources and using analytical tools and techniques to interpret the information."

David, the eager young developer, interjected, "How do we ensure the accuracy of our data?"

"We validate," Michael affirmed, "We validate our data by cross-referencing multiple sources and using reliable data collection methods. We also implement data quality controls to ensure that the information we use for analysis is accurate, consistent, and reliable."

Visualizing Performance

Angela steered the conversation towards visualizing performance, "While collecting and analyzing data is crucial, it's also important to visualize our performance in a way that is clear and actionable. This involves using dashboards, scorecards, and other visual tools to present our data in an accessible and meaningful format."

David leaned forward, "How do we create effective performance visualizations?"

"We design," Angela explained, "We design our visualizations to highlight key insights and trends, using charts, graphs, and other visual elements to make the data easy to understand. We also ensure that our visualizations are tailored to the needs of our audience, providing them with the information they need to make informed decisions."

Feedback and Continuous Improvement

Michael emphasized the importance of feedback and continuous improvement, "Performance measurement systems are not just about tracking our progress; they're also about using the insights we gain to drive continuous improvement. This involves seeking feedback, identifying areas for improvement, and making the necessary adjustments to enhance our performance."

Linda inquired, "How do we incorporate feedback into our performance measurement systems?"

"We engage," Michael replied, "We engage with our team

members and stakeholders, seeking their input and feedback on our performance and the effectiveness of our strategies. We use this feedback to identify areas for improvement and to make informed adjustments to our plans and initiatives."

Strategic Integration

With the understanding of performance measurement systems unveiled, Angela and Michael emphasized the importance of strategic integration, "By establishing effective performance metrics, collecting and analyzing data, visualizing our performance, and incorporating feedback, we create a comprehensive framework for evaluating our progress and driving continuous improvement. Let us leverage these systems to navigate our course with precision and clarity."

Embarking on the Journey

Armed with a deep understanding of performance measurement systems, the team embarked on a journey of evaluation and improvement. They approached performance measurement with rigor and determination, knowing that their success depended on their ability to measure their progress and make informed decisions.

As they leveraged performance metrics, data analysis, and visualizations to guide their journey, the air crackled with anticipation and focus. With each insight they gained, they drew closer to their strategic goals, propelled by the power of performance measurement and strategic alignment.

In the heart of Lusaka, amidst the dynamic landscape of innovation and competition, GlobalTech Solutions stood poised on the brink of greatness. Armed with a comprehensive understanding of performance measurement systems, they were ready to gauge the wind and adjust their sails for success with precision, resilience, and unwavering determination.

Balanced Scorecard Approach

Balancing the Compass: A Holistic View of Success

In the heart of GlobalTech Solutions, the strategic command center was abuzz with focused energy as the team delved into the intricacies of the balanced scorecard approach. This approach, promising a comprehensive view of their strategic journey, would serve as a multifaceted compass guiding them towards balanced success. Angela and Michael, the seasoned navigators, prepared to lead their team through this crucial exploration.

Angela's voice, resonating with determination, addressed the team, "Good morning, everyone. Today, we delve into the balanced scorecard approach, a holistic tool that will provide us with a multidimensional view of our strategic performance. Let us embrace this approach to balance our focus across various critical aspects of our business and navigate towards success with clarity and precision."

Michael, nodding in agreement, added, "Indeed. The balanced scorecard approach allows us to integrate our strategic objectives with measurable outcomes across different perspectives. This balance ensures that we are not overly focused on any single aspect of our business but are progressing holistically. Let us proceed with a commitment to leveraging this tool for comprehensive strategic management."

The Four Perspectives

Angela began by explaining the core of the balanced scorecard approach, "At the heart of the balanced scorecard approach are four perspectives that provide a balanced view of our organizational performance: Financial, Customer, Internal Processes, and Learning and Growth. Each perspective offers unique insights and contributes to our overall success."

Linda, the perceptive marketing lead, sought clarification, "How do these perspectives work together?"

Angela responded, "Each perspective aligns with specific strategic objectives and performance metrics. The financial perspective focuses on profitability and value creation, the customer perspective on customer satisfaction and market share, the internal processes perspective on operational efficiency, and the learning and growth perspective on innovation and employee development. Together, they ensure we have a holistic view of our performance."

Financial Perspective

Michael directed the team's attention to the financial perspective, "The financial perspective measures our ability to create value for our shareholders. It includes metrics such as revenue growth, profitability, and return on investment. By focusing on financial performance, we ensure that our strategic initiatives translate into financial success."

David, the eager young developer, interjected, "How do we balance financial goals with other objectives?"

"We integrate," Michael affirmed, "We integrate financial goals with our broader strategic objectives, ensuring that our pursuit of financial success does not compromise our focus on customer satisfaction, operational excellence, and innovation. Financial metrics provide us with a clear picture of our value creation."

Customer Perspective

Angela steered the conversation towards the customer perspective, "The customer perspective measures our ability to meet and exceed customer expectations. It includes metrics such as customer satisfaction, loyalty, and market share. By focusing on the customer perspective, we ensure that we are delivering value and building strong relationships with our customers."

David leaned forward, "How do we measure customer satisfaction?"

"We listen," Angela explained, "We listen to our customers through surveys, feedback, and engagement. We analyze customer data to understand their needs and preferences, and we use this information to improve our products and services, ensuring that we are meeting their expectations and building loyalty."

Internal Processes Perspective

Michael emphasized the importance of the internal processes perspective, "The internal processes perspective measures our operational efficiency and effectiveness. It includes metrics such as process improvement, cycle time, and quality control. By focusing on internal processes, we ensure that we are operating efficiently and delivering high-quality products and services."

Linda inquired, "How do we identify areas for improvement in our internal processes?"

"We analyze," Michael replied, "We analyze our processes through data collection, performance metrics, and benchmarking. We identify bottlenecks, inefficiencies, and areas for improvement, and we implement process improvements to enhance our operational performance and quality."

Learning and Growth Perspective

Angela concluded with the learning and growth perspective, "The learning and growth perspective measures our ability to innovate and develop our employees. It includes metrics such as employee training, skill development, and innovation. By focusing on learning and growth, we ensure that we are building a culture of continuous improvement and innovation."

David asked, "How do we foster a culture of learning and growth?"

"We invest," Angela explained, "We invest in our employees through training, development programs, and opportunities for growth. We encourage innovation and creativity, providing our team with the resources and support they need to develop new ideas and solutions. This perspective ensures that we are building a sustainable future."

Strategic Integration

With the understanding of the balanced scorecard approach unveiled, Angela and Michael emphasized the importance of strategic integration, "By leveraging the balanced scorecard approach, we create a comprehensive framework for measuring our performance across multiple perspectives. This balance ensures that we are progressing holistically and achieving our strategic goals."

Embarking on the Journey

Armed with a deep understanding of the balanced scorecard approach, the team embarked on a journey of balanced success. They approached strategic control with a holistic view, knowing that their success depended on their ability to measure and manage performance across multiple dimensions.

As they integrated the financial, customer, internal processes, and learning and growth perspectives into their strategic management, the air crackled with anticipation and focus. With each balanced decision they made, they drew closer to their strategic goals, propelled by the power of the balanced scorecard and strategic alignment.

In the heart of Lusaka, amidst the dynamic landscape of innovation and competition, GlobalTech Solutions stood poised on the brink of greatness. Armed with a comprehensive understanding of the balanced scorecard approach, they were ready to navigate their journey towards balanced success with precision, resilience, and unwavering determination.

Continuous Improvement and Feedback Loops

The Echo of Progress: Embracing Continuous Improvement and Feedback Loops

In the strategic command center of GlobalTech Solutions, the atmosphere was one of focused anticipation. The team was delving into the heart of strategic control and evaluation, exploring the concept of continuous improvement and the critical role of feedback loops in refining their strategic initiatives. Angela and Michael, the seasoned navigators, stood ready to guide their team through this vital phase of their journey.

Angela's voice, filled with determination, resonated as she addressed the team, "Good morning, everyone. Today, we explore the concept of continuous improvement and the importance of feedback loops. These principles are essential for ensuring that our strategic initiatives remain dynamic, responsive, and effective in an ever-changing environment."

Michael, nodding in agreement, added, "Indeed. Continuous improvement and feedback loops allow us to adapt and refine our strategies based on real-time insights and feedback. This process is crucial for maintaining our competitive edge and achieving sustained success. Let us proceed with a commitment to embracing these principles in our strategic management."

The Concept of Continuous Improvement

Angela began by explaining the concept of continuous improvement, "Continuous improvement is the ongoing effort to enhance our processes, products, and services. It's about making incremental changes and improvements that, over time, lead to significant advancements in our performance and outcomes."

Linda, the perceptive marketing lead, sought clarification, "How do we implement continuous improvement in our organization?"

Angela responded, "We implement continuous improvement by fostering a culture of innovation and excellence. This involves encouraging our team members to identify areas for improvement, experimenting with new ideas, and learning from our experiences. It's about creating an environment where continuous improvement is an integral part of our daily operations."

Establishing Feedback Loops

Michael directed the team's attention to the importance of feedback loops, "Feedback loops are the mechanisms that allow us to collect, analyze, and act on feedback from various sources. They provide us with the information we need to make informed decisions and drive continuous improvement."

David, the eager young developer, interjected, "How do we establish effective feedback loops?"

"We listen," Michael affirmed, "We listen to feedback from our customers, employees, and stakeholders. We use surveys, interviews, and other feedback mechanisms to gather insights and data. We then analyze this information to identify trends, issues, and opportunities for improvement."

Acting on Feedback

Angela steered the conversation towards the process of acting on feedback, "Collecting feedback is only the first step. We must also act on the feedback we receive, implementing changes and improvements based on the insights we gain. This involves prioritizing actions, allocating resources, and ensuring that we follow through on our commitments."

David leaned forward, "How do we prioritize actions based on feedback?"

"We evaluate," Angela explained, "We evaluate the feedback based on its impact, feasibility, and alignment with our strategic goals. We prioritize actions that offer the greatest potential for improvement and allocate resources to ensure that these actions are effectively implemented."

Monitoring and Reviewing Progress

Michael emphasized the importance of monitoring and reviewing progress, "Continuous improvement is an ongoing process, and it's important to monitor our progress and review the outcomes of our actions. This involves tracking key performance indicators (KPIs), conducting regular reviews, and making adjustments as needed."

Linda inquired, "How do we ensure that our monitoring and review processes are effective?"

"We assess," Michael replied, "We assess our monitoring

and review processes by setting clear objectives, using reliable data, and engaging our team members in the review process. We also ensure that our reviews are regular and systematic, providing us with the insights we need to make informed adjustments."

Creating a Culture of Continuous Improvement

Angela concluded by emphasizing the importance of creating a culture of continuous improvement, "To truly embrace continuous improvement, we must create a culture that values and supports this principle. This involves fostering an environment of trust, collaboration, and innovation, where team members feel empowered to contribute to our ongoing success."

David asked, "How do we foster such a culture?"

"We nurture," Angela explained, "We nurture a culture of continuous improvement by recognizing and rewarding contributions, providing opportunities for learning and development, and encouraging open communication and collaboration. This culture ensures that continuous improvement becomes an integral part of our organizational DNA."

Strategic Integration

With the understanding of continuous improvement and feedback loops unveiled, Angela and Michael emphasized the importance of strategic integration, "By embracing continuous improvement and establishing effective feedback loops, we create a dynamic framework for refining our strategies and achieving sustained success. Let us leverage these principles to navigate our journey with agility and resilience."

Embarking on the Journey

Armed with a deep understanding of continuous improvement and feedback loops, the team embarked on a journey of dynamic refinement. They approached strategic control with a commitment to ongoing improvement, knowing that their success depended on their ability to adapt and evolve.

As they integrated continuous improvement and feedback loops into their strategic management, the air crackled with anticipation and focus. With each feedback loop they established and each improvement they implemented, they drew closer to their strategic goals, propelled by the power of dynamic refinement and strategic alignment.

In the heart of Lusaka, amidst the dynamic landscape of innovation and competition, GlobalTech Solutions stood poised on the brink of greatness. Armed with a comprehensive understanding of continuous improvement and feedback loops, they were ready to navigate their journey towards sustained success with precision, resilience, and unwavering determination.

Corrective Action and Strategy Adjustment

Course Corrections: The Art of Strategic Adaptation

In the bustling strategic command center of GlobalTech Solutions, a palpable sense of purpose filled the room. The team was delving into the final subpoint of their exploration of strategic control and evaluation: the critical process of taking corrective action and adjusting strategies. Angela and Michael, the seasoned leaders guiding this strategic voyage, prepared to impart the knowledge essential for making timely and effective adjustments to their plans.

Angela's voice, clear and resolute, set the tone for the discussion, "Good morning, everyone. Today, we focus on the art of strategic adaptation, specifically the processes of corrective action and strategy adjustment. These practices are crucial for ensuring that our strategies remain relevant and effective in a dynamic environment."

Michael, nodding in agreement, added, "Indeed. The ability to take corrective action and adjust our strategies is what enables us to stay on course and achieve our objectives, even in the face of unforeseen challenges and changes. Let us embrace this process with a commitment to agility and resilience."

Identifying the Need for Corrective Action

Angela began by explaining the importance of identifying the need for corrective action, "The first step in taking corrective action is recognizing when it's necessary. This involves monitoring our performance metrics and key performance indicators (KPIs) to identify any deviations from our strategic goals."

Linda, the perceptive marketing lead, sought clarification, "How do we determine when corrective action is needed?"

Angela responded, "We look for significant deviations from our expected performance. If our KPIs indicate that we're not meeting our targets or if we identify trends that suggest we're veering off course, it's a clear signal that corrective action is needed. This proactive approach allows us to address issues before they escalate."

Analyzing the Root Causes

Michael directed the team's attention to the process of analyzing the root causes, "Once we've identified the need for corrective action, the next step is to analyze the root causes of the deviations. This involves digging deeper into the data to understand why we're not meeting our targets and identifying the underlying issues."

David, the eager young developer, interjected, "How do we conduct a root cause analysis?"

"We investigate," Michael affirmed, "We investigate by using techniques such as the '5 Whys' method, fishbone diagrams, and data analysis. These tools help us to systematically explore the factors contributing to the deviations and identify the root causes. Understanding these causes is essential for developing effective corrective actions."

Developing Corrective Actions

Angela steered the conversation towards the development of corrective actions, "After identifying the root causes, we need to develop corrective actions to address them. This involves creating targeted interventions that address the specific issues and prevent them from recurring."

David leaned forward, "How do we ensure that our corrective actions are effective?"

"We design," Angela explained, "We design our corrective actions based on a thorough understanding of the root causes. This involves developing specific, actionable steps that address the issues directly. We also ensure that our corrective actions are realistic, feasible, and aligned with our overall strategic goals."

Implementing Corrective Actions

Michael emphasized the importance of implementing corrective actions, "Developing corrective actions is only part of the process; we must also implement them effectively. This involves allocating the necessary resources, assigning responsibilities, and ensuring that the actions are carried out as planned."

Linda inquired, "How do we ensure successful implementation?"

"We execute," Michael replied, "We execute by creating a detailed implementation plan, setting clear timelines, and monitoring the progress of the corrective actions. Effective communication and coordination are also crucial to ensure that everyone involved understands their roles and responsibilities."

Adjusting Strategies

Angela concluded by emphasizing the need for strategy adjustment, "In addition to taking corrective action, we must also be prepared to adjust our overall strategies when necessary. This involves revisiting our strategic plans, reassessing our goals, and making adjustments to ensure that we remain on track."

David asked, "How do we approach strategy adjustment?"

"We adapt," Angela explained, "We adapt by regularly reviewing our strategic plans and being open to making changes based on new information and insights. This requires a flexible mindset and a willingness to pivot when needed. Adjusting our strategies ensures that we can respond effectively to changing conditions and continue to move towards our goals."

Strategic Integration

With the understanding of corrective action and strategy adjustment unveiled, Angela and Michael emphasized the importance of strategic integration, "By effectively identifying the need for corrective action, analyzing root causes, developing and implementing corrective actions, and adjusting our strategies, we create a robust framework for maintaining our strategic alignment and achieving our objectives."

Embarking on the Journey

Armed with a deep understanding of corrective action and strategy adjustment, the team embarked on a journey of strategic adaptation. They approached strategic control with a commitment to agility and resilience, knowing that their success depended on their ability to make timely and effective adjustments.

As they integrated corrective actions and strategy adjustments into their strategic management, the air crackled with anticipation and focus. With each adjustment they made and each corrective action they implemented, they drew closer to their strategic goals, propelled by the power of dynamic refinement and strategic alignment.

In the heart of Lusaka, amidst the dynamic landscape of innovation and competition, GlobalTech Solutions stood poised on the brink of greatness. Armed with a comprehensive understanding of corrective action and strategy adjustment, they were ready to navigate their journey towards sustained success with precision, resilience, and unwavering determination.

8

Chapter 8: Corporate Governance and Ethics in Strategic Management

Role of Corporate Governance in Strategy

Guardians of Integrity: The Pillars of Corporate Governance

In the sleek, glass-walled boardroom of GlobalTech Solutions, the morning sun cast a warm glow, illuminating the serious faces around the table. Today's agenda was a crucial one—understanding the role of corporate governance in strategic management. Angela and Michael, the seasoned leaders guiding the company's strategic journey, were ready to impart the wisdom of governance to their attentive team.

Angela's voice, calm yet authoritative, set the stage, "Good morning, everyone. Today, we delve into the cornerstone of our strategic management process—corporate governance. Effective corporate governance is not just about compliance; it is about ensuring that our strategic decisions are made with integrity, transparency, and accountability."

Michael, nodding in agreement, added, "Indeed. Corporate governance provides the framework within which our strategies are developed and executed. It ensures that our decisions are made in the best interests of all our stakeholders, fostering trust and sustainable success. Let's explore how this framework guides our strategic management."

The Foundation of Corporate Governance

Angela began by explaining the foundation of corporate governance, "Corporate governance encompasses the systems, processes, and practices that ensure our company is managed effectively and ethically. It involves a set of relationships between the company's management, its board of directors, its shareholders, and other stakeholders."

Linda, the perceptive marketing lead, sought clarification, "How does corporate governance influence our strategy?"

Angela responded, "Corporate governance influences our strategy by providing a structured framework for decision-making. It ensures that our strategies are aligned with our ethical values, regulatory requirements, and the long-term interests of our stakeholders. This alignment is crucial for sustainable success."

The Role of the Board of Directors

Michael directed the team's attention to the role of the board of directors, "The board of directors plays a central role in corporate governance. They are responsible for overseeing the company's strategic direction, ensuring that our strategies are sound and aligned with our governance principles."

David, the eager young developer, interjected, "What specific responsibilities does the board have in strategic management?"

"The board," Michael affirmed, "The board is responsible for setting the company's strategic vision, approving major strategic initiatives, and monitoring the implementation of these strategies. They provide oversight and guidance to ensure that our strategies are ethical, viable, and aligned with our long-term goals."

Accountability and Transparency

Angela steered the conversation towards the principles of accountability and transparency, "Accountability and transparency are key principles of corporate governance. They ensure that our strategic decisions are made openly and that we are accountable to our stakeholders for our actions and outcomes."

David leaned forward, "How do we ensure transparency in our strategic management?"

"We disclose," Angela explained, "We ensure transparency by providing clear, accurate, and timely information about our strategic plans and performance to our stakeholders. This involves regular reporting, open communication, and engaging with our stakeholders to build trust and confidence in our strategic direction."

Ethical Decision-Making

Michael emphasized the importance of ethical decision-making, "Ethical decision-making is at the heart of corporate governance. It ensures that our strategies are not only effective but also align with our core values and ethical standards."

Linda inquired, "How do we incorporate ethics into our strategic decisions?"

"We integrate," Michael replied, "We integrate ethics into our strategic decisions by embedding our core values into our strategic planning process. This involves considering the ethical implications of our decisions, promoting a culture of integrity, and ensuring that our actions reflect our commitment to ethical conduct."

Risk Management and Compliance

Angela concluded by highlighting the importance of risk management and compliance, "Effective corporate governance also involves robust risk management and compliance frameworks. These frameworks help us identify, assess, and mitigate risks associated with our strategies, ensuring that we comply with relevant laws and regulations."

David asked, "How do we implement effective risk management and compliance?"

"We assess and monitor," Angela explained, "We implement effective risk management by regularly assessing potential risks to our strategies and developing mitigation plans. Compliance involves staying up-to-date with regulatory requirements and ensuring that our practices adhere to these standards. This proactive approach protects our company and supports our strategic goals."

Strategic Integration

With the understanding of corporate governance unveiled, Angela and Michael emphasized the importance of strategic integration, "By embracing corporate governance principles, we create a framework for ethical, accountable, and transparent strategic management. This framework ensures that our strategies are aligned with our values and long-term interests."

Embarking on the Journey

Armed with a deep understanding of corporate governance, the team embarked on a journey of integrity and accountability. They approached strategic management with a commitment to ethical decision-making, knowing that their success depended on their ability to uphold these principles.

As they integrated corporate governance into their strategic management, the air crackled with anticipation and focus. With each ethical decision they made and each transparent action they took, they drew closer to their strategic goals, propelled by the power of integrity and strategic alignment.

In the heart of Lusaka, amidst the dynamic landscape of innovation and competition, GlobalTech Solutions stood poised on the brink of greatness. Armed with a comprehensive understanding of corporate governance, they were ready to navigate their journey towards sustained success with precision, resilience, and unwavering determination.

Ethical Considerations in Strategic Decisions

Navigating the Ethical Landscape: Guiding Principles for Strategic Decisions

In the sleek, sunlit boardroom of GlobalTech Solutions, the team gathered with a sense of gravitas. Today's discussion was crucial—integrating ethical considerations into strategic decisions. Angela and Michael, the stalwart leaders, stood ready to guide their team through the nuanced landscape of ethics in strategic management.

Angela's voice, steady and earnest, began the session, "Good morning, everyone. Today, we address a fundamental aspect of our strategic management—ethical considerations. Ethical decision-making is essential not only for our reputation but also for long-term sustainability. Our strategies must be grounded in our core values and ethical principles."

Michael, with a thoughtful nod, added, "Indeed. Ethical considerations guide us in making choices that are not only effective but also just and responsible. Let's delve into how we can ensure our strategic decisions uphold the highest ethical standards."

Defining Ethical Decision-Making

Angela started by defining ethical decision-making, "Ethical decision-making involves evaluating our choices based on moral principles and values. It's about doing what is right, fair, and just, even when it might not be the easiest or most profitable option."

Linda, the perceptive marketing lead, asked, "How do we

ensure our decisions are ethical?"

Angela responded, "We ensure our decisions are ethical by integrating our core values into every step of our strategic planning process. This means considering the impact of our decisions on all stakeholders and making choices that align with our commitment to integrity and responsibility."

Incorporating Stakeholder Interests

Michael highlighted the importance of incorporating stakeholder interests, "Ethical strategic decisions must take into account the interests of all our stakeholders, including employees, customers, suppliers, the community, and shareholders. This holistic approach ensures that our actions are fair and considerate of the broader impact."

David, the eager young developer, interjected, "How do we balance conflicting interests among stakeholders?"

"We balance," Michael affirmed, "We balance by engaging with our stakeholders to understand their perspectives and priorities. This involves open communication, empathy, and sometimes making compromises to achieve a fair outcome that respects the diverse interests involved."

Addressing Ethical Dilemmas

Angela steered the conversation towards addressing ethical dilemmas, "Ethical dilemmas are situations where we must choose between competing values or interests. Navigating these dilemmas requires a clear understanding of our ethical principles and a structured approach to decision-making."

David leaned forward, "What steps do we take when faced

with an ethical dilemma?"

"We analyze," Angela explained, "We analyze the situation by identifying the ethical issues, considering the possible consequences of different actions, and evaluating these actions against our core values. This structured approach helps us to make informed and principled decisions."

Ensuring Transparency and Accountability

Michael emphasized the importance of transparency and accountability, "Ethical decision-making requires transparency and accountability. We must be open about our decision-making processes and accountable for the outcomes of our decisions."

Linda inquired, "How do we ensure transparency in our decisions?"

"We communicate," Michael replied, "We ensure transparency by clearly communicating our decisions and the reasoning behind them to all stakeholders. This openness builds trust and demonstrates our commitment to ethical conduct."

Fostering an Ethical Culture

Angela concluded by highlighting the importance of fostering an ethical culture, "Creating a culture of ethics involves setting a positive example at the leadership level and promoting ethical behavior throughout the organization. This culture ensures that ethical considerations are embedded in our strategic decisions."

David asked, "How do we foster such a culture?"

"We lead," Angela explained, "We foster an ethical culture by leading with integrity, providing ethics training, encouraging open dialogue about ethical issues, and recognizing and rewarding ethical behavior. This culture supports our strategic goals and reinforces our commitment to doing what is right."

Strategic Integration

With the understanding of ethical considerations in strategic decisions unveiled, Angela and Michael emphasized the importance of strategic integration, "By embedding ethical considerations into our strategic decisions, we ensure that our actions reflect our core values and support our long-term success. Let us commit to making ethical decision-making a cornerstone of our strategic management."

Embarking on the Ethical Journey

Armed with a deep understanding of ethical considerations, the team embarked on a journey of principled decision-making. They approached strategic management with a commitment to integrity, knowing that their success depended on their ability to uphold the highest ethical standards.

As they integrated ethical considerations into their strategic decisions, the air crackled with anticipation and focus. With each principled choice they made and each transparent action they took, they drew closer to their strategic goals, propelled by the power of integrity and ethical alignment.

In the heart of Lusaka, amidst the dynamic landscape of innovation and competition, GlobalTech Solutions stood poised on the brink of greatness. Armed with a comprehensive understanding of ethical considerations in strategic decisions, they were ready to navigate their journey towards sustained success with precision, resilience, and unwavering determination.

Corporate Social Responsibility (CSR) and Sustainability

Beyond Profits: Embracing CSR and Sustainability

In the modern boardroom of GlobalTech Solutions, the team gathered once more, their focus now turning to an integral aspect of strategic management—Corporate Social Responsibility (CSR) and sustainability. Angela and Michael, the trusted leaders guiding their strategic journey, were ready to delve into how these principles could shape their corporate strategy.

Angela's voice, filled with conviction, began the session, "Good morning, everyone. Today, we explore Corporate Social Responsibility and sustainability. These concepts are more than just buzzwords; they are fundamental to how we conduct business. By embracing CSR and sustainability, we not only enhance our reputation but also contribute to the well-being of our community and environment."

Michael, with a firm nod, added, "Indeed. CSR and sustainability are about creating long-term value for our stakeholders and ensuring that our business practices support the greater good. Let's explore how these principles can be woven into our strategic framework."

Understanding Corporate Social Responsibility (CSR)

Angela started by defining CSR, "Corporate Social Responsibility involves a company's commitment to manage the social, environmental, and economic effects of its operations responsibly and in line with public expectations. It's about going beyond profit-making to contribute positively to society."

Linda, the perceptive marketing lead, asked, "How does CSR influence our strategic decisions?"

Angela responded, "CSR influences our strategic decisions by ensuring that we consider the broader impact of our actions on society and the environment. This means integrating ethical practices into our business model and striving to make a positive difference in the communities where we operate."

The Role of Sustainability in Strategy

Michael highlighted the importance of sustainability, "Sustainability is about meeting the needs of the present without compromising the ability of future generations to meet their own needs. It involves adopting practices that protect the environment, conserve resources, and promote long-term ecological balance."

David, the eager young developer, interjected, "How do we incorporate sustainability into our strategy?"

"We incorporate," Michael affirmed, "We incorporate sustainability by developing strategies that minimize our environmental footprint, promote resource efficiency, and support sustainable development. This involves investing in green technologies, reducing waste, and supporting renewable energy initiatives."

CSR Initiatives and Programs

Angela steered the conversation towards CSR initiatives, "Implementing effective CSR initiatives involves identifying areas where we can make the most significant impact. This could include community development programs, environmental conservation projects, and initiatives to improve employee well-being."

David leaned forward, "Can you give an example of a successful CSR initiative?"

"We act," Angela explained, "One example could be partnering with local schools to support education through scholarships and infrastructure development. This not only benefits the community but also enhances our corporate image and builds strong local relationships."

Measuring CSR and Sustainability Impact

Michael emphasized the importance of measuring impact, "To ensure the effectiveness of our CSR and sustainability efforts, we need to measure their impact. This involves setting clear objectives, tracking progress, and reporting on outcomes."

Linda inquired, "How do we measure the impact of our CSR initiatives?"

"We measure," Michael replied, "We measure by developing key performance indicators (KPIs) for our CSR and sustainability programs. This could include metrics on carbon footprint reduction, community engagement levels, and employee satisfaction. Regular reporting and feedback help us refine our initiatives and demonstrate our commitment."

Engaging Stakeholders in CSR

Angela concluded by highlighting the importance of stakeholder engagement, "Engaging our stakeholders in our CSR and sustainability efforts ensures that our initiatives are aligned with their needs and expectations. This involves open dialogue, collaboration, and transparency."

David asked, "How do we effectively engage our stakeholders?"

"We engage," Angela explained, "We engage by actively listening to our stakeholders' concerns and involving them in the planning and implementation of our CSR initiatives. This creates a sense of shared purpose and helps us build stronger, more trustful relationships."

Strategic Integration

With the understanding of CSR and sustainability unveiled, Angela and Michael emphasized the importance of strategic integration, "By embedding CSR and sustainability into our strategic framework, we ensure that our business practices are ethical, responsible, and aligned with the broader good. Let us commit to making these principles central to our strategic management."

Embarking on the CSR Journey

Armed with a deep understanding of CSR and sustainability, the team embarked on a journey of responsible corporate citizenship. They approached strategic management with a commitment to ethical practices, knowing that their success depended on their ability to make a positive impact on society and the environment.

As they integrated CSR and sustainability into their strategic decisions, the air crackled with anticipation and focus. With each responsible choice they made and each sustainable action they took, they drew closer to their strategic goals, propelled by the power of integrity and social responsibility.

In the heart of Lusaka, amidst the dynamic landscape of innovation and competition, GlobalTech Solutions stood poised on the brink of greatness. Armed with a comprehensive understanding of CSR and sustainability, they were ready to navigate their journey towards sustained success with precision, resilience, and unwavering determination.

Stakeholder Theory and Management

Harmonizing Interests: Embracing Stakeholder Theory in Strategic Management

In the sophisticated boardroom of GlobalTech Solutions, the team convened once more, their focus now turning to an essential component of strategic management—Stakeholder Theory and Management. Angela and Michael, the experienced leaders, were ready to guide their team through the complexities of managing diverse stakeholder interests.

Angela's voice, clear and insightful, began the session, "Good morning, everyone. Today, we explore Stakeholder Theory and its significance in strategic management. Understanding and managing stakeholder relationships is crucial for our success. By considering the needs and expectations of all our stakeholders, we can create strategies that are more inclusive and sustainable."

Michael, with a contemplative nod, added, "Indeed. Stakeholder Theory emphasizes that our business does not exist in isolation. We are interconnected with various groups that influence and are influenced by our actions. Let's delve into how we can harmonize these interests to achieve our strategic goals."

Understanding Stakeholder Theory

Angela started by explaining Stakeholder Theory, "Stakeholder Theory suggests that companies should consider the interests of all stakeholders, not just shareholders. This includes employees, customers, suppliers, community members, and anyone else affected by our operations."

Linda, the perceptive marketing lead, asked, "How does Stakeholder Theory influence our strategic decisions?"

Angela responded, "Stakeholder Theory influences our strategic decisions by broadening our perspective. We evaluate how our actions impact different groups and strive to balance these interests. This approach fosters trust and cooperation, which are essential for long-term success."

Identifying Key Stakeholders

Michael highlighted the importance of identifying key stakeholders, "To effectively manage stakeholder relationships, we need to identify who our key stakeholders are. This involves mapping out all the groups that affect or are affected by our business activities."

David, the eager young developer, interjected, "How do we

identify our key stakeholders?"

"We map," Michael affirmed, "We map our stakeholders by conducting a thorough analysis of our business environment. This involves listing all possible stakeholders and categorizing them based on their influence and interest in our operations. This helps us prioritize our engagement efforts."

Engaging with Stakeholders

Angela steered the conversation towards engaging with stakeholders, "Engaging with our stakeholders involves active communication and collaboration. It's about understanding their needs, addressing their concerns, and involving them in our decision-making processes."

David leaned forward, "Can you give an example of effective stakeholder engagement?"

"We collaborate," Angela explained, "One example could be forming a community advisory board where local residents and community leaders can voice their concerns and provide input on our projects. This helps us build stronger relationships and ensures that our strategies are aligned with community interests."

Balancing Stakeholder Interests

Michael emphasized the importance of balancing stakeholder interests, "Balancing the diverse interests of our stakeholders can be challenging, but it is essential for creating sustainable strategies. This involves finding common ground and making compromises that benefit the majority."

Linda inquired, "How do we balance conflicting interests

among stakeholders?"

"We negotiate," Michael replied, "We balance interests by facilitating open dialogue and negotiation. We listen to each stakeholder group, understand their priorities, and work towards solutions that address the most critical concerns. This collaborative approach helps us find equitable solutions."

Measuring Stakeholder Satisfaction

Angela highlighted the importance of measuring stakeholder satisfaction, "To ensure our stakeholder management efforts are effective, we need to measure stakeholder satisfaction. This involves gathering feedback and assessing how well we are meeting their needs and expectations."

David asked, "How do we measure stakeholder satisfaction?"

"We survey," Angela explained, "We measure satisfaction by conducting regular surveys and feedback sessions with our stakeholders. This helps us identify areas for improvement and adjust our strategies to better align with their expectations. Transparent reporting on our performance also builds trust."

Strategic Integration

With the understanding of Stakeholder Theory and Management unveiled, Angela and Michael emphasized the importance of strategic integration, "By incorporating Stakeholder Theory into our strategic framework, we ensure that our business decisions are inclusive and consider the broader impact on all our stakeholders. Let us commit to managing our stakeholder relationships with integrity and transparency."

Embarking on the Stakeholder Journey

Armed with a deep understanding of Stakeholder Theory, the team embarked on a journey of inclusive and responsible decision-making. They approached strategic management with a commitment to balancing diverse interests, knowing that their success depended on their ability to harmonize stakeholder relationships.

As they integrated Stakeholder Theory into their strategic decisions, the air crackled with anticipation and focus. With each collaborative choice they made and each inclusive action they took, they drew closer to their strategic goals, propelled by the power of cooperation and mutual respect.

In the heart of Lusaka, amidst the dynamic landscape of innovation and competition, GlobalTech Solutions stood poised on the brink of greatness. Armed with a comprehensive understanding of Stakeholder Theory and Management, they were ready to navigate their journey towards sustained success with precision, resilience, and unwavering determination.

Legal and Regulatory Compliance

Upholding Integrity: Navigating Legal and Regulatory Compliance

In the elegant boardroom of GlobalTech Solutions, the team assembled once more, their attention now turned to a critical aspect of strategic management—Legal and Regulatory Compliance. Angela and Michael, the seasoned leaders, were prepared to guide their team through the intricate landscape of legal obligations and regulatory standards.

Angela's voice, resolute and assured, initiated the discussion, "Good morning, everyone. Today, we delve into the realm of legal and regulatory compliance. Upholding integrity and abiding by the law are non-negotiable principles of our strategic management. By navigating legal requirements effectively, we safeguard our reputation and ensure the sustainability of our business."

Michael, with a firm nod, added, "Indeed. Legal and regulatory compliance is not just about avoiding penalties; it's about conducting business ethically and responsibly. Let's explore how we can integrate compliance into our strategic framework."

Understanding Legal and Regulatory Compliance

Angela began by defining legal and regulatory compliance, "Legal and regulatory compliance involves adhering to laws, regulations, and standards set forth by government authorities and industry bodies. It encompasses a wide range of areas, including labor laws, environmental regulations, data protection, and financial reporting."

Linda, the perceptive marketing lead, inquired, "How

does legal and regulatory compliance impact our strategic decisions?"

Angela responded, "Legal and regulatory compliance influences our strategic decisions by providing a framework within which we must operate. It sets boundaries and standards that guide our actions, ensuring that we conduct business in a lawful and ethical manner."

Navigating Complex Regulations

Michael highlighted the challenge of navigating complex regulations, "The regulatory landscape is constantly evolving and can be overwhelming. However, it's essential that we stay informed about changes in laws and regulations that affect our industry and operations."

David, the eager young developer, interjected, "How do we ensure we're compliant with all relevant regulations?"

"We educate," Michael affirmed, "We ensure compliance by educating ourselves and our team about applicable laws and regulations. This involves regular training, staying updated on changes in legislation, and consulting with legal experts when necessary."

Embedding Compliance into Processes

Angela emphasized the importance of embedding compliance into processes, "To ensure consistent compliance, we need to integrate it into our organizational processes and procedures. This means establishing clear policies, implementing robust controls, and conducting regular audits to monitor adherence."

David leaned forward, "How do we embed compliance into our day-to-day operations?"

"We integrate," Angela explained, "We integrate compliance by incorporating it into our business practices from the ground up. This involves designing systems and workflows that incorporate compliance checks and controls at every stage. By making compliance a priority, we minimize the risk of non-compliance."

Mitigating Legal Risks

Michael underscored the importance of mitigating legal risks, "Identifying and mitigating legal risks is essential for protecting our business from potential liabilities. This requires conducting thorough risk assessments, addressing any compliance gaps, and implementing measures to mitigate identified risks."

Linda inquired, "How do we prioritize which legal risks to address?"

"We assess," Michael replied, "We prioritize legal risks based on their potential impact on our business and the likelihood of occurrence. This involves evaluating the severity of consequences, the probability of occurrence, and any legal precedents or trends in our industry."

Reporting and Transparency

Angela concluded by highlighting the importance of reporting and transparency, "Maintaining transparency and open communication about our compliance efforts is essential for building trust with our stakeholders. This involves disclosing relevant information about our compliance programs, performance, and any incidents or violations."

David asked, "How do we ensure transparency in our compliance reporting?"

"We communicate," Angela explained, "We ensure transparency by providing clear and accurate reporting on our compliance efforts and performance. This may include publishing annual compliance reports, holding regular meetings with stakeholders to discuss compliance matters, and responding promptly to any inquiries or concerns."

Strategic Integration

With the understanding of legal and regulatory compliance unveiled, Angela and Michael emphasized the importance of strategic integration, "By integrating legal and regulatory compliance into our strategic framework, we uphold our commitment to integrity, ethics, and responsible business conduct. Let us remain vigilant in navigating the complex regulatory landscape with diligence and integrity."

Embarking on the Compliance Journey

Armed with a deep understanding of legal and regulatory compliance, the team embarked on a journey of ethical and lawful business practices. They approached strategic management with a commitment to upholding integrity, knowing that their success depended on their ability to navigate legal requirements effectively.

As they integrated compliance into their strategic decisions, the air crackled with diligence and determination. With each compliant choice they made and each transparent action they took, they drew closer to their strategic goals, propelled by the power of ethical conduct and regulatory adherence.

In the heart of Lusaka, amidst the dynamic landscape of innovation and competition, GlobalTech Solutions stood poised on the brink of greatness. Armed with a comprehensive understanding of legal and regulatory compliance, they were ready to navigate their journey towards sustained success with precision, resilience, and unwavering determination.

Building an Ethical Organizational Culture

Cultivating Integrity: Fostering an Ethical Organizational Culture

In the serene boardroom of GlobalTech Solutions, the team reconvened once again, shifting their focus to a pivotal aspect of strategic management—Building an Ethical Organizational Culture. Angela and Michael, the stalwart leaders, were prepared to lead their team through the transformative journey of nurturing integrity and ethical conduct within the organization.

Angela's voice, imbued with conviction and purpose, initiated the discussion, "Good morning, everyone. Today, we embark on a profound exploration of building an ethical organizational culture. At the heart of our strategic management lies the foundation of integrity and ethical conduct. By fostering a culture that prioritizes ethics and values, we cultivate an environment where our team can thrive and our business can prosper sustainably."

Michael, with a firm nod, added, "Indeed. An ethical

organizational culture is not just a lofty ideal; it is the bedrock upon which our success is built. Let us delve into how we can sow the seeds of integrity and nurture a culture that inspires trust, transparency, and accountability."

Defining Ethical Organizational Culture

Angela began by defining ethical organizational culture, "Ethical organizational culture refers to the shared values, beliefs, and behaviors that guide the actions of individuals within an organization. It is characterized by a commitment to honesty, integrity, respect, and accountability in all aspects of business operations."

Linda, the perceptive marketing lead, inquired, "How does ethical organizational culture influence our strategic decisions?"

Angela responded, "Ethical organizational culture shapes our strategic decisions by providing a moral compass that guides our actions. It ensures that our decisions are aligned with our values and principles, even in the face of challenges or temptations."

Leading by Example

Michael highlighted the role of leadership in shaping culture, "Leadership plays a crucial role in fostering an ethical organizational culture. Leaders must lead by example, demonstrating integrity, transparency, and ethical behavior in their actions and decisions."

David, the eager young developer, interjected, "How do we ensure our leaders embody ethical values?"

"We model," Michael affirmed, "We ensure our leaders embody ethical values by providing training and development opportunities that reinforce ethical leadership skills. This includes promoting open communication, ethical decision-making frameworks, and accountability mechanisms."

Creating a Culture of Transparency

Angela emphasized the importance of transparency in culture, "Transparency is a cornerstone of an ethical organizational culture. It fosters trust and accountability by ensuring that information is accessible, communication is open, and decisions are made with integrity."

David leaned forward, "How do we promote transparency in our culture?"

"We communicate," Angela explained, "We promote transparency by establishing clear communication channels, providing regular updates on company performance and initiatives, and encouraging open dialogue between employees and leadership. Transparency builds trust and empowers employees to act with integrity."

Embedding Ethics into Processes

Michael underscored the importance of integrating ethics into processes, "To sustain an ethical organizational culture, we must embed ethics into our day-to-day operations and decision-making processes. This involves establishing ethical guidelines, conducting ethics training, and integrating ethical considerations into performance evaluations."

Linda inquired, "How do we ensure ethics are integrated

into our processes?"

"We integrate," Michael replied, "We ensure ethics are integrated by designing systems and workflows that incorporate ethical checks and controls at every stage. This includes establishing clear policies and procedures, conducting regular ethics audits, and providing channels for reporting ethical concerns."

Fostering Accountability and Responsibility

Angela concluded by highlighting the importance of accountability, "Accountability is essential for maintaining an ethical organizational culture. It ensures that individuals are held responsible for their actions and decisions, fostering a sense of ownership and commitment to ethical conduct."

David asked, "How do we promote accountability in our culture?"

"We hold," Angela explained, "We promote accountability by establishing clear expectations, setting performance goals that align with ethical values, and holding individuals accountable for their actions. This includes recognizing and rewarding ethical behavior and addressing instances of misconduct promptly and fairly."

Strategic Integration

With the understanding of building an ethical organizational culture unveiled, Angela and Michael emphasized the importance of strategic integration, "By embedding ethics into our organizational culture, we create a foundation of integrity and trust that underpins our strategic management. Let us remain steadfast in our commitment to fostering an environment where ethics are valued, practiced, and celebrated."

Embarking on the Ethical Journey

Armed with a deep understanding of ethical organizational culture, the team embarked on a transformative journey of cultivating integrity within the organization. They approached strategic management with a commitment to upholding ethical values, knowing that their success depended on their ability to nurture a culture of trust and accountability.

As they integrated ethics into their organizational practices, the air crackled with purpose and resolve. With each ethical choice they made and each transparent action they took, they drew closer to their strategic goals, propelled by the power of integrity and ethical leadership.

In the heart of Lusaka, amidst the dynamic landscape of innovation and competition, GlobalTech Solutions stood poised on the brink of greatness. Armed with a comprehensive understanding of ethical organizational culture, they were ready to navigate their journey towards sustained success with integrity, resilience, and unwavering determination.

9

Chapter 9: Innovation and Strategic Management

Importance of Innovation in Strategic Management

Igniting Transformation: Unleashing the Power of Innovation

In the vibrant meeting room of GlobalTech Solutions, the atmosphere buzzed with anticipation as the team gathered to explore a crucial aspect of strategic management—Innovation. Angela and Michael, the visionary leaders, were poised to illuminate the significance of innovation in shaping the company's strategic direction.

Angela's voice, filled with enthusiasm and conviction, initiated the discussion, "Good morning, everyone. Today, we embark on an exhilarating exploration of innovation and its pivotal role in strategic management. Innovation is the lifeblood of progress, the catalyst for transformation, and the cornerstone of our success. By embracing innovation, we unlock boundless opportunities to propel our business forward and stay ahead in a rapidly evolving landscape."

Michael, with a spark of inspiration in his eyes, added, "Indeed. Innovation is not just about creating new products or technologies; it's about challenging the status quo, fostering creativity, and driving continuous improvement. Let us delve into how innovation can fuel our strategic journey towards greater heights of success."

Transforming Vision into Reality

Angela began by emphasizing the transformative power of innovation, "Innovation is the engine that drives progress and propels organizations towards their strategic vision. It enables us to challenge conventional thinking, identify new opportunities, and adapt to changing market dynamics."

Linda, the perceptive marketing lead, inquired, "How does innovation influence our strategic decisions?"

Angela responded, "Innovation influences our strategic decisions by inspiring us to think boldly and creatively about the future. It encourages us to explore new business models, develop innovative products and services, and seize emerging opportunities that align with our strategic objectives."

Staying Ahead of the Curve

Michael highlighted the importance of staying ahead in a competitive landscape, "In today's fast-paced world, innovation is not just a choice; it's a necessity for survival. Organizations that fail to innovate risk being left behind by their competitors. Innovation allows us to anticipate market trends, disrupt industries, and maintain a competitive edge."

David, the eager young developer, interjected, "How do we ensure we stay ahead of the curve with our innovation efforts?"

"We anticipate," Michael affirmed, "We stay ahead by fostering a culture of curiosity and experimentation within our organization. This involves encouraging employees to explore new ideas, take calculated risks, and embrace failure as a stepping stone to success. By fostering an environment where innovation thrives, we position ourselves to lead the way in our industry."

Driving Customer Value

Angela emphasized the importance of innovation in delivering value to customers, "Innovation is not just about creating novelty; it's about solving real problems and meeting the evolving needs of our customers. By innovating continuously, we can develop products and services that deliver superior value and enhance customer satisfaction."

Linda inquired, "How do we ensure our innovation efforts are customer-centric?"

"We listen," Angela explained, "We ensure our innovation efforts are customer-centric by actively listening to customer feedback, understanding their pain points, and anticipating their future needs. This customer-centric approach ensures that our innovation initiatives are aligned with market demand and deliver tangible benefits to our customers."

Embracing a Culture of Innovation

Michael concluded by highlighting the importance of fostering a culture of innovation, "At the heart of successful innovation lies a culture that encourages creativity, collaboration, and experimentation. As leaders, it is our responsibility to nurture this culture and empower our team to innovate fearlessly."

David asked, "How do we foster a culture of innovation within our organization?"

"We empower," Michael replied, "We foster a culture of innovation by empowering employees at all levels to contribute ideas, experiment with new approaches, and challenge the status quo. This involves providing resources, recognition, and support for innovative endeavors, and celebrating both successes and failures as valuable learning experiences."

Igniting the Innovation Journey

Armed with a renewed understanding of the importance of innovation in strategic management, the team embarked on a transformative journey of exploration and discovery. They approached strategic decision-making with a fresh perspective, fueled by the conviction that innovation held the key to unlocking their full potential.

As they embraced the spirit of innovation, the air crackled with excitement and possibility. With each bold idea they pursued and each innovative solution they crafted, they propelled themselves closer to their strategic goals, propelled by the boundless potential of innovation to shape their future.

In the heart of Lusaka, amidst the dynamic landscape of

innovation and competition, GlobalTech Solutions stood poised on the brink of greatness. Armed with a comprehensive understanding of the importance of innovation in strategic management, they were ready to navigate their journey towards sustained success with creativity, resilience, and unwavering determination.

Types of Innovation: Product, Process, Business Model

Innovating Across Frontiers: Exploring the Spectrum of Innovation

In the dynamic boardroom of GlobalTech Solutions, the team's enthusiasm soared as they delved deeper into the realm of innovation, exploring its diverse manifestations and implications for strategic management. Angela and Michael, the visionary leaders, were prepared to illuminate the different types of innovation and their strategic significance.

Angela's voice, vibrant with energy and curiosity, initiated the discussion, "Good morning, everyone. Today, we embark on an exhilarating exploration of innovation's multifaceted nature. Innovation is not a monolithic concept but a rich tapestry of creativity and ingenuity that manifests in various forms. By understanding the different types of innovation, we can harness their transformative power to drive our strategic objectives forward."

Michael, with a gleam of anticipation in his eyes, added, "Indeed. Innovation comes in many shapes and sizes, each offering unique opportunities for growth and differentiation. Let us explore the three primary types of innovation—Product, Process, and Business Model—and their implications for our strategic management."

Unleashing Product Innovation

Angela began by highlighting the importance of product innovation, "Product innovation involves the development of new or improved products and services that offer unique features, functionalities, or benefits to customers. It is about creating value by delivering innovative solutions that address unmet needs and exceed customer expectations."

Linda, the perceptive marketing lead, inquired, "How does product innovation contribute to our strategic objectives?"

Angela responded, "Product innovation plays a pivotal role in driving revenue growth, enhancing market competitiveness, and building brand differentiation. By continuously innovating our products and services, we can capture new market segments, retain existing customers, and stay ahead of emerging trends."

Optimizing Process Innovation

Michael highlighted the significance of process innovation, "Process innovation involves reimagining and optimizing the way we do things internally to improve efficiency, reduce costs, and enhance quality. It is about streamlining workflows, adopting new technologies, and implementing best practices to drive operational excellence."

David, the eager young developer, interjected, "How does process innovation impact our strategic performance?"

"We transform," Michael affirmed, "Process innovation enables us to enhance our competitive advantage by increasing productivity, minimizing waste, and accelerating time-to-market. By continuously innovating our processes, we can adapt to changing market conditions, scale our operations efficiently, and deliver value to customers more effectively."

Reinventing Business Model Innovation

Angela emphasized the transformative power of business model innovation, "Business model innovation involves reimagining the way we create, deliver, and capture value in the marketplace. It is about challenging traditional paradigms, exploring new revenue streams, and reshaping industry dynamics to unlock new growth opportunities."

Linda inquired, "How does business model innovation shape our strategic direction?"

"We evolve," Angela explained, "Business model innovation enables us to reinvent our business model to better align with shifting customer preferences, emerging technologies, and evolving market trends. By exploring new business models, such as subscription services, platform-based ecosystems, or value-added partnerships, we can diversify our revenue streams, expand our market reach, and create sustainable competitive advantages."

Harnessing the Power of Innovation

With a deeper understanding of the different types of innovation, Angela and Michael emphasized the importance of strategic integration, "By harnessing the power of product, process, and business model innovation, we can unlock new growth opportunities, drive operational excellence, and shape the future of our organization. Let us remain committed to fostering a culture of innovation that empowers us to continuously push the boundaries of possibility."

Embarking on the Innovation Journey

Armed with a comprehensive understanding of the spectrum of innovation, the team embarked on a transformative journey of exploration and discovery. They approached strategic management with renewed vigor, fueled by the realization that innovation was not just a goal but a mindset—a relentless pursuit of excellence and advancement.

As they embraced the diverse forms of innovation, the air crackled with excitement and possibility. With each product enhancement they devised, each process optimization they implemented, and each business model they reinvented, they propelled themselves closer to their strategic goals, propelled by the transformative power of innovation to shape their destiny.

In the heart of Lusaka, amidst the dynamic landscape of innovation and competition, GlobalTech Solutions stood poised on the brink of greatness. Armed with a comprehensive understanding of the spectrum of innovation, they were ready to navigate their journey towards sustained success with creativity, resilience, and unwavering determination.

Fostering an Innovative Culture

Cultivating Creativity: Nurturing an Innovative Culture

In the bustling conference room of GlobalTech Solutions, anticipation filled the air as the team delved deeper into the discussion on innovation, exploring how to cultivate a culture that fosters creativity and ingenuity. Angela and Michael, the visionary leaders, were ready to unveil the secrets of nurturing an innovative culture within the organization.

Angela's voice, infused with warmth and encouragement, initiated the discussion, "Good morning, everyone. Today, we embark on an inspiring journey to explore the importance of fostering an innovative culture within our organization. Innovation is not just about ideas; it's about creating an environment where creativity flourishes, risks are embraced, and experimentation is encouraged. By cultivating an innovative culture, we can unlock the full potential of our team and drive our strategic initiatives forward."

Michael, with a reassuring smile, added, "Indeed. An innovative culture is the lifeblood of our organization—it fuels our creativity, drives our progress, and propels us towards our strategic goals. Let us delve into how we can foster a culture that celebrates innovation and empowers our team to unleash their full creative potential."

Embracing a Growth Mindset

Angela began by highlighting the importance of a growth mindset, "At the heart of an innovative culture lies a growth mindset—a belief that challenges are opportunities for growth, failures are valuable learning experiences, and success is the result of perseverance and resilience. By cultivating a growth mindset within our organization, we can inspire our team to embrace change, take risks, and pursue excellence."

Linda, the perceptive marketing lead, inquired, "How do we cultivate a growth mindset within our team?"

Angela responded, "We inspire," "We cultivate a growth mindset by celebrating curiosity, embracing experimentation, and encouraging continuous learning and development. This involves providing opportunities for skill-building, fostering a culture of mentorship and feedback, and recognizing and celebrating achievements and milestones along the way."

Creating Psychological Safety

Michael highlighted the importance of psychological safety in fostering innovation, "Psychological safety is essential for creating an environment where individuals feel empowered to express their ideas, take risks, and challenge the status quo without fear of judgment or reprisal. By creating a culture of psychological safety, we can unleash the full creative potential of our team and foster a spirit of collaboration and innovation."

David, the eager young developer, interjected, "How do we establish psychological safety within our team?"

"We trust," Michael affirmed, "We establish psychological safety by building trust and mutual respect among team members, creating open channels of communication, and encouraging constructive feedback and dialogue. This involves fostering an inclusive and supportive environment where every voice is valued and every idea is given the opportunity to flourish."

Encouraging Collaboration and Diversity

Angela emphasized the importance of collaboration and diversity in driving innovation, "Innovation thrives in environments where diverse perspectives are embraced, and collaboration is encouraged. By bringing together individuals from different backgrounds, experiences, and areas of expertise, we can spark creativity, stimulate new ideas, and drive breakthrough innovation."

Linda inquired, "How do we encourage collaboration and diversity within our team?"

"We embrace," Angela explained, "We encourage collaboration and diversity by fostering a culture of inclusivity, respect, and openness to new ideas and perspectives. This involves creating cross-functional teams, organizing brainstorming sessions and innovation workshops, and providing opportunities for employees to share their insights, experiences, and expertise."

Empowering Autonomy and Creativity

Michael concluded by highlighting the importance of autonomy and creativity in fostering innovation, "Innovation flourishes when individuals are empowered to pursue their passions, explore new ideas, and take ownership of their work. By fostering a culture of autonomy and creativity, we can unleash the full creative potential of our team and drive meaningful change and innovation."

David asked, "How do we empower autonomy and creativity within our team?"

"We empower," Michael replied, "We empower autonomy

and creativity by providing individuals with the freedom to experiment, take risks, and pursue their ideas, while providing guidance, support, and resources to help them succeed. This involves fostering a culture of ownership and accountability, where individuals are encouraged to take initiative, think outside the box, and push the boundaries of possibility."

Cultivating an Innovative Culture

With a renewed understanding of the importance of fostering an innovative culture, Angela and Michael emphasized the importance of strategic integration, "By cultivating a culture that celebrates innovation, creativity, and collaboration, we can unlock the full potential of our team and drive our strategic initiatives forward. Let us remain committed to nurturing an environment where innovation thrives, and our team is empowered to unleash their full creative potential."

Embarking on the Innovation Journey

Armed with a renewed sense of purpose and determination, the team embarked on a transformative journey of cultivating creativity and innovation within the organization. They approached strategic management with a fresh perspective, fueled by the realization that innovation was not just a goal but a mindset—a relentless pursuit of excellence and ingenuity.

As they embraced the principles of growth mindset, psychological safety, collaboration, and autonomy, the air crackled with excitement and possibility. With each idea they shared, each risk they took, and each collaboration they forged, they propelled themselves closer to their strategic goals, propelled by the transformative power of innovation to shape their future.

In the heart of Lusaka, amidst the dynamic landscape of innovation and competition, GlobalTech Solutions stood poised on the brink of greatness. Armed with a comprehensive understanding of the importance of fostering an innovative culture, they were ready to navigate their journey towards sustained success with creativity, resilience, and unwavering determination.

R&D and Strategic Alliances

Forging Pathways: R&D and Strategic Alliances in Innovation

In the vibrant hub of GlobalTech Solutions, anticipation filled the room as the team delved deeper into the exploration of innovation, uncovering the strategic significance of research and development (R&D) and strategic alliances in driving forward the company's innovative endeavors. Angela and Michael, the guiding forces, were prepared to illuminate the pathways of R&D and strategic alliances in the realm of innovation.

Angela's voice, resonating with determination and foresight, initiated the discussion, "Good morning, everyone. Today, we venture into the realm of research and development (R&D) and strategic alliances, two pillars that underpin our journey of innovation. R&D fuels our quest for groundbreaking discoveries, while strategic alliances amplify our capabilities and extend our reach. By harnessing the power of R&D and strategic alliances, we can accelerate our innovation efforts and propel our organization towards new horizons of success."

Michael, with a gleam of optimism in his eyes, added, "Indeed. R&D and strategic alliances are not just investments; they are strategic imperatives that drive our innovation agenda forward. Let us explore how these avenues can amplify our innovation capabilities and position us for sustained growth and competitiveness."

Pioneering Research and Development (R&D)

Angela began by highlighting the importance of R&D in driving innovation, "Research and Development (R&D) is the engine that powers our innovation journey, fueling our quest for breakthrough discoveries, technological advancements, and novel solutions to complex challenges. It is about pushing the boundaries of possibility, exploring uncharted territories, and transforming ideas into tangible realities."

Linda, the perceptive marketing lead, inquired, "How does R&D contribute to our strategic objectives?"

Angela responded, "R&D plays a pivotal role in driving our strategic objectives by fostering a culture of experimentation, driving continuous improvement, and fueling our pipeline of innovative products and solutions. By investing in R&D, we can stay ahead of the curve, anticipate market trends, and maintain our position as a market leader in our industry."

Forging Strategic Alliances

Michael highlighted the significance of strategic alliances in amplifying innovation efforts, "Strategic alliances are essential for extending our innovation capabilities, accessing new markets, and leveraging complementary strengths and resources. They enable us to pool our expertise, share risks and rewards, and capitalize on synergies to drive collective growth and competitiveness."

David, the eager young developer, interjected, "How do strategic alliances enhance our innovation efforts?"

"We collaborate," Michael affirmed, "Strategic alliances enhance our innovation efforts by fostering collaboration with external partners, such as industry leaders, research institutions, and startups. By forging strategic partnerships, we can access new technologies, insights, and expertise, accelerate our time-to-market, and expand our market reach."

Empowering Innovation through Collaboration

Angela emphasized the importance of collaboration in driving innovation, "Collaboration is at the heart of successful innovation. By partnering with external stakeholders, we can leverage their expertise, resources, and networks to amplify our innovation capabilities and drive meaningful impact. Strategic alliances enable us to tap into a diverse ecosystem of talent and ideas, fostering a culture of open innovation and collaboration."

Linda inquired, "How do we foster effective collaboration through strategic alliances?"

"We align," Angela explained, "We foster effective collaboration through strategic alliances by aligning our goals, values, and expectations with our partners, establishing clear communication channels, and building trust and mutual respect. This involves identifying partners who share our vision and complement our strengths, negotiating mutually beneficial agreements, and fostering an environment of transparency and accountability."

Driving Innovation through Strategic Integration

Michael concluded by highlighting the importance of strategic integration in driving innovation, "At the heart of successful innovation lies strategic integration—seamlessly integrating R&D efforts and strategic alliances into our overall innovation strategy. By aligning our R&D initiatives with our strategic objectives and leveraging strategic alliances to augment our innovation capabilities, we can maximize our impact and achieve sustainable growth and competitiveness."

Forging Ahead with Innovation

Armed with a deeper understanding of the strategic significance of R&D and strategic alliances in driving innovation, Angela and Michael emphasized the importance of strategic integration, "By harnessing the power of R&D and strategic alliances, we can accelerate our innovation efforts, amplify our impact, and position ourselves for sustained growth and competitiveness. Let us remain committed to forging new pathways of innovation and driving our organization towards new horizons of success."

Embarking on the Innovation Journey

With a renewed sense of purpose and determination, the team embarked on a transformative journey of exploration and discovery, armed with the knowledge that R&D and strategic alliances were not just investments but strategic imperatives that would drive their innovation agenda forward. As they embraced the power of collaboration and strategic integration, the air crackled with excitement and possibility, propelling them towards new frontiers of innovation and growth.

In the heart of Lusaka, amidst the dynamic landscape of innovation and competition, GlobalTech Solutions stood poised on the brink of greatness. Armed with a comprehensive understanding of the strategic significance of R&D and strategic alliances in driving innovation, they were ready to navigate their journey towards sustained success with creativity, resilience, and unwavering determination.

Managing Technological Change

Embracing Tomorrow: Navigating Technological Change

In the dynamic corridors of GlobalTech Solutions, anticipation filled the air as the team delved into the discussion on managing technological change, exploring the strategic implications of embracing innovation and navigating the evolving landscape of technology. Angela and Michael, the guiding lights, were prepared to illuminate the pathways of managing technological change in the context of strategic management.

Angela's voice, filled with conviction and foresight, initiated the discussion, "Good morning, everyone. Today, we embark on an exhilarating exploration of managing technological change—a journey that will shape the future of our organization and redefine our strategic landscape. Technology is not just a tool; it is a catalyst for transformation, a harbinger of progress, and a driver of innovation. By embracing technological change, we can unlock new possibilities, drive strategic growth, and position ourselves as leaders in our industry."

Michael, with a reassuring smile, added, "Indeed. Managing technological change is not just about adopting new technologies; it is about embracing a mindset of agility, adaptability, and foresight. Let us explore how we can navigate the complexities of technological change and harness its transformative power to drive our strategic objectives forward."

Embracing Disruption

Angela began by highlighting the importance of embracing disruption in managing technological change, "In today's fast-paced world, technological change is inevitable. Disruption is not a threat; it is an opportunity—a chance to reimagine our business models, reinvent our processes, and revolutionize our products and services. By embracing disruption, we can stay ahead of the curve, anticipate market trends, and position ourselves as innovators in our industry."

Linda, the perceptive marketing lead, inquired, "How do we embrace disruption and stay ahead in a rapidly changing landscape?"

Angela responded, "We adapt," "We embrace disruption by fostering a culture of adaptability, resilience, and innovation within our organization. This involves staying abreast of emerging technologies, monitoring market trends, and proactively seeking out opportunities for innovation and growth. By embracing change as a constant, we can navigate the complexities of technological change and seize new opportunities for strategic advancement."

Harnessing Emerging Technologies

Michael highlighted the significance of harnessing emerging technologies in driving strategic growth, "Emerging technologies, such as artificial intelligence, blockchain, and the Internet of Things, hold immense potential to transform our business processes, enhance our products and services, and create new avenues for value creation. By harnessing these technologies strategically, we can unlock new sources of competitive advantage, drive operational efficiencies, and deliver superior value to our customers."

David, the eager young developer, interjected, "How do we harness emerging technologies effectively?"

"We innovate," Michael affirmed, "We harness emerging technologies effectively by fostering a culture of innovation and experimentation, investing in R&D, and collaborating with technology partners and startups. This involves identifying use cases for emerging technologies that align with our strategic objectives, piloting new initiatives, and iterating based on feedback and results. By embracing a mindset of continuous learning and improvement, we can leverage emerging technologies to drive strategic growth and differentiation."

Navigating Digital Transformation

Angela emphasized the importance of navigating digital transformation in managing technological change, "Digital transformation is not just about digitizing existing processes; it is about reimagining the way we do business, from the ground up. It is about leveraging digital technologies to create seamless, connected experiences for our customers, optimize our operations, and unlock new revenue streams. By embracing digital transformation, we can position ourselves as leaders in the digital age and drive sustainable growth and competitiveness."

Linda inquired, "How do we navigate digital transformation effectively?"

"We transform," Angela explained, "We navigate digital transformation effectively by adopting a holistic approach that encompasses people, processes, and technology. This involves empowering our employees with digital skills and capabilities, redesigning our business processes to leverage digital technologies, and investing in scalable, flexible IT infrastructure. By aligning our digital transformation initiatives with our strategic objectives and fostering a culture of collaboration and innovation, we can navigate the complexities of technological change and drive meaningful impact."

Forging Ahead with Technological Change

Armed with a deeper understanding of managing technological change, Angela and Michael emphasized the importance of strategic integration, "By embracing disruption, harnessing emerging technologies, and navigating digital transformation, we can unlock new opportunities, drive strategic growth, and position ourselves as leaders in our industry. Let us remain committed to embracing a mindset of agility, adaptability, and foresight as we navigate the complexities of technological change and shape the future of our organization."

Embarking on the Technological Journey

With a renewed sense of purpose and determination, the team embarked on a transformative journey of navigating technological change, armed with the knowledge that disruption was not a threat but an opportunity to innovate and thrive. As they embraced the complexities of technological change, the air crackled with excitement and possibility, propelling them towards new frontiers of innovation and growth.

In the heart of Lusaka, amidst the dynamic landscape of innovation and competition, GlobalTech Solutions stood poised on the brink of greatness. Armed with a comprehensive understanding of managing technological change, they were ready to navigate their journey towards sustained success with creativity, resilience, and unwavering determination.

Case Studies of Innovation-Driven Strategies

Pioneers of Innovation: Real-World Case Studies

In the vibrant corridors of GlobalTech Solutions, the team gathered with anticipation as they delved into real-world case studies of innovation-driven strategies, exploring the transformative power of innovation in driving strategic success. Angela and Michael, the visionary leaders, were prepared to unveil the stories of pioneering organizations that had embraced innovation as a strategic imperative.

Angela's voice, resonating with enthusiasm and inspiration, initiated the discussion, "Good morning, everyone. Today, we embark on an enlightening journey as we explore real-world case studies of innovation-driven strategies—stories of organizations that have defied convention, pushed the boundaries of possibility, and redefined their industries through innovation. By studying these examples, we can glean valuable insights and inspiration to fuel our own innovation journey."

Michael, with a nod of agreement, added, "Indeed. Real-world case studies offer invaluable lessons in innovation and strategic management, showcasing the power of creativity, resilience, and foresight in driving transformative change. Let us delve into these stories and uncover the secrets of their success."

Case Study 1: Apple Inc. - Transforming Industries through Disruptive Innovation

Angela began by highlighting the groundbreaking innovations of Apple Inc., "Apple Inc. is synonymous with innovation, known for revolutionizing industries through disruptive products and technologies. From the iconic iPhone that redefined the smartphone market to the revolutionary iPad that transformed the tablet industry, Apple has consistently pushed the boundaries of innovation, creating products that not only meet customer needs but anticipate them."

Linda, the perceptive marketing lead, interjected, "What sets Apple apart in terms of innovation?"

Angela responded, "Apple's success lies in its relentless pursuit of excellence, its focus on user experience, and its commitment to design and aesthetics. By combining cutting-edge technology with intuitive design and seamless integration, Apple has created a unique ecosystem of products and services that delight customers and set new standards for innovation in the tech industry."

Case Study 2: Tesla, Inc. - Driving Sustainable Innovation in the Automotive Industry

Michael highlighted the transformative innovations of Tesla, Inc., "Tesla, Inc. is leading the charge in sustainable innovation, pioneering electric vehicles, renewable energy solutions, and autonomous driving technology. From the groundbreaking Tesla Model S to the innovative Powerwall energy storage system, Tesla has demonstrated a commitment to sustainability, innovation, and excellence in everything it does."

David, the eager young developer, inquired, "How has Tesla achieved success in such a competitive industry?"

"We innovate," Michael affirmed, "Tesla's success can be attributed to its relentless focus on innovation, its agile approach to product development, and its visionary leadership under Elon Musk. By challenging the status quo, disrupting traditional business models, and embracing a culture of experimentation and risk-taking, Tesla has positioned itself as a leader in the automotive industry and a driving force for change in the world."

Case Study 3: Amazon.com, Inc. - Transforming Retail through Digital Disruption

Angela explored the innovative strategies of Amazon.com, Inc., "Amazon.com, Inc. has redefined the retail landscape through digital disruption, leveraging technology to create seamless, personalized shopping experiences for customers. From its pioneering e-commerce platform to its revolutionary Prime membership program, Amazon has transformed the way people shop, consume media, and access goods and services."

Linda inquired, "What has been Amazon's key to success in driving innovation?"

"Amazon's success lies in its customer-centric approach, its culture of innovation, and its relentless focus on long-term growth," Angela explained. "By prioritizing customer needs, investing in technology and infrastructure, and fostering a culture of experimentation and risk-taking, Amazon has been able to stay ahead of the curve, anticipate market trends, and drive continuous innovation in the retail industry."

Drawing Inspiration from Innovation

As the team delved deeper into the case studies of Apple Inc., Tesla, Inc., and Amazon.com, Inc., they were inspired by the stories of innovation, resilience, and transformation. Each case study offered valuable lessons and insights into the strategic importance of innovation, the power of creativity, and the impact of visionary leadership in driving strategic success.

Armed with newfound inspiration and insights, the team was ready to embark on their own innovation journey, fueled by the belief that with creativity, determination, and strategic foresight, they too could shape the future of their organization and drive meaningful impact in their industry.

In the heart of Lusaka, amidst the dynamic landscape of innovation and competition, GlobalTech Solutions stood poised on the brink of greatness. Armed with real-world case studies of innovation-driven strategies, they were ready to navigate their journey towards sustained success with confidence, courage, and unwavering determination.

10

Chapter 10: Digital Transformation and Strategic Management

Impact of Digital Technologies on Strategy

Unveiling Tomorrow: The Digital Revolution in Strategic Management

In the bustling headquarters of GlobalTech Solutions, anticipation filled the room as the team gathered to explore the profound impact of digital technologies on strategy, unraveling the transformative power of the digital revolution in strategic management. Angela and Michael, the visionary leaders, were poised to unveil the future of strategic management in the digital age.

Angela's voice, infused with excitement and anticipation, initiated the discussion, "Good morning, everyone. Today, we embark on a journey into the heart of the digital revolution—a revolution that is reshaping industries, redefining business models, and revolutionizing the way we think about strategy.

Digital technologies are not just tools; they are enablers of transformation, catalysts for innovation, and drivers of strategic change. By understanding the impact of digital technologies on strategy, we can unlock new pathways to success and navigate the complexities of the digital landscape with confidence and clarity."

Michael, with a nod of agreement, added, "Indeed. The digital revolution has ushered in a new era of strategic management—one characterized by agility, adaptability, and innovation. Let us delve into the impact of digital technologies on strategy and uncover the opportunities and challenges that lie ahead."

Empowering Strategic Agility

Angela began by highlighting the transformative impact of digital technologies on strategic agility, "In today's fast-paced world, strategic agility is more important than ever. Digital technologies empower organizations to sense and respond to market changes in real time, adapt their strategies on the fly, and seize new opportunities as they arise. By embracing digital technologies, we can foster a culture of agility and innovation, enabling us to stay ahead of the curve and drive strategic growth in an ever-evolving landscape."

Linda, the perceptive marketing lead, inquired, "How do digital technologies enhance strategic agility?"

Angela responded, "Digital technologies enhance strategic agility by providing real-time insights into market trends, customer preferences, and competitive dynamics. This enables organizations to make informed decisions, iterate on their strategies, and pivot quickly in response to changing market conditions. By leveraging data analytics, artificial intelligence, and predictive modeling, we can anticipate opportunities and threats, optimize our strategies, and stay one step ahead of the competition."

Unlocking Customer-Centricity

Michael highlighted the role of digital technologies in unlocking customer-centricity in strategic management, "In the digital age, customer expectations are higher than ever. Digital technologies enable organizations to gather rich data about customer behavior, preferences, and needs, allowing them to tailor their products, services, and experiences to meet customer expectations. By embracing digital technologies, we can become more customer-centric in our strategic approach, driving customer loyalty, satisfaction, and advocacy."

David, the eager young developer, inquired, "How do digital technologies enable customer-centricity?"

"We engage," Michael affirmed, "Digital technologies enable customer-centricity by providing insights into customer preferences, behavior, and sentiment across multiple channels. This allows organizations to personalize their interactions with customers, deliver targeted marketing campaigns, and provide seamless omnichannel experiences. By leveraging digital technologies such as customer relationship management (CRM) systems, social media listening tools, and predictive analytics, we can deepen our understanding of our customers and deliver value at every touchpoint."

Fostering Innovation and Experimentation

Angela emphasized the role of digital technologies in fostering innovation and experimentation, "Innovation is the lifeblood of strategic management, driving growth, differentiation, and competitive advantage. Digital technologies provide organizations with the tools and platforms to experiment, iterate, and innovate at scale. By embracing digital technologies, we can create a culture of innovation, where experimentation is encouraged, failure is seen as a learning opportunity, and creativity flourishes."

Linda inquired, "How do digital technologies foster innovation and experimentation?"

"We innovate," Angela explained, "Digital technologies foster innovation and experimentation by providing access to cutting-edge tools, platforms, and technologies that enable rapid prototyping, testing, and iteration. This allows organizations to explore new ideas, products, and business models with minimal risk and investment. By embracing digital technologies such as cloud computing, collaboration tools, and open innovation platforms, we can empower our teams to think creatively, experiment boldly, and drive breakthrough innovation."

Forging Ahead in the Digital Age

As the team delved deeper into the impact of digital technologies on strategy, they were inspired by the possibilities that lay ahead. The digital revolution was not just a challenge; it was an opportunity to reimagine strategic management, redefine business models, and unlock new pathways to success in the digital age.

Armed with newfound insights and inspiration, the team was ready to embrace the digital revolution and navigate their journey towards sustained success with confidence, creativity, and unwavering determination.

In the heart of Lusaka, amidst the dynamic landscape of innovation and competition, GlobalTech Solutions stood poised on the brink of greatness. Armed with a comprehensive understanding of the impact of digital technologies on strategy, they were ready to embrace the future of strategic management in the digital age and shape their destiny in a world of endless possibilities.

Digital Business Models

Reinventing Tomorrow: The Evolution of Digital Business Models

In the bustling headquarters of GlobalTech Solutions, excitement permeated the air as the team gathered to explore the evolution of digital business models, unraveling the intricacies of reinventing strategic approaches in the digital landscape. Angela and Michael, the visionary leaders, were poised to guide their team through the transformative journey of digital business models.

Angela's voice, brimming with anticipation and curiosity, initiated the discussion, "Good morning, everyone. Today, we embark on a journey into the heart of digital business models—a journey that will redefine the way we think about strategy, innovation, and value creation. In the digital age, business models are not just about products and services;

they are about ecosystems, platforms, and experiences. By understanding the evolution of digital business models, we can unlock new pathways to growth and prosperity in the digital economy."

Michael, with a nod of agreement, added, "Indeed. Digital business models are reshaping industries, disrupting traditional value chains, and redefining the rules of competition. Let us delve into the evolution of digital business models and uncover the strategies that will drive success in the digital economy."

From Products to Platforms

Angela began by highlighting the shift from products to platforms in digital business models, "In the digital age, platforms are the new battleground for competition. Traditional business models focused on creating and selling products; however, digital platforms enable organizations to create ecosystems where users can interact, transact, and co-create value. By embracing platform-based business models, organizations can unlock new revenue streams, scale their operations, and foster innovation in ways that were previously unimaginable."

Linda, the perceptive marketing lead, inquired, "How do platforms redefine value creation?"

Angela responded, "Platforms redefine value creation by enabling network effects, where the value of the platform increases as more users join and engage with it. This creates a virtuous cycle of growth, where the platform becomes more valuable to users, attracting more participants and further enhancing its value proposition. By leveraging network effects, organizations can create powerful ecosystems that drive sustainable growth and competitive advantage."

Embracing the Sharing Economy

Michael highlighted the emergence of the sharing economy in digital business models, "The sharing economy has transformed the way we consume goods and services, enabling peer-to-peer transactions, resource sharing, and collaborative consumption. Digital platforms such as Airbnb, Uber, and TaskRabbit have disrupted traditional industries by connecting individuals with underutilized assets to those in need of them. By embracing the sharing economy, organizations can unlock new sources of value, optimize resource utilization, and create more sustainable business models."

David, the eager young developer, inquired, "How do organizations succeed in the sharing economy?"

"We collaborate," Michael affirmed, "Organizations succeed in the sharing economy by building trust, fostering collaboration, and delivering seamless experiences to users. This involves creating platforms that facilitate secure transactions, transparent communication, and frictionless interactions between users. By focusing on building vibrant communities and delivering value to both providers and consumers, organizations can thrive in the sharing economy and unlock new opportunities for growth."

Harnessing Data as a Strategic Asset

Angela emphasized the importance of data as a strategic asset in digital business models, "In the digital economy, data is the new currency. Digital technologies enable organizations to collect, analyze, and leverage vast amounts of data to gain insights into customer behavior, market trends, and competitive dynamics. By harnessing data as a strategic asset, organizations can personalize their offerings, optimize their operations, and drive innovation in ways that were previously impossible."

Linda inquired, "How do organizations leverage data effectively?"

"We innovate," Angela explained, "Organizations leverage data effectively by investing in data analytics capabilities, developing advanced algorithms, and adopting a data-driven decision-making culture. This involves collecting relevant data from multiple sources, analyzing it to extract actionable insights, and using those insights to inform strategic decisions and drive continuous improvement. By embracing data as a strategic asset, organizations can unlock new opportunities, drive innovation, and stay ahead of the competition in the digital age."

Forging Ahead in the Digital Economy

As the team delved deeper into the evolution of digital business models, they were inspired by the possibilities that lay ahead. The digital economy was not just a challenge; it was an opportunity to reinvent strategic approaches, reimagine value creation, and shape the future of their organization in a world of endless possibilities.

Armed with newfound insights and inspiration, the team was ready to embrace the evolution of digital business models and navigate their journey towards sustained success with confidence, creativity, and unwavering determination.

In the heart of Lusaka, amidst the dynamic landscape of innovation and competition, GlobalTech Solutions stood poised on the brink of greatness. Armed with a comprehensive understanding of digital business models, they were ready to embrace the future of strategic management in the digital age and shape their destiny in a world of endless opportunities.

Big Data and Analytics in Strategic Decision-Making

Illuminating Insights: Harnessing Big Data for Strategic Excellence

In the dynamic meeting room of GlobalTech Solutions, a sense of anticipation filled the air as the team gathered to explore the transformative potential of big data and analytics in strategic decision-making. Angela and Michael, the guiding lights of innovation, were ready to unveil the power of data-driven insights in shaping strategic excellence.

Angela's voice, brimming with enthusiasm and conviction, initiated the discussion, "Good morning, everyone. Today, we embark on a journey into the realm of big data and analytics— a journey that will illuminate the path to strategic excellence and redefine the way we make decisions in the digital age. In today's data-driven world, insights are the currency of success, and organizations that harness the power of data will unlock new opportunities for growth, innovation, and competitive advantage."

Michael, with a nod of agreement, added, "Indeed. Big data and analytics have the potential to revolutionize strategic decision-making, enabling organizations to gain deeper insights into market trends, customer behavior, and competitive dynamics. Let us delve into the world of big data and analytics and uncover the strategies that will drive success in the digital economy."

Unlocking Actionable Insights

Angela began by highlighting the transformative power of big data in unlocking actionable insights, "In the digital age, data is abundant, but insights are scarce. Big data and analytics enable organizations to extract meaningful insights from vast amounts of data, empowering them to make informed decisions, anticipate market trends, and seize new opportunities for growth. By harnessing the power of big data, we can transform raw data into actionable insights that drive strategic excellence and business success."

Linda, the perceptive marketing lead, inquired, "How do organizations unlock actionable insights from big data?"

Angela responded, "We analyze," "Organizations unlock actionable insights from big data by leveraging advanced analytics techniques such as data mining, machine learning, and predictive modeling. This involves collecting and aggregating data from diverse sources, processing it to identify patterns and trends, and applying statistical algorithms to generate actionable insights. By leveraging the power of big data analytics, organizations can gain a deeper understanding of their customers, markets, and operations, enabling them to make data-driven decisions that drive strategic success."

Anticipating Market Trends

Michael highlighted the role of big data in anticipating market trends, "In today's fast-paced business environment, staying ahead of the competition requires more than just reacting to market changes; it requires anticipating them. Big data and analytics enable organizations to identify emerging trends, predict future demand, and capitalize on new opportunities before their competitors. By harnessing the power of big data, we can gain a competitive edge in the marketplace and drive strategic growth with confidence and foresight."

David, the eager young developer, inquired, "How do organizations anticipate market trends using big data?"

"We predict," Michael affirmed, "Organizations anticipate market trends using big data by leveraging predictive analytics techniques to forecast future demand, identify emerging customer preferences, and anticipate shifts in market dynamics. This involves analyzing historical data, identifying relevant patterns and correlations, and using statistical models to predict future outcomes. By leveraging the power of predictive analytics, organizations can anticipate market trends, mitigate risks, and capitalize on new opportunities for growth and innovation."

Optimizing Decision-Making

Angela emphasized the role of big data in optimizing decision-making processes, "In the digital age, strategic decisions are only as good as the insights that inform them. Big data and analytics enable organizations to optimize their decision-making processes by providing timely, relevant, and actionable insights that drive strategic alignment and business success. By harnessing the power of big data, we can make faster, smarter, and more informed decisions that drive competitive advantage and drive sustainable growth."

Linda inquired, "How do organizations optimize decision-making using big data?"

"We decide," Angela explained, "Organizations optimize decision-making using big data by integrating data analytics into their decision-making processes, establishing data-driven governance frameworks, and fostering a culture of evidence-based decision-making. This involves aligning data analytics initiatives with strategic objectives, empowering decision-makers with access to timely and relevant data insights, and embedding analytics capabilities into everyday workflows. By leveraging the power of big data to inform decision-making, organizations can drive strategic excellence and achieve their business objectives with greater efficiency and effectiveness."

Forging Ahead with Data-Driven Excellence

As the team delved deeper into the world of big data and analytics, they were inspired by the transformative potential of data-driven insights in shaping strategic excellence. In the digital age, data was not just a resource; it was a strategic asset—a source of competitive advantage, innovation, and growth.

Armed with newfound insights and inspiration, the team was ready to embrace the power of big data and analytics and navigate their journey towards strategic excellence with confidence, creativity, and unwavering determination.

In the heart of Lusaka, amidst the dynamic landscape of innovation and competition, GlobalTech Solutions stood poised on the brink of greatness. Armed with a comprehensive understanding of big data and analytics, they were ready to harness the power of data-driven insights and shape the future of their organization in a world of endless possibilities.

Cybersecurity and Risk Management

Safeguarding Tomorrow: Navigating the Cybersecurity Landscape

In the fortified conference room of GlobalTech Solutions, a sense of vigilance permeated the air as the team gathered to explore the critical importance of cybersecurity and risk management in the digital era. Angela and Michael, the vigilant guardians of innovation, were prepared to navigate the complexities of the cybersecurity landscape and safeguard the future of their organization.

Angela's voice, resolute and commanding, initiated the discussion, "Good morning, everyone. Today, we confront one of the greatest challenges of the digital age—cybersecurity. In an interconnected world where data is the lifeblood of business, protecting our assets, our customers, and our reputation from cyber threats is paramount. By understanding the intricacies of cybersecurity and risk management, we can fortify our defenses, mitigate vulnerabilities, and navigate the digital landscape with confidence and resilience."

Michael, with a stern gaze, added, "Indeed. Cyber threats

are ever-evolving, constantly adapting, and relentlessly targeting organizations of all sizes and industries. Let us delve into the world of cybersecurity and risk management and uncover the strategies that will safeguard our organization from harm."

Securing the Digital Perimeter

Angela began by highlighting the importance of securing the digital perimeter, "In the digital age, the perimeter of our organization extends beyond physical walls to encompass networks, devices, and cloud-based systems. Cybersecurity measures such as firewalls, intrusion detection systems, and access controls are essential for protecting our digital assets from unauthorized access, malicious attacks, and data breaches. By securing the digital perimeter, we can create a strong foundation for our cybersecurity strategy and defend against external threats."

Linda, the perceptive marketing lead, inquired, "How do we ensure the security of our digital perimeter?"

Angela responded, "We fortify," "Securing the digital perimeter requires a multi-layered approach, incorporating technical controls, security protocols, and employee awareness training. This involves implementing robust security measures such as encryption, multi-factor authentication, and regular security audits to identify and address vulnerabilities. By fortifying our digital perimeter, we can create a resilient defense against cyber threats and protect our organization's sensitive data and assets."

Managing Insider Threats

Michael highlighted the importance of managing insider threats, "While external threats pose a significant risk to our organization, insider threats can be just as damaging. Employees, contractors, and partners with access to sensitive information can inadvertently or maliciously compromise our cybersecurity defenses, leading to data leaks, intellectual property theft, and reputational damage. By implementing effective insider threat detection and mitigation measures, we can identify and address potential risks before they escalate into security incidents."

David, the eager young developer, inquired, "How do we manage insider threats effectively?"

"We educate," Michael affirmed, "Managing insider threats requires a combination of technical controls, policy enforcement, and employee education. This involves implementing access controls to limit the exposure of sensitive information, monitoring user activity for suspicious behavior, and providing regular cybersecurity training to employees to raise awareness of potential threats and best practices for safeguarding data. By educating our workforce and fostering a culture of security awareness, we can minimize the risk of insider threats and protect our organization from harm."

Embracing a Culture of Security

Angela emphasized the importance of embracing a culture of security, "In the digital age, cybersecurity is not just a technical challenge; it is a cultural imperative. A strong culture of security empowers employees to take ownership of cybersecurity risks, prioritize security in their day-to-day activities, and report potential security incidents promptly. By fostering a culture of security, we can create a united front against cyber threats and cultivate a resilient organization that is prepared to defend against any challenge."

Linda inquired, "How do we cultivate a culture of security within our organization?"

"We lead," Angela explained, "Cultivating a culture of security requires leadership commitment, employee engagement, and ongoing communication. This involves setting clear expectations for security standards and behaviors, providing resources and training to support employees in their security responsibilities, and recognizing and rewarding individuals who demonstrate exemplary security practices. By leading by example and fostering open communication channels, we can cultivate a culture of security that permeates every aspect of our organization and strengthens our defenses against cyber threats."

Navigating the Digital Frontier

As the team delved deeper into the world of cybersecurity and risk management, they were acutely aware of the challenges and responsibilities that lay ahead. In the digital age, cybersecurity was not just a technology issue; it was a business imperative—a critical component of organizational resilience, reputation, and trust.

Armed with newfound insights and determination, the team was ready to navigate the digital frontier and safeguard the future of their organization with unwavering vigilance, resilience, and resolve.

In the heart of Lusaka, amidst the dynamic landscape of innovation and competition, GlobalTech Solutions stood poised on the frontline of cybersecurity. Armed with a comprehensive understanding of cybersecurity and risk management, they were prepared to defend their organization against cyber threats and emerge stronger, more resilient, and more secure in the face of adversity.

Leveraging Social Media and Digital Marketing

The Digital Dialogue: Harnessing the Power of Social Media

In the vibrant hub of GlobalTech Solutions, anticipation filled the air as the team convened to explore the transformative potential of social media and digital marketing in shaping strategic excellence. Angela and Michael, the visionary leaders of innovation, were ready to embark on a journey into the dynamic realm of digital engagement and brand storytelling.

Angela's voice, brimming with enthusiasm and insight, initiated the discussion, "Good morning, everyone. Today, we embark on a voyage into the heart of social media and digital marketing—a voyage that will redefine the way we connect with our audience, tell our story, and build our brand in the digital age. Social media is not just a platform for communication; it is a catalyst for engagement, a gateway to innovation, and a driver of strategic growth. By understanding the power of social media and digital marketing, we can amplify our voice, extend our reach, and forge deeper connections with our audience."

Michael, with a nod of agreement, added, "Indeed. Social media has transformed the way organizations engage with their customers, enabling real-time communication, personalized interactions, and immersive brand experiences. Let us delve into the world of social media and digital marketing and uncover the strategies that will drive success in the digital economy."

Building Brand Authenticity

Angela began by highlighting the importance of building brand authenticity in the digital age, "In today's hyperconnected world, authenticity is the currency of trust. Social media provides organizations with a platform to showcase their values, personality, and purpose authentically, fostering trust, loyalty, and advocacy among their audience. By cultivating a genuine and transparent presence on social media, we can humanize our brand, resonate with our audience on a deeper level, and build lasting relationships that drive strategic growth."

Linda, the perceptive marketing lead, inquired, "How do we build brand authenticity on social media?"

Angela responded, "We engage," "Building brand authenticity on social media requires active engagement, genuine interactions, and transparent communication. This involves listening to our audience, understanding their needs and preferences, and responding to their feedback in a timely and authentic manner. By engaging with our audience authentically, we can demonstrate our commitment to transparency, accountability, and customer-centricity, earning their trust and loyalty in the process."

Creating Compelling Content

Michael highlighted the importance of creating compelling content in digital marketing, "In the digital age, content is king. Social media provides organizations with a platform to create and share compelling content that resonates with their audience, captures their attention, and drives meaningful engagement. By leveraging storytelling, visual imagery, and interactive experiences, we can create a powerful narrative that showcases our brand values, highlights our unique selling propositions, and inspires action among our audience."

David, the eager young developer, inquired, "How do we create compelling content that stands out?"

"We innovate," Michael affirmed, "Creating compelling content requires creativity, innovation, and a deep understanding of our audience's preferences and interests. This involves experimenting with different content formats, storytelling techniques, and visual elements to find what resonates best with our audience. By embracing innovation and pushing the boundaries of creativity, we can create content that captures the imagination, sparks conversation, and drives engagement on social media."

Driving Strategic Engagement

Angela emphasized the role of social media in driving strategic engagement, "In the digital age, engagement is the cornerstone of strategic success. Social media provides organizations with a platform to foster meaningful conversations, solicit feedback, and build communities around their brand. By leveraging social media as a two-way communication channel, we can deepen our relationships with our audience, gather valuable insights, and drive strategic growth through authentic engagement."

Linda inquired, "How do we drive strategic engagement on social media?"

"We connect," Angela explained, "Driving strategic engagement on social media requires building meaningful connections with our audience, fostering conversations around relevant topics, and providing value-added content that resonates with their interests and needs. This involves listening to our audience, responding to their comments and messages, and proactively engaging with them in a genuine and meaningful way. By connecting with our audience authentically, we can build trust, loyalty, and advocacy, driving strategic growth and success in the digital age."

Forging Ahead in the Digital Dialogue

As the team delved deeper into the world of social media and digital marketing, they were inspired by the transformative potential of digital engagement in shaping strategic excellence. In the digital age, social media was not just a channel for communication; it was a platform for connection—a bridge that connected organizations with their audience in meaningful and impactful ways.

Armed with newfound insights and determination, the team was ready to harness the power of social media and digital marketing and navigate their journey towards strategic excellence with confidence, creativity, and unwavering commitment.

In the heart of Lusaka, amidst the dynamic landscape of

innovation and competition, GlobalTech Solutions stood poised on the forefront of the digital dialogue. Armed with a comprehensive understanding of social media and digital marketing, they were prepared to amplify their voice, extend their reach, and forge deeper connections with their audience in the digital age.

Digital Transformation Case Studies

Embracing Digital Evolution: Lessons from Industry Leaders

In the illuminated boardroom of GlobalTech Solutions, anticipation filled the air as the team gathered to explore real-world examples of digital transformation and strategic innovation. Angela and Michael, the visionary architects of change, were ready to unveil the transformative journeys of industry leaders who had embraced digital evolution to drive strategic success.

Angela's voice, resonant with anticipation and curiosity, initiated the discussion, "Good morning, everyone. Today, we embark on a journey into the heart of digital transformation—a journey that will illuminate the pathways to success and inspire us to reimagine our strategic approach in the digital age. By examining the experiences of industry leaders who have embraced digital evolution, we can glean valuable insights, uncover best practices, and chart a course towards strategic excellence in the digital era."

Michael, with a nod of agreement, added, "Indeed. Digital transformation is not just about adopting new technologies; it is about reimagining business models, transforming organizational culture, and driving innovation across every aspect of the organization. Let us delve into the world of digital transformation case studies and uncover the strategies that have propelled industry leaders to success."

1. Amazon: Reinventing Retail

Angela began by highlighting the transformative journey of Amazon, "In the retail industry, Amazon has redefined the rules of engagement, leveraging digital technologies to create seamless shopping experiences, personalized recommendations, and frictionless transactions. By embracing digital innovation, Amazon has transformed from an online bookstore into a global e-commerce powerhouse, disrupting traditional retail models and reshaping consumer expectations."

Michael elaborated, "Amazon's success lies in its relentless focus on customer-centricity, innovation, and agility. By investing in advanced technologies such as artificial intelligence, machine learning, and cloud computing, Amazon has created a scalable infrastructure that enables it to deliver personalized experiences, optimize operations, and drive continuous innovation. Through strategic acquisitions, partnerships, and investments, Amazon has expanded its ecosystem to encompass a wide range of products and services, from e-commerce and digital content to cloud computing and logistics."

2. Netflix: Revolutionizing Entertainment

Angela continued with the case study of Netflix, "In the entertainment industry, Netflix has revolutionized the way we consume content, leveraging digital technologies to deliver streaming services that offer personalized recommendations, on-demand access, and original programming. By embracing digital disruption, Netflix has disrupted traditional media models, challenged incumbents, and pioneered a new era of content consumption."

Michael added, "Netflix's success is built on its data-driven approach to content creation, distribution, and recommendation. By leveraging big data and analytics, Netflix analyzes viewer behavior, preferences, and trends to personalize recommendations, optimize content delivery, and inform its content acquisition and production decisions. Through strategic investments in original programming and global expansion, Netflix has built a loyal subscriber base and established itself as a dominant player in the entertainment industry."

3. Tesla: Driving Innovation in Automotive

Angela shifted focus to the case study of Tesla, "In the automotive industry, Tesla has emerged as a leader in electric vehicles, leveraging digital technologies to reinvent the driving experience, accelerate innovation, and promote sustainability. By embracing digital disruption, Tesla has challenged traditional automakers, disrupted the status quo, and reshaped the future of mobility."

Michael elaborated, "Tesla's success lies in its relentless

focus on innovation, technology, and design. By leveraging advanced technologies such as electric propulsion, autonomous driving, and over-the-air updates, Tesla has created a differentiated value proposition that resonates with consumers seeking sustainable, high-performance vehicles. Through its direct-to-consumer sales model, digital marketing efforts, and cult-like brand following, Tesla has disrupted traditional dealership models and established a direct connection with its customers, driving loyalty and advocacy."

Charting Our Course

As the team delved deeper into the world of digital transformation case studies, they were inspired by the transformative journeys of industry leaders who had embraced digital evolution to drive strategic success. In the digital age, success was not just about adopting new technologies; it was about reimagining business models, transforming organizational culture, and driving innovation across every aspect of the organization.

Armed with newfound insights and inspiration, the team was ready to chart their course towards digital transformation with confidence, creativity, and unwavering commitment.

In the heart of Lusaka, amidst the dynamic landscape of innovation and competition, GlobalTech Solutions stood poised on the brink of digital transformation. Armed with a comprehensive understanding of industry best practices and real-world case studies, they were prepared to embrace the challenges and opportunities of the digital era and emerge as leaders in the digital landscape.

11

Chapter 11: Strategic Management in Small and Medium Enterprises (SMEs)

Unique Challenges and Opportunities for SMEs

Navigating the Terrain: Strategic Management in SMEs

In the cozy conference room of GlobalTech Solutions, a sense of camaraderie filled the air as the team gathered to explore the unique challenges and opportunities of strategic management in small and medium enterprises (SMEs). Angela and Michael, the pragmatic advocates of innovation, were ready to delve into the intricacies of SME strategy and uncover the keys to success in the competitive landscape.

Angela's voice, tinged with empathy and insight, initiated the discussion, "Good morning, everyone. Today, we embark on a journey into the world of small and medium enterprises—

a journey that will shine a light on the challenges, opportunities, and strategies for success in the SME landscape. SMEs are the backbone of the global economy, driving innovation, creating jobs, and fostering entrepreneurship. By understanding the unique dynamics of SMEs and tailoring our strategic approach accordingly, we can unlock new avenues for growth, resilience, and success."

Michael, with a nod of agreement, added, "Indeed. SMEs face a distinct set of challenges and opportunities that require a tailored approach to strategic management. Let us delve into the world of SME strategy and uncover the strategies that will empower SMEs to thrive in today's competitive marketplace."

Embracing Agility and Flexibility

Angela began by highlighting the importance of agility and flexibility in SME strategy, "In the fast-paced world of SMEs, agility and flexibility are essential for survival and success. Unlike large corporations, SMEs often operate in dynamic and uncertain environments, facing rapid changes in market conditions, customer preferences, and competitive landscapes. By embracing agility and flexibility, SMEs can adapt quickly to changing circumstances, seize new opportunities, and navigate challenges with resilience and resourcefulness."

Michael elaborated, "SMEs have the advantage of agility—the ability to pivot, iterate, and innovate at a rapid pace. By leveraging their nimbleness, SMEs can respond swiftly to market shifts, experiment with new ideas, and capitalize on emerging trends. Through a culture of experimentation, continuous learning, and adaptation, SMEs can stay ahead of the curve, outmaneuver larger competitors, and carve out a niche for themselves in the marketplace."

Maximizing Resource Efficiency

Angela highlighted the importance of resource efficiency in SME strategy, "In SMEs, resources are often limited and precious—requiring careful stewardship and strategic allocation. Unlike large corporations with vast reserves of capital and manpower, SMEs must make every resource count, maximizing efficiency, and effectiveness in every aspect of their operations. By optimizing resource allocation, minimizing waste, and leveraging economies of scale, SMEs can achieve greater productivity, profitability, and sustainability."

Michael added, "SMEs have the advantage of resourcefulness— the ability to do more with less. By leveraging their creativity, ingenuity, and entrepreneurial spirit, SMEs can find innovative solutions to resource constraints, harnessing the power of technology, outsourcing, and collaboration to achieve their strategic objectives. Through strategic partnerships, lean processes, and frugal innovation, SMEs can unlock new efficiencies, drive cost savings, and enhance their competitive position in the marketplace."

Fostering Entrepreneurial Leadership

Angela emphasized the importance of entrepreneurial leadership in SME strategy, "In SMEs, leadership plays a pivotal role in shaping organizational culture, driving strategic direction, and inspiring innovation. Unlike large corporations with hierarchical structures and formalized processes, SMEs require entrepreneurial leaders who are visionary, adaptable, and hands-on—willing to take risks, challenge the status quo, and lead by example. By fostering a culture of entrepreneurship, empowerment, and accountability, SMEs can unleash the full potential of their workforce, foster innovation, and drive strategic growth."

Michael added, "SMEs have the advantage of entrepreneurial spirit—the drive, passion, and resilience to overcome obstacles and pursue bold ideas. By cultivating a culture of experimentation, autonomy, and ownership, SMEs can empower their employees to take initiative, embrace change, and contribute their unique talents and perspectives to the organization. Through visionary leadership, mentorship, and empowerment, SMEs can cultivate a dynamic and adaptive organization that thrives in today's competitive marketplace."

Charting a Path to Success

As the team delved deeper into the world of strategic management in SMEs, they were inspired by the resilience, ingenuity, and entrepreneurial spirit that defined the SME landscape. In the dynamic world of SMEs, success was not just about size or scale; it was about agility, resourcefulness, and visionary leadership—a testament to the power of innovation, determination, and perseverance.

Armed with newfound insights and inspiration, the team was ready to chart their path to success in the SME landscape with confidence, creativity, and unwavering determination.

In the heart of Lusaka, amidst the vibrant tapestry of entrepreneurship and innovation, GlobalTech Solutions stood poised on the frontier of SME strategy. Armed with a comprehensive understanding of the unique challenges and opportunities of SMEs, they were prepared to embrace the journey ahead, navigate the terrain with agility and resilience, and emerge as leaders in the dynamic and ever-evolving SME landscape.

Strategic Planning for SMEs

Forging the Path: Strategic Planning in the SME Landscape

In the bustling headquarters of GlobalTech Solutions, a sense of purpose filled the air as the team reconvened to explore the intricacies of strategic planning in small and medium enterprises (SMEs). Angela and Michael, the pragmatic architects of progress, were ready to navigate the complexities of SME strategy and illuminate the pathways to success in the dynamic business landscape.

Angela's voice, infused with determination and clarity, initiated the discussion, "Good morning, everyone. Today, we embark on a journey into the heart of strategic planning—a journey that will unveil the blueprint for success in the SME landscape. Strategic planning is the compass that guides our actions, aligns our resources, and propels us towards our goals. By understanding the principles of strategic planning and tailoring our approach to the unique needs of SMEs, we can chart a course to success and unlock the full potential of our organization."

Michael, with a nod of agreement, added, "Indeed. Strategic planning is essential for SMEs to navigate the complexities of the business landscape, seize opportunities, and mitigate risks. Let us delve into the world of strategic planning in SMEs and uncover the strategies that will drive success in the competitive marketplace."

Defining Vision and Mission

Angela began by highlighting the importance of defining vision and mission in SME strategic planning, "In SMEs, vision and mission serve as the North Star—the guiding principles that define our purpose, aspirations, and values. Unlike large corporations with established legacies and global footprints, SMEs must articulate a clear and compelling vision and mission to inspire their stakeholders, attract talent, and differentiate themselves in the marketplace. By defining a vision that encapsulates our long-term aspirations and a mission that articulates our core purpose and values, we can rally our team, align our efforts, and chart a course towards strategic success."

Michael elaborated, "Vision and mission provide SMEs with a sense of direction, purpose, and identity. By engaging stakeholders in the visioning process, soliciting feedback, and fostering buy-in, SMEs can cultivate a shared sense of purpose and commitment that propels the organization forward. Through regular communication, reinforcement, and alignment with strategic goals and objectives, SMEs can ensure that their vision and mission remain relevant, inspiring, and actionable, guiding their decisions and actions in pursuit of strategic excellence."

Setting SMART Goals

Angela highlighted the importance of setting SMART goals in SME strategic planning, "In the fast-paced world of SMEs, goals serve as the milestones that mark our progress, guide our actions, and measure our success. Unlike large corporations with vast resources and established market positions, SMEs must set SMART goals that are Specific, Measurable, Achievable, Relevant, and Time-bound to focus their efforts, allocate resources effectively, and track their performance against strategic objectives. By setting SMART goals that align with our vision, mission, and strategic priorities, we can channel our efforts, prioritize initiatives, and drive meaningful progress towards our long-term objectives."

Michael added, "SMART goals provide SMEs with a roadmap for success—a clear and actionable plan that defines the steps required to achieve our strategic objectives. By breaking down our goals into smaller, manageable tasks, assigning responsibilities, and establishing timelines, SMEs can create accountability, foster collaboration, and drive execution excellence throughout the organization. Through regular monitoring, evaluation, and course correction, SMEs can ensure that their goals remain relevant, achievable, and aligned with their evolving needs and aspirations."

Adapting to Change

Angela emphasized the importance of adapting to change in SME strategic planning, "In the dynamic world of SMEs, change is inevitable—a constant force that shapes our environment, disrupts our plans, and presents new opportunities and challenges. Unlike large corporations with established processes and hierarchies, SMEs must embrace change as a catalyst for innovation, growth, and adaptation. By fostering a culture of agility, resilience, and continuous improvement, SMEs can navigate uncertainty, seize opportunities, and thrive in the face of adversity."

Michael added, "Adapting to change requires SMEs to be proactive, responsive, and flexible—willing to experiment, iterate, and pivot in response to shifting market dynamics, customer preferences, and competitive pressures. By monitoring market trends, gathering feedback, and staying attuned to emerging opportunities and threats, SMEs can anticipate change, seize opportunities, and mitigate risks before they escalate into crises. Through strategic foresight, scenario planning, and contingency measures, SMEs can prepare for uncertainty and position themselves for success in the ever-evolving business landscape."

Charting the Course Ahead

As the team delved deeper into the world of strategic planning in SMEs, they were inspired by the clarity, focus, and resilience that defined the SME landscape. In the dynamic world of SMEs, success was not just about size or scale; it was about vision, agility, and strategic alignment—a testament to the power of vision, planning, and execution.

Armed with newfound insights and determination, the team was ready to chart their course towards strategic success in the SME landscape with confidence, creativity, and unwavering commitment.

In the heart of Lusaka, amidst the vibrant tapestry of entrepreneurship and innovation, GlobalTech Solutions stood poised on the brink of strategic transformation. Armed with a comprehensive understanding of strategic planning in SMEs, they were prepared to embrace the challenges and opportunities of the SME landscape, navigate the terrain with agility and resilience, and emerge as leaders in the dynamic and ever-evolving SME landscape.

Resource Constraints and Strategic Innovation

Thriving in Constraint: Strategic Innovation in SMEs

In the vibrant corridors of GlobalTech Solutions, a spirit of ingenuity filled the air as the team reconvened to explore the intersection of resource constraints and strategic innovation in small and medium enterprises (SMEs). Angela and Michael, the resilient champions of progress, were ready to unlock the potential of innovation in the face of adversity and scarcity.

Angela's voice, infused with determination and optimism, initiated the discussion, "Good morning, everyone. Today, we embark on a journey into the world of strategic innovation—a journey that will illuminate the pathways to success in the face of resource constraints. In SMEs, scarcity breeds creativity, adversity fuels innovation, and constraints become catalysts for transformation. By embracing the power of strategic innovation, we can overcome limitations, unlock new opportunities, and thrive in the competitive marketplace."

Michael, with a nod of agreement, added, "Indeed. In the dynamic world of SMEs, innovation is not just a luxury; it is a necessity—a survival strategy that enables organizations to adapt, evolve, and thrive amidst uncertainty and change.

Let us delve into the world of strategic innovation in SMEs and uncover the strategies that will drive success in the face of resource constraints."

Embracing Frugal Innovation

Angela began by highlighting the importance of frugal innovation in SMEs, "In the resource-constrained world of SMEs, frugal innovation is a game-changer—a mindset that challenges conventional wisdom, fosters creativity, and drives value creation on a shoestring budget. Unlike large corporations with vast resources and R&D budgets, SMEs must find innovative ways to do more with less, leveraging creativity, ingenuity, and resourcefulness to overcome limitations and seize opportunities. By embracing frugal innovation, we can unlock new efficiencies, drive cost savings, and create differentiated value propositions that resonate with customers and stakeholders."

Michael elaborated, "Frugal innovation empowers SMEs to think outside the box, challenge the status quo, and reimagine solutions to complex problems. By leveraging low-cost materials, technologies, and processes, SMEs can develop innovative products, services, and business models that address unmet needs, capture market share, and disrupt incumbent players. Through a culture of experimentation, iteration, and adaptation, SMEs can cultivate a dynamic and agile organization that thrives in the face of resource constraints, driving sustainable growth and competitive advantage."

Harnessing Digital Technologies

Angela highlighted the transformative potential of digital technologies in driving strategic innovation in SMEs, "In the digital age, technology has leveled the playing field, democratizing access to tools, platforms, and resources that were once exclusive to large corporations. SMEs can leverage digital technologies such as cloud computing, artificial intelligence, and automation to streamline operations, enhance efficiency, and unlock new growth opportunities. By harnessing the power of digital technologies, SMEs can overcome resource constraints, scale their operations, and compete effectively in the digital marketplace."

Michael added, "Digital technologies enable SMEs to innovate at speed and scale, leveraging data-driven insights, predictive analytics, and real-time connectivity to drive strategic decision-making, optimize processes, and enhance customer experiences. By embracing digital transformation, SMEs can adapt to changing market dynamics, anticipate customer needs, and differentiate themselves in the marketplace. Through strategic investments in technology, talent, and infrastructure, SMEs can build a foundation for sustainable growth and resilience in the digital era."

Cultivating a Culture of Innovation

Angela emphasized the importance of cultivating a culture of innovation in SMEs, "Innovation is not just about technology; it is about mindset—a culture of curiosity, experimentation, and collaboration that empowers employees to challenge the status quo, explore new ideas, and drive change. Unlike large corporations with hierarchical structures and formalized processes, SMEs have the advantage of agility—the ability to adapt quickly, iterate rapidly, and pivot in response to feedback and market signals. By fostering a culture of innovation, SMEs can unleash the full potential of their workforce, inspire creativity, and drive strategic growth."

Michael added, "Cultivating a culture of innovation requires SMEs to embrace risk-taking, failure, and learning as essential elements of the innovation process. By providing employees with the autonomy, resources, and support they need to experiment, iterate, and explore new ideas, SMEs can unleash their creativity and drive breakthrough innovation that propels the organization forward. Through strategic leadership, visionary guidance, and a commitment to continuous improvement, SMEs can create a dynamic and adaptive organization that thrives in the face of adversity and uncertainty."

Forging Ahead

As the team delved deeper into the world of strategic innovation in SMEs, they were inspired by the resilience, creativity, and entrepreneurial spirit that defined the SME landscape. In the dynamic world of SMEs, success was not just about size or scale; it was about agility, innovation, and strategic alignment—a testament to the power of resourcefulness, ingenuity, and determination.

Armed with newfound insights and determination, the team was ready to forge ahead on their journey towards strategic innovation with confidence, creativity, and unwavering commitment.

In the heart of Lusaka, amidst the vibrant tapestry of entrepreneurship and innovation, GlobalTech Solutions stood poised on the frontier of strategic transformation. Armed with a comprehensive understanding of strategic innovation in SMEs, they were prepared to embrace the challenges and opportunities of the SME landscape, harness the power of innovation, and emerge as leaders in the dynamic and ever-evolving SME landscape.

Networking and Strategic Alliances

Forging Connections: Networking and Alliances in SMEs

In the bustling offices of GlobalTech Solutions, a sense of anticipation filled the air as the team gathered to explore the transformative power of networking and strategic alliances in small and medium enterprises (SMEs). Angela and Michael, the visionary architects of collaboration, were ready to unlock the potential of partnerships and connections in driving strategic success.

Angela's voice, vibrant with enthusiasm and conviction, initiated the discussion, "Good morning, everyone. Today, we embark on a journey into the world of networking and strategic alliances—a journey that will illuminate the pathways to success through collaboration and partnership. In SMEs, relationships are the currency of success, connections are the conduits of opportunity, and alliances are the engines of growth. By embracing the power of networking and strategic alliances, we can expand our reach, leverage complementary strengths, and unlock new possibilities for innovation and growth."

Michael, with a nod of agreement, added, "Indeed. In the dynamic world of SMEs, partnerships and alliances play a crucial role in driving strategic success, enabling organizations to access new markets, resources, and capabilities that may be beyond their reach. Let us delve into the world of networking and strategic alliances in SMEs and uncover the strategies that will propel us towards collaborative excellence."

Forging Strategic Partnerships

Angela began by highlighting the importance of forging strategic partnerships in SMEs, "In the interconnected world of business, partnerships are the linchpin of success—a strategic alliance between two or more organizations that share complementary strengths, resources, and objectives. Unlike large corporations with extensive networks and resources, SMEs must leverage strategic partnerships to expand their reach, access new markets, and amplify their impact. By forging strategic partnerships with like-minded organizations, SMEs can create synergies, pool resources, and achieve mutual goals that would be difficult to attain alone."

Michael elaborated, "Strategic partnerships enable SMEs to leverage the strengths and capabilities of their partners, complementing their own offerings and expanding their value proposition to customers. By collaborating with partners who bring unique expertise, resources, or distribution channels to the table, SMEs can enhance their competitive position, accelerate their growth, and mitigate risks associated with market entry or expansion. Through strategic alignment, clear communication, and mutual trust, SMEs can cultivate a network of trusted partners that enables them to navigate the complexities of the business landscape and seize new opportunities for strategic success."

Fostering Industry Networks

Angela highlighted the importance of fostering industry networks in SMEs, "In the interconnected ecosystem of industries, networks are the lifeblood of innovation and growth—a community of peers, collaborators, and stakeholders who share common interests, challenges, and aspirations. Unlike large corporations with established industry presence and influence, SMEs must actively participate in industry networks to stay informed, connected, and competitive. By fostering industry networks, SMEs can access valuable insights, build relationships, and stay ahead of emerging trends and opportunities in their respective industries."

Michael added, "Industry networks provide SMEs with access to a wealth of resources, knowledge, and opportunities that may not be available through traditional channels. By participating in industry associations, trade shows, and networking events, SMEs can connect with potential customers, partners, and suppliers, expanding their network and enhancing their visibility in the marketplace. Through active engagement, collaboration, and thought leadership, SMEs can position themselves as key players in their industry, driving innovation, and shaping the future of their respective sectors."

Navigating the Ecosystem

As the team delved deeper into the world of networking and strategic alliances in SMEs, they were inspired by the transformative potential of collaboration and partnership. In the dynamic world of SMEs, success was not just about individual achievement; it was about collective effort, shared vision, and collaborative action—a testament to the power of relationships, connections, and mutual support.

Armed with newfound insights and determination, the team was ready to navigate the ecosystem of networking and strategic alliances with confidence, creativity, and unwavering commitment.

In the heart of Lusaka, amidst the vibrant tapestry of entrepreneurship and innovation, GlobalTech Solutions stood poised on the frontier of collaborative excellence. Armed with a comprehensive understanding of networking and strategic alliances in SMEs, they were prepared to embrace the power of partnerships, leverage the strength of their network, and emerge as leaders in the dynamic and ever-evolving SME landscape.

Case Studies of Successful SME Strategies

Learning from the Trailblazers: Case Studies of SME Success

In the innovation hub of GlobalTech Solutions, a sense of anticipation filled the air as the team gathered to explore the real-world success stories of small and medium enterprises (SMEs) that had defied the odds, overcome challenges, and achieved remarkable success through strategic management. Angela and Michael, the avid storytellers of progress, were ready to uncover the lessons and insights hidden within the journeys of these trailblazing organizations.

Angela's voice, resonant with curiosity and admiration, initiated the discussion, "Good morning, everyone. Today, we embark on a journey into the world of SME success—a journey that will unveil the stories of perseverance, innovation, and strategic excellence that have propelled these organizations to greatness. In SMEs, success is not just about size or scale; it is about vision, resilience, and strategic alignment. By studying the experiences of these trailblazing organizations, we can extract valuable insights and lessons that will inspire and inform our own journey towards strategic success."

Michael, with a nod of agreement, added, "Indeed. In the dynamic world of SMEs, there is much to be learned from the experiences of our peers and predecessors—their triumphs, their challenges, and their strategies for success. Let us delve into the world of SME success stories and uncover the strategies that have driven these organizations to achieve remarkable results."

Case Study 1: Patagonia

Angela began by highlighting the success story of Patagonia, an outdoor apparel company known for its commitment to environmental sustainability and social responsibility. "Patagonia's journey to success is a testament to the power of purpose-driven strategy—a strategic approach that aligns business objectives with social and environmental values. Founded by Yvon Chouinard in 1973, Patagonia set out to create high-quality outdoor gear while minimizing its environmental impact—a mission that has guided the company's decisions and actions ever since. By integrating sustainability into its business model, Patagonia has not only cultivated a loyal customer base but also achieved remarkable financial success, demonstrating that doing good can be good for business."

Michael added, "Patagonia's success is a shining example of the potential for SMEs to drive positive change through purpose-driven strategy. By aligning their business objectives with social and environmental values, SMEs can differentiate themselves in the marketplace, attract like-minded customers and employees, and build a resilient and sustainable business model that delivers long-term value to all stakeholders."

Case Study 2: Warby Parker

Angela continued with the success story of Warby Parker, an eyewear company that disrupted the industry by offering high-quality, affordable glasses online. "Warby Parker's journey to success is a testament to the power of disruptive innovation—a strategic approach that challenges the status quo, reimagines traditional business models, and delivers value to customers in new and unexpected ways. Founded by Neil Blumenthal, Dave Gilboa, Andrew Hunt, and Jeffrey Raider in 2010, Warby Parker set out to revolutionize the eyewear industry by offering stylish, affordable glasses direct to consumers—a mission that resonated with millennials and digital natives seeking an alternative to traditional brick-and-mortar retailers. By leveraging technology, data analytics, and a direct-to-consumer business model, Warby Parker has not only disrupted the eyewear industry but also achieved remarkable growth and profitability, demonstrating that innovation can drive strategic success in SMEs."

Michael added, "Warby Parker's success is a testament to the potential for SMEs to disrupt traditional industries through innovation and entrepreneurship. By challenging the status quo, identifying unmet needs, and leveraging technology and data analytics, SMEs can carve out a niche for themselves in the marketplace, differentiate their offerings, and create value for customers in new and innovative ways."

Case Study 3: Airbnb

Angela concluded with the success story of Airbnb, a global online marketplace for lodging and travel experiences. "Airbnb's journey to success is a testament to the power of platform-based business models—a strategic approach that leverages technology and network effects to connect buyers and sellers in new and innovative ways. Founded by Brian Chesky, Joe Gebbia, and Nathan Blecharczyk in 2008, Airbnb set out to disrupt the hospitality industry by allowing individuals to rent out their homes to travelers—a concept that has transformed the way people travel and experience new destinations. By creating a platform that facilitates peer-to-peer transactions, Airbnb has not only revolutionized the travel industry but also achieved remarkable growth and valuation, demonstrating the potential for SMEs to create value through platform-based business models."

Michael concluded, "Airbnb's success is a testament to the transformative potential of platform-based business models in driving strategic success in SMEs. By leveraging technology, network effects, and the sharing economy, SMEs can create new marketplaces, unlock untapped resources, and connect buyers and sellers in new and innovative ways, driving growth, and profitability."

Extracting Lessons

As the team delved deeper into the success stories of Patagonia, Warby Parker, and Airbnb, they were inspired by the resilience, innovation, and strategic vision that defined these trailblazing organizations. In the dynamic world of SMEs, success was not just about size or scale; it was about purpose, innovation, and strategic alignment—a testament to the power of vision, resilience, and strategic execution.

Armed with newfound insights and inspiration, the team was ready to apply the lessons learned from these success stories to their own journey towards strategic success, with confidence, creativity, and unwavering determination.

In the heart of Lusaka, amidst the vibrant tapestry of entrepreneurship and innovation, GlobalTech Solutions stood poised on the brink of greatness. Armed with a comprehensive understanding of successful SME strategies, they were prepared to chart their course towards strategic success, leveraging the lessons learned from the trailblazers to create a brighter future for themselves and their organization.

Government Support and Policy Implications

Empowering Growth: Government Support for SMEs

In the boardroom of GlobalTech Solutions, a sense of anticipation filled the air as the team gathered to explore the critical role of government support and policy implications in fostering the growth and success of small and medium enterprises (SMEs). Angela and Michael, the advocates of collaboration and advocacy, were ready to delve into the complexities of public-private partnerships and the impact of policy decisions on SMEs.

Angela's voice, infused with passion and advocacy, initiated the discussion, "Good morning, everyone. Today, we embark on a journey into the realm of government support and policy implications—a journey that will illuminate the critical role of public policy in creating an enabling environment for SMEs to thrive. In SMEs, success is not just about individual effort; it is about collaboration, partnership, and a supportive ecosystem that fosters innovation, growth, and sustainability. By understanding the impact of government support and policy decisions on SMEs, we can advocate for change, drive meaningful reform, and create a brighter future for all."

Michael, with a nod of agreement, added, "Indeed. In the dynamic world of SMEs, government support and policy decisions play a crucial role in shaping the business environment, influencing market dynamics, and determining the success or failure of SMEs. Let us delve into the world of government support and policy implications in SMEs and uncover the strategies that will empower SMEs to achieve their full potential."

Fostering a Supportive Ecosystem

Angela began by highlighting the importance of fostering a supportive ecosystem for SMEs through government initiatives and policy interventions, "In the competitive landscape of business, SMEs face a myriad of challenges—from access to finance and markets to regulatory compliance and skills development. Government support and policy interventions can play a crucial role in addressing these challenges, creating an enabling environment for SMEs to thrive. By providing financial incentives, access to markets, and support services such as mentorship, training, and networking opportunities, governments can empower SMEs to overcome barriers to growth, unleash their potential, and contribute to economic development and job creation."

Michael elaborated, "Government support for SMEs is not just about providing financial assistance; it is about creating a conducive business environment that fosters entrepreneurship, innovation, and sustainable growth. By streamlining regulatory processes, reducing bureaucratic red tape, and promoting a culture of innovation and risk-taking, governments can create an ecosystem that enables SMEs to flourish, drive economic growth, and enhance global competitiveness. Through strategic partnerships between the public and private sectors, governments can leverage their resources and expertise to address the unique needs and challenges of SMEs, driving inclusive and sustainable development."

Policy Implications for Growth

Angela highlighted the importance of policy implications for SME growth, "Policy decisions have far-reaching implications for the growth and success of SMEs, shaping market dynamics, investor confidence, and business competitiveness. Tax policies, trade agreements, and regulatory frameworks can either facilitate or hinder SME growth, influencing investment decisions, market entry strategies, and operational efficiency. By aligning policy objectives with the needs and aspirations of SMEs, governments can create an environment that promotes entrepreneurship, innovation, and job creation, driving economic growth and prosperity for all."

Michael added, "Policy decisions must be informed by evidence-based research, stakeholder consultation, and a deep understanding of the challenges and opportunities facing SMEs. By engaging with SMEs, industry associations, and other stakeholders, governments can develop policies that are responsive to the needs of the business community, foster innovation, and drive sustainable development. Through strategic planning, monitoring, and evaluation, governments can ensure that their policies are effective, efficient, and equitable, creating an environment that enables SMEs to thrive and contribute to inclusive economic growth."

Advocating for Change

As the team delved deeper into the world of government support and policy implications for SMEs, they were inspired by the potential for collaboration and advocacy to drive meaningful change and create a brighter future for SMEs.

Armed with newfound insights and determination, the team was ready to advocate for policies that empower SMEs, drive economic growth, and enhance global competitiveness, with confidence, creativity, and unwavering commitment.

In the heart of Lusaka, amidst the vibrant tapestry of entrepreneurship and innovation, GlobalTech Solutions stood poised on the frontier of advocacy and change. Armed with a comprehensive understanding of government support and policy implications for SMEs, they were prepared to be champions for SMEs, driving meaningful reform and creating a supportive ecosystem that empowers SMEs to achieve their full potential and contribute to sustainable development and inclusive prosperity.

12

Chapter 12: Globalization and International Strategies

Understanding Globalization and its Impact

Embracing the World: Navigating Globalization's Terrain

In the conference room of GlobalTech Solutions, a sense of anticipation permeated the air as the team gathered to explore the intricacies of globalization and its profound impact on business strategies. Angela and Michael, the intrepid explorers of global markets, were ready to embark on a journey into the interconnected world of commerce and culture.

Angela's voice, resonant with curiosity and enthusiasm, initiated the discussion, "Good morning, everyone. Today, we embark on a journey into the realm of globalization—a journey that will illuminate the opportunities and challenges of navigating the global marketplace. In the interconnected world of business, globalization has transformed the landscape, reshaping markets, supply chains, and consumer preferences. By understanding the dynamics of globalization and its impact on business strategies, we can unlock new opportunities for growth and success in the global marketplace."

Michael, with a nod of agreement, added, "Indeed. In the dynamic world of globalization, businesses must adapt and evolve to thrive in an increasingly interconnected and competitive environment. Let us delve into the world of globalization and international strategies and uncover the strategies that will empower us to navigate this complex terrain with confidence and agility."

The Age of Interconnection

Angela began by highlighting the transformative impact of globalization on the business landscape, "Globalization has ushered in an era of unprecedented interconnectedness, breaking down barriers to trade, investment, and communication. In today's global marketplace, businesses can no longer afford to operate in isolation; they must embrace globalization and leverage its opportunities to expand their reach, access new markets, and drive sustainable growth. By understanding the forces driving globalization—such as advances in technology, liberalization of trade, and increased mobility of capital and labor—businesses can position themselves to capitalize on emerging trends and opportunities in the global marketplace."

Michael elaborated, "Globalization has blurred the boundaries between markets, creating new opportunities for businesses to tap into diverse customer segments, supply chains, and talent pools around the world. By embracing globalization, businesses can access new sources of innovation, talent, and capital, driving productivity, efficiency, and competitiveness. However, globalization also presents challenges, such as increased competition, regulatory complexity, and cultural differences, which businesses must navigate effectively to succeed in the global marketplace. By adopting a global mindset, investing in cross-cultural competence, and building strategic partnerships, businesses can mitigate risks and unlock the full potential of globalization."

Navigating Global Dynamics

As the team delved deeper into the dynamics of globalization, they were struck by the interconnectedness of the global marketplace and the opportunities it presented for growth and expansion.

Armed with newfound insights and determination, the team was ready to embrace the challenges and opportunities of globalization, navigating its complex terrain with confidence, creativity, and unwavering commitment.

In the heart of Lusaka, amidst the vibrant tapestry of globalization and innovation, GlobalTech Solutions stood poised on the cusp of new horizons. Armed with a comprehensive understanding of globalization and international strategies, they were prepared to chart their course towards global success, leveraging the opportunities of the interconnected world to drive sustainable growth and prosperity.

International Market Entry Strategies

Breaking Borders: Crafting International Market Entry Strategies

In the strategic planning room of GlobalTech Solutions, a palpable sense of anticipation filled the air as the team convened to explore the diverse strategies for entering international markets. Angela and Michael, the architects of expansion, were poised to unveil the pathways to global success.

Angela's voice, infused with determination and foresight, initiated the discussion, "Good morning, everyone. Today, we embark on a journey into the realm of international market entry strategies—a journey that will illuminate the diverse approaches for breaking into new markets and expanding our global footprint. In the interconnected world of business, international expansion is no longer a luxury but a necessity for sustainable growth and competitiveness. By understanding the intricacies of international market entry strategies, we can navigate the complexities of global expansion and unlock new avenues for success."

Michael, with a nod of agreement, added, "Indeed. In the dynamic world of globalization, businesses must adopt tailored strategies for entering international markets, taking into account factors such as market attractiveness, competitive dynamics, and regulatory environment. Let us delve into the world of international market entry strategies and uncover the strategies that will empower us to expand our reach and capture new opportunities in the global marketplace."

The Pathways to Global Expansion

Angela began by highlighting the diverse approaches to international market entry, "International expansion presents businesses with a myriad of pathways for entering new markets, each with its own opportunities and challenges. From exporting and licensing to joint ventures and wholly-owned subsidiaries, businesses must carefully evaluate their options and choose the approach that best aligns with their strategic objectives, resources, and capabilities. By understanding the trade-offs associated with each entry mode—such as control, risk, and investment requirements—businesses can craft a tailored strategy that maximizes their chances of success in the global marketplace."

Michael elaborated, "Exporting is often the simplest and least resource-intensive entry mode, allowing businesses to enter new markets quickly and cost-effectively by selling their products or services abroad. Licensing and franchising offer businesses the opportunity to leverage the expertise and resources of local partners, while retaining control over their intellectual property. Joint ventures and strategic alliances enable businesses to share risks and resources with local partners, while gaining access to their knowledge of the market and distribution networks. Wholly-owned subsidiaries provide businesses with maximum control and flexibility but require significant investment and commitment. By carefully evaluating these entry modes and considering factors such as market potential, competitive dynamics, and regulatory environment, businesses can choose the approach that best positions them for success in international markets."

Tailoring Strategies to Market Dynamics

As the team delved deeper into the nuances of international market entry strategies, they were struck by the importance of tailoring their approach to the unique dynamics of each market and industry.

Armed with newfound insights and determination, the team was ready to embark on their global expansion journey, crafting tailored strategies that would enable them to break borders, seize new opportunities, and achieve sustainable growth in the global marketplace.

In the heart of Lusaka, amidst the dynamic landscape of globalization and innovation, GlobalTech Solutions stood poised on the brink of international success. Armed with a comprehensive understanding of international market entry strategies, they were prepared to chart their course towards global expansion, leveraging the diverse pathways to international markets to drive sustainable growth and prosperity.

Cross-cultural Management and Strategy

Bridging Worlds: Navigating Cross-cultural Management

In the multicultural conference room of GlobalTech Solutions, a sense of anticipation permeated the air as the team gathered to explore the intricacies of cross-cultural management and its profound impact on global strategy. Angela and Michael, the ambassadors of cultural fluency, were poised to unveil the keys to bridging cultural divides and fostering synergy in diverse environments.

Angela's voice, rich with empathy and insight, initiated the discussion, "Good morning, everyone. Today, we embark on a journey into the realm of cross-cultural management—a journey that will illuminate the importance of cultural intelligence in navigating the complexities of global business. In the interconnected world of globalization, cultural differences can either be a barrier or a bridge to success. By understanding the nuances of cross-cultural management and strategy, we can foster collaboration, innovation, and harmony across diverse teams and markets."

Michael, with a nod of agreement, added, "Indeed. In the dynamic world of international business, cultural intelligence is a critical skill for leaders and teams to develop. Let us delve into the world of cross-cultural management and uncover the strategies that will empower us to navigate cultural differences and leverage diversity as a source of competitive advantage."

Embracing Cultural Diversity

Angela began by highlighting the importance of embracing cultural diversity in global business, "In today's interconnected world, businesses operate in increasingly diverse environments, with teams and customers spanning different cultures, languages, and backgrounds. Cultural diversity can be a source of strength, creativity, and innovation, but it can also present challenges such as miscommunication, misunderstanding, and conflict. By embracing cultural diversity and fostering an inclusive culture, businesses can unlock the full potential of their teams, harnessing the richness of diverse perspectives, experiences, and ideas to drive innovation and competitiveness in the global marketplace."

Michael elaborated, "Cross-cultural management requires leaders and teams to develop cultural intelligence—the ability to understand, adapt to, and leverage cultural differences in diverse environments. By developing empathy, curiosity, and open-mindedness, leaders can bridge cultural divides, build trust, and foster collaboration across diverse teams and markets. Through effective communication, cross-cultural training, and intercultural sensitivity, businesses can create an environment where diversity is celebrated, respected, and leveraged as a source of strength and competitive advantage."

Building Bridges Across Cultures

As the team delved deeper into the intricacies of cross-cultural management, they were struck by the transformative potential of cultural intelligence in bridging divides and fostering synergy in diverse environments.

Armed with newfound insights and determination, the team was ready to embrace cultural diversity as a source of competitive advantage, fostering an inclusive culture that celebrates the richness of human experience and drives innovation and success in the global marketplace.

In the heart of Lusaka, amidst the mosaic of cultures and perspectives, GlobalTech Solutions stood poised on the frontier of cross-cultural management. Armed with a comprehensive understanding of cultural intelligence and its impact on global strategy, they were prepared to build bridges across cultures, forge connections, and create a harmonious and inclusive environment where diversity thrives and success knows no borders.

Global Supply Chain Management

Connecting Continents: Mastering Global Supply Chains

In the command center of GlobalTech Solutions, a sense of purpose filled the air as the team convened to explore the intricacies of global supply chain management and its pivotal role in international strategy. Angela and Michael, the architects of connectivity, were poised to unveil the keys to orchestrating seamless operations across continents.

Angela's voice, charged with efficiency and precision, initiated the discussion, "Good morning, everyone. Today, we embark on a journey into the realm of global supply chain management—a journey that will illuminate the importance of agility, resilience, and collaboration in managing complex networks of suppliers, manufacturers, and distributors across the globe. In the interconnected world of globalization, supply chains are the lifeline of business, enabling the flow of goods, services, and information across borders. By mastering global supply chain management, we can optimize efficiency, reduce costs, and enhance competitiveness in the global marketplace."

Michael, with a nod of agreement, added, "Indeed. In the dynamic world of international business, supply chain management is a strategic imperative for businesses to master. Let us delve into the world of global supply chain management and uncover the strategies that will empower us to build agile, resilient, and efficient supply chains that span continents and deliver value to customers around the world."

Creating Seamless Connections

Angela began by highlighting the importance of creating seamless connections in global supply chains, "In today's interconnected world, businesses operate in increasingly complex and dynamic supply chain networks, with suppliers, manufacturers, and distributors spanning multiple countries and continents. Global supply chain management is the art of orchestrating these networks to ensure the efficient flow of goods, services, and information from raw materials to end customers. By optimizing processes, leveraging technology, and fostering collaboration with partners, businesses can create seamless connections in their supply chains, reducing lead times, minimizing costs, and enhancing customer satisfaction."

Michael elaborated, "Global supply chain management requires businesses to adopt a holistic and integrated approach to managing their supply chain networks. From strategic sourcing and procurement to production planning and distribution, businesses must coordinate activities across the entire supply chain to optimize efficiency and responsiveness. By leveraging technologies such as cloud computing, big data analytics, and blockchain, businesses can gain real-time visibility into their supply chains, enabling them to identify bottlenecks, mitigate risks, and make data-driven decisions that drive continuous improvement and innovation."

Building Resilience and Agility

As the team delved deeper into the intricacies of global supply chain management, they were struck by the importance of building resilience and agility in the face of uncertainty and disruption.

Armed with newfound insights and determination, the team was ready to optimize their global supply chain, building seamless connections that span continents and deliver value to customers around the world.

In the heart of Lusaka, amidst the dynamic pulse of globalization and innovation, GlobalTech Solutions stood poised on the frontier of global supply chain management. Armed with a comprehensive understanding of supply chain dynamics and best practices, they were prepared to master the complexities of global commerce, building agile, resilient, and efficient supply chains that connect continents and drive sustainable growth and success in the global marketplace.

Risk Management in International Business

Navigating Uncertainty: Safeguarding International Ventures

In the strategy room of GlobalTech Solutions, a palpable sense of vigilance filled the air as the team gathered to explore the intricacies of risk management in international business and its critical role in safeguarding global ventures. Angela and Michael, the guardians of resilience, were poised to unveil the keys to navigating uncertainty in the global arena.

Angela's voice, steady and resolute, initiated the discussion,

"Good morning, everyone. Today, we embark on a journey into the realm of risk management in international business—a journey that will illuminate the importance of foresight, preparedness, and resilience in mitigating the myriad risks that accompany global expansion. In the dynamic world of globalization, businesses face a multitude of risks—from political instability and economic volatility to supply chain disruptions and regulatory compliance. By mastering risk management, we can safeguard our international ventures, protect our assets, and ensure continuity in the face of uncertainty."

Michael, with a nod of agreement, added, "Indeed. In the interconnected world of international business, risk management is a strategic imperative for businesses to embrace. Let us delve into the world of risk management and uncover the strategies that will empower us to identify, assess, and mitigate risks in our global operations, safeguarding our investments and preserving our competitive advantage."

Anticipating and Assessing Risks

Angela began by highlighting the importance of anticipating and assessing risks in international business, "In today's volatile and uncertain world, businesses must adopt a proactive approach to risk management, anticipating and assessing potential risks before they materialize. From geopolitical tensions and currency fluctuations to natural disasters and cybersecurity threats, the landscape of risks in international business is vast and ever-changing. By conducting comprehensive risk assessments, businesses can identify and prioritize risks based on their likelihood and potential impact, enabling them to develop targeted strategies for mitigation and contingency planning."

Michael elaborated, "Risk management in international business requires businesses to adopt a multi-dimensional approach, considering factors such as political, economic, social, technological, legal, and environmental risks. By leveraging tools such as risk matrices, scenario planning, and simulation modeling, businesses can quantify and prioritize risks, enabling them to allocate resources effectively and develop risk mitigation strategies that are tailored to their specific circumstances. By fostering a culture of risk awareness and resilience, businesses can empower their teams to identify and respond to emerging risks in real-time, ensuring agility and adaptability in the face of uncertainty."

Mitigating and Managing Risks

As the team delved deeper into the intricacies of risk management in international business, they were struck by the importance of adopting a proactive and holistic approach to mitigating and managing risks.

Armed with newfound insights and determination, the team was ready to embrace the challenges of global expansion, safeguarding their international ventures through foresight, preparedness, and resilience.

In the heart of Lusaka, amidst the ebb and flow of global commerce and competition, GlobalTech Solutions stood poised on the frontier of risk management. Armed with a comprehensive understanding of international risks and best practices in risk mitigation, they were prepared to navigate uncertainty with confidence, safeguarding their investments and preserving their competitive advantage in the global marketplace.

Case Studies of Successful International Strategies

Trailblazers of Global Success: Lessons from Industry Leaders

In the boardroom of GlobalTech Solutions, a sense of excitement filled the air as the team gathered to delve into case studies of successful international strategies, eager to glean insights from industry leaders who had navigated the complexities of global expansion with aplomb. Angela and Michael, the seekers of wisdom, were poised to uncover the secrets of global success.

Angela's voice, brimming with curiosity and anticipation, initiated the discussion, "Good morning, everyone. Today, we embark on a journey into the world of successful international strategies—a journey that will illuminate the pathways to global success as charted by industry leaders who have dared to venture beyond borders and conquer new markets. In the dynamic world of globalization, learning from the experiences of others is invaluable, providing us with inspiration, guidance, and practical insights that we can apply to our own global endeavors. Let us delve into the case studies of successful international strategies and uncover the lessons that will empower us to chart our course towards global success."

Michael, with a nod of agreement, added, "Indeed. In the interconnected world of international business, success is not just about having a great product or service—it is about understanding the nuances of global markets, adapting to diverse cultures, and navigating regulatory landscapes. Let us explore the case studies of industry leaders who have demonstrated exceptional acumen and agility in expanding their presence across borders, capturing new opportunities, and creating value for their stakeholders."

Case Study 1: Coca-Cola Company

Angela began by presenting the case study of Coca-Cola Company, "Coca-Cola Company is a shining example of a global brand that has successfully penetrated markets around the world, becoming synonymous with refreshment and enjoyment. Through strategic partnerships, localized marketing campaigns, and product innovation, Coca-Cola has adapted its offerings to suit the preferences and tastes of diverse cultures, capturing the hearts and minds of consumers across continents. By embracing cultural diversity and leveraging its global distribution network, Coca-Cola has achieved unparalleled success in the international marketplace, demonstrating the importance of agility, adaptability, and customer-centricity in global expansion."

Case Study 2: Amazon

Michael followed with the case study of Amazon, "Amazon is a trailblazer in the world of e-commerce, revolutionizing the way people shop and consume goods around the world. Through relentless innovation, customer obsession, and strategic acquisitions, Amazon has expanded its presence beyond its home market in the United States, establishing a formidable global footprint. By investing in logistics infrastructure, digital technology, and customer service excellence, Amazon has overcome the challenges of cross-border trade, enabling seamless transactions and delivery experiences for customers worldwide. Amazon's success highlights the importance of bold vision, relentless execution, and customer-centricity in driving global expansion and creating value in the digital age."

Case Study 3: Toyota

Angela concluded with the case study of Toyota, "Toyota is a global automotive powerhouse, renowned for its commitment to quality, innovation, and sustainability. Through a combination of strategic partnerships, localized production, and market segmentation, Toyota has established itself as a leader in the global automotive industry, capturing market share and mindshare in diverse markets around the world. By leveraging its global supply chain network, research and development capabilities, and brand reputation for reliability, Toyota has navigated the complexities of global competition with agility and resilience, demonstrating the importance of continuous improvement, innovation, and customer satisfaction in sustaining global success."

Extracting Insights

As the team delved deeper into the case studies of successful international strategies, they were struck by the common themes of agility, adaptability, and customer-centricity that underpinned their success.

Armed with newfound insights and inspiration, the team was ready to apply the lessons learned from industry leaders to their own global endeavors, charting a course towards success in the interconnected world of international business.

In the heart of Lusaka, amidst the tapestry of globalization and innovation, GlobalTech Solutions stood poised on the brink of global success. Armed with a comprehensive understanding of successful international strategies, they were prepared to emulate the achievements of industry leaders, leveraging their wisdom and experience to navigate the complexities of global expansion and create value for their stakeholders in the global marketplace.

13

Chapter 13: Strategic Leadership

Characteristics of Effective Strategic Leaders

Guiding Lights: The Essence of Strategic Leadership

In the executive suite of GlobalTech Solutions, a sense of reverence filled the air as the team gathered to explore the essence of strategic leadership and the characteristics that distinguish exceptional leaders in the dynamic world of business. Angela and Michael, the architects of inspiration, were poised to unveil the traits that elevate leaders to greatness.

Angela's voice, infused with reverence and wisdom, initiated the discussion, "Good morning, everyone. Today, we embark on a journey into the heart of strategic leadership—a journey that will illuminate the qualities and attributes of effective leaders who inspire, empower, and guide their teams to greatness. In the ever-changing landscape of business, leadership is not merely about directing operations or making decisions—it is about envisioning the future, navigating uncertainty, and mobilizing collective efforts towards a common purpose. Let us delve into the characteristics of effective strategic leaders and uncover the essence of leadership excellence."

Michael, with a nod of agreement, added, "Indeed. In the tumultuous seas of business, strategic leaders are the guiding lights that steer organizations towards success, even in the face of adversity. Let us explore the traits that define strategic leaders and inspire others to follow in their footsteps."

Visionary Thinking

Angela began by highlighting the importance of visionary thinking in strategic leadership, "At the heart of strategic leadership lies the ability to envision the future—to see opportunities where others see challenges, to anticipate trends before they emerge, and to chart a course towards a compelling vision. Visionary leaders possess clarity of purpose and conviction of belief, inspiring others to rally behind a shared vision and pursue ambitious goals with passion and determination. By articulating a clear and compelling vision, strategic leaders create a sense of direction and purpose that energizes and motivates their teams to achieve greatness."

Courageous Decision-Making

Michael elaborated, "Strategic leadership requires courage—the courage to make tough decisions in the face of uncertainty, the courage to challenge the status quo and embrace change, and the courage to take calculated risks in pursuit of strategic objectives. Courageous leaders demonstrate resilience in the face of adversity, remaining steadfast in their convictions and leading by example in times of crisis. By fostering a culture of courage and innovation, strategic leaders empower their teams to embrace change, learn from failure, and seize opportunities for growth and transformation."

Empowering Others

As the team delved deeper into the characteristics of effective strategic leaders, they were struck by the importance of empowering others and fostering a culture of collaboration and trust.

Armed with newfound insights and inspiration, the team was ready to embrace the mantle of leadership, embodying the qualities of vision, courage, and empowerment as they guided GlobalTech Solutions towards a future of innovation, growth, and excellence.

In the heart of Lusaka, amidst the corridors of power and possibility, GlobalTech Solutions stood poised on the threshold of leadership greatness. Armed with a comprehensive understanding of strategic leadership, they were prepared to chart their course towards success, guided by the timeless principles of visionary thinking, courageous decision-making, and empowering others to achieve their full potential in the pursuit of shared goals.

Strategic Decision-Making and Leadership

Decisive Paths: The Nexus of Strategy and Leadership

In the command center of GlobalTech Solutions, a sense of purpose filled the air as the team gathered to explore the nexus of strategic decision-making and leadership, recognizing the pivotal role that leaders play in shaping the destiny of organizations in the turbulent waters of business. Angela and Michael, the architects of clarity, were poised to unveil the essence of strategic decision-making in the realm of leadership.

Angela's voice, imbued with resolve and insight, initiated the discussion, "Good morning, everyone. Today, we embark on a journey into the heart of strategic decision-making and leadership—a journey that will illuminate the art and science of making bold and informed decisions in the pursuit of organizational goals. In the dynamic landscape of business, leaders are called upon to navigate complexity, uncertainty, and ambiguity with wisdom and foresight, charting decisive paths towards a prosperous future. Let us delve into the intersection of strategic decision-making and leadership and uncover the strategies that empower leaders to make impactful decisions that drive organizational success."

Michael, with a nod of agreement, added, "Indeed. In the crucible of leadership, strategic decision-making is both an art and a science—a delicate balance of intuition and analysis, experience and insight. Let us explore the principles that guide effective decision-making and empower leaders to steer their organizations towards greatness."

Strategic Thinking

Angela began by highlighting the importance of strategic thinking in leadership, "At the core of strategic decision-making lies the ability to think strategically—to assess situations from a holistic perspective, anticipate consequences, and align actions with long-term objectives. Strategic leaders possess the foresight to anticipate trends and disruptions, enabling them to make proactive decisions that position their organizations for success in the face of uncertainty. By cultivating a strategic mindset and encouraging creative thinking, leaders can foster a culture of innovation and adaptability that empowers their teams to tackle complex challenges and seize opportunities for growth and transformation."

Data-Informed Insights

Michael elaborated, "Strategic decision-making is informed by data—the lifeblood of modern organizations. Leaders must leverage data and analytics to gain insights into market trends, customer preferences, and competitive dynamics, enabling them to make informed decisions that drive sustainable growth and competitive advantage. By harnessing the power of data, leaders can identify patterns, forecast outcomes, and optimize strategies to achieve desired outcomes. However, data alone is not enough—leaders must also possess the judgment and intuition to interpret data effectively, recognizing both its limitations and its potential to inform strategic choices."

Risk Management and Resilience

As the team delved deeper into the principles of strategic decision-making and leadership, they were struck by the importance of risk management and resilience in guiding organizations through uncertainty.

Armed with newfound insights and determination, the team was ready to embrace the challenges of leadership, embodying the qualities of strategic thinking, data-informed insights, and risk management as they navigated GlobalTech Solutions towards a future of innovation, growth, and excellence.

In the heart of Lusaka, amidst the crucible of leadership and possibility, GlobalTech Solutions stood poised on the brink of greatness. Armed with a comprehensive understanding of strategic decision-making and leadership, they were prepared to chart their course towards success, guided by the timeless principles of vision, courage, and resilience in the pursuit of organizational excellence.

Building and Leading High-Performance Teams

Forging Excellence: The Art of Team Leadership

In the collaborative hub of GlobalTech Solutions, a sense of camaraderie filled the air as the team gathered to explore the intricacies of building and leading high-performance teams, recognizing the transformative power of cohesive and motivated teams in achieving organizational success. Angela and Michael, the architects of synergy, were poised to unveil the secrets of team leadership excellence.

Angela's voice, resonant with warmth and encouragement, initiated the discussion, "Good morning, everyone. Today, we embark on a journey into the heart of team leadership—a journey that will illuminate the art and science of building and leading high-performance teams that exceed expectations and drive organizational success. In the interconnected world of business, teams are the engines of innovation, collaboration, and productivity, propelling organizations towards their goals with passion and purpose. Let us delve into the essence of team leadership and uncover the strategies that empower leaders to inspire, motivate, and guide their teams to greatness."

Michael, with a nod of agreement, added, "Indeed. In the dynamic landscape of business, effective team leadership is essential for harnessing the collective talents and energies of individuals towards common objectives. Let us explore the principles that guide team leadership and empower leaders to cultivate a culture of excellence and collaboration within their teams."

Visionary Alignment

Angela began by highlighting the importance of visionary alignment in team leadership, "At the heart of team leadership lies the ability to align individuals with a common vision and purpose—to inspire them with a shared sense of mission and direction that transcends individual interests and fosters collaboration and cohesion. Effective team leaders articulate a compelling vision that resonates with team members, instilling a sense of purpose and belonging that motivates them to give their best effort towards collective goals. By fostering a culture of shared ownership and accountability, leaders can empower their teams to overcome challenges, seize opportunities, and achieve remarkable results."

Empowerment and Trust

Michael elaborated, "Team leadership is about empowerment and trust—empowering team members with autonomy, responsibility, and authority to make decisions and take ownership of their work, and trusting them to deliver results with excellence and integrity. Effective leaders create a supportive and inclusive environment where team members feel valued, respected, and empowered to contribute their unique perspectives and talents towards shared objectives. By fostering open communication, collaboration, and trust, leaders can unleash the full potential of their teams, driving innovation, creativity, and performance to new heights."

Continuous Development

As the team delved deeper into the principles of team leadership, they were struck by the importance of continuous development and growth in nurturing high-performance teams.

Armed with newfound insights and determination, the team was ready to embrace the challenges of team leadership, embodying the qualities of visionary alignment, empowerment, and trust as they guided GlobalTech Solutions towards a future of collaboration, excellence, and success.

In the heart of Lusaka, amidst the spirit of teamwork and possibility, GlobalTech Solutions stood poised on the cusp of greatness. Armed with a comprehensive understanding of team leadership, they were prepared to foster a culture of excellence and collaboration, cultivating high-performance teams that drive innovation, productivity, and success in the dynamic landscape of business.

Leading Change and Innovation

Catalysts of Transformation: Leading Change and Innovation

In the innovation hub of GlobalTech Solutions, a sense of anticipation filled the air as the team gathered to explore the dynamic interplay between leadership, change, and innovation, recognizing the transformative potential of visionary leaders in driving organizational evolution and growth. Angela and Michael, the architects of transformation, were poised to unveil the keys to leading change and fostering innovation within the organization.

Angela's voice, charged with energy and enthusiasm, initiated the discussion, "Good morning, everyone. Today, we embark on a journey into the realm of change and innovation leadership—a journey that will illuminate the pivotal role of leaders in driving organizational transformation and fostering a culture of innovation and adaptability. In the fast-paced world of business, change is inevitable, and innovation is essential for staying ahead of the curve. Let us delve into the essence of change and innovation leadership and uncover the strategies that empower leaders to inspire, motivate, and guide their teams towards creative breakthroughs and sustainable growth."

Michael, with a nod of agreement, added, "Indeed. In the landscape of constant disruption and technological advancement, leaders must embrace change as a catalyst for growth and innovation as a driver of competitiveness. Let us explore the principles that guide change and innovation leadership and empower leaders to navigate uncertainty, inspire creativity, and drive organizational success."

Embracing Ambiguity

Angela began by highlighting the importance of embracing ambiguity in leading change and innovation, "At the heart of change and innovation leadership lies the ability to embrace ambiguity—to navigate uncertainty, complexity, and volatility with confidence and resilience. Effective leaders understand that change is not linear but rather a journey filled with twists and turns, requiring adaptability, flexibility, and agility to navigate successfully. By fostering a growth mindset and encouraging experimentation and risk-taking, leaders can create an environment where failure is seen as a learning opportunity and change is embraced as a pathway to innovation and growth."

Fostering a Culture of Innovation

Michael elaborated, "Change and innovation leadership is about fostering a culture of innovation—a culture where creativity, curiosity, and collaboration are valued and celebrated, and where employees are empowered to challenge the status quo, experiment with new ideas, and pursue bold initiatives. Effective leaders set the tone for innovation by championing creativity, providing resources and support for experimentation, and recognizing and rewarding innovative contributions. By creating a safe space for innovation and encouraging diverse perspectives and approaches, leaders can unleash the creative potential of their teams, driving breakthrough innovations that propel the organization forward."

Leading by Example

As the team delved deeper into the principles of change and innovation leadership, they were struck by the importance of leading by example and fostering a spirit of continuous improvement and learning.

Armed with newfound insights and determination, the team was ready to embrace the challenges of change and innovation leadership, embodying the qualities of adaptability, creativity, and resilience as they guided GlobalTech Solutions towards a future of innovation, growth, and excellence.

In the heart of Lusaka, amidst the spirit of innovation and possibility, GlobalTech Solutions stood poised on the brink of transformation. Armed with a comprehensive understanding of change and innovation leadership, they were prepared to embrace change as an opportunity for growth and innovation as a driver of competitiveness, driving organizational success and shaping the future of business in the dynamic landscape of the 21st century.

Leadership Development and Succession Planning

CHAPTER 13: STRATEGIC LEADERSHIP

Nurturing Tomorrow's Leaders: The Legacy of Leadership Development

In the mentorship chambers of GlobalTech Solutions, a sense of legacy filled the air as the team gathered to explore the timeless principles of leadership development and succession planning, recognizing the importance of cultivating a pipeline of future leaders to sustain organizational excellence and continuity. Angela and Michael, the custodians of leadership legacy, were poised to unveil the strategies for nurturing tomorrow's leaders.

Angela's voice, resonating with wisdom and foresight, initiated the discussion, "Good morning, everyone. Today, we embark on a journey into the realm of leadership development and succession planning—a journey that will illuminate the importance of investing in the next generation of leaders to ensure the long-term success and sustainability of our organization. In the ever-changing landscape of business, leadership is the cornerstone of organizational excellence, and developing a strong bench of future leaders is essential for navigating the challenges of tomorrow. Let us delve into the essence of leadership development and succession planning and uncover the strategies that empower leaders to identify, nurture, and groom the leaders of tomorrow."

Michael, with a nod of agreement, added, "Indeed. In the journey of leadership, succession planning is not just about filling vacancies—it is about ensuring continuity of vision, values, and culture, and preparing the next generation of leaders to take the reins with confidence and competence. Let us explore the principles that guide leadership development and succession planning and empower leaders to build a legacy of leadership excellence within our organization."

Identifying High-Potential Talent

Angela began by highlighting the importance of identifying high-potential talent in leadership development, "At the heart of leadership development lies the ability to identify high-potential talent—individuals who possess not only the requisite skills and competencies but also the passion, drive, and potential to lead with distinction. Effective leaders invest time and resources in talent identification processes, leveraging assessments, performance evaluations, and feedback mechanisms to identify individuals with leadership potential. By fostering a culture of talent development and recognition, leaders can create pathways for growth and advancement, inspiring aspiring leaders to reach their full potential and contribute to the organization's success."

Tailored Development Programs

Michael elaborated, "Leadership development is about more than just training—it is about creating tailored development programs that cater to the unique needs and aspirations of individual leaders. Effective leaders take a personalized approach to leadership development, providing opportunities for experiential learning, mentorship, and coaching that align with each leader's development goals and aspirations. By offering a mix of formal training, on-the-job experiences, and stretch assignments, leaders can cultivate well-rounded leaders who are prepared to tackle the challenges of leadership with confidence and competence."

Succession Planning and Continuity

As the team delved deeper into the principles of leadership development and succession planning, they were struck by the importance of continuity and legacy in shaping the future of leadership within the organization.

Armed with newfound insights and determination, the team was ready to embrace the challenges of leadership development and succession planning, embodying the qualities of mentorship, empowerment, and legacy-building as they groomed the leaders of tomorrow to carry the torch of leadership forward.

In the heart of Lusaka, amidst the spirit of mentorship and growth, GlobalTech Solutions stood poised on the threshold of leadership excellence. Armed with a comprehensive understanding of leadership development and succession planning, they were prepared to build a legacy of leadership excellence that would endure for generations, shaping the future of business and leadership in the dynamic landscape of the 21st century.

Profiles of Strategic Leaders

Icons of Leadership: Profiles of Strategic Visionaries

In the boardroom of GlobalTech Solutions, a sense of reverence filled the air as the team gathered to explore the profiles of strategic leaders who had left an indelible mark on the world of business, recognizing their exemplary vision, courage, and impact on shaping the course of history. Angela and Michael, the chroniclers of leadership legacy, were poised to unveil the profiles of these strategic visionaries.

Angela's voice, infused with admiration and respect, initiated the discussion, "Good morning, everyone. Today, we pay tribute to the icons of leadership—visionaries whose pioneering spirit, unwavering resolve, and transformative vision have inspired generations and reshaped the landscape of business. In the annals of history, these strategic leaders stand as beacons of inspiration, guiding us with their wisdom and fortitude. Let us delve into the profiles of these strategic visionaries and draw lessons from their remarkable journeys."

Michael, with a nod of agreement, added, "Indeed. In the tapestry of leadership, these icons shine brightly, illuminating the path forward with their innovative thinking, bold decision-making, and unwavering commitment to excellence. Let us explore the profiles of these strategic leaders and uncover the timeless principles that have guided them to greatness."

Steve Jobs: The Visionary Trailblazer

Angela began by highlighting the profile of Steve Jobs, the visionary trailblazer who revolutionized the technology industry with his passion, creativity, and relentless pursuit of excellence. "Steve Jobs, the co-founder of Apple Inc., is widely regarded as one of the most visionary leaders of our time. With his insatiable curiosity, boundless creativity, and uncompromising standards, Jobs transformed Apple into one of the most innovative and iconic companies in the world. His relentless pursuit of perfection, coupled with his ability to anticipate and shape consumer trends, enabled Apple to disrupt entire industries and redefine the way we live, work, and communicate. Jobs' legacy serves as a testament to the power of vision, passion, and perseverance in driving organizational success and creating a lasting impact on the world."

Indra Nooyi: The Inspirational Trailblazer

Michael continued with the profile of Indra Nooyi, the inspirational trailblazer who shattered glass ceilings and redefined leadership in the corporate world. "Indra Nooyi, the former CEO of PepsiCo, is a trailblazer in every sense of the word. As one of the few women of color to lead a Fortune 500 company, Nooyi defied stereotypes and expectations, demonstrating that diversity and inclusion are not just moral imperatives but also strategic advantages. Under her leadership, PepsiCo experienced unprecedented growth and innovation, expanding its product portfolio, embracing sustainability, and championing diversity and empowerment. Nooyi's unwavering commitment to purpose-driven leadership and her ability to navigate complexity with grace and resilience serve as an inspiration to leaders around the world, reminding us that true leadership knows no bounds."

Profiles of Leadership Excellence

As the team delved deeper into the profiles of strategic leaders, they were captivated by the diverse journeys and remarkable achievements of these visionary trailblazers.

Armed with newfound inspiration and admiration, the team was ready to embrace the challenges of leadership, embodying the qualities of vision, courage, and innovation as they charted their course towards excellence and impact in the dynamic landscape of business.

In the heart of Lusaka, amidst the echoes of leadership greatness, GlobalTech Solutions stood poised on the threshold of transformation. Armed with the wisdom and insights gleaned from the profiles of strategic leaders, they were prepared to forge their own path towards leadership excellence, guided by the timeless principles of vision, courage, and impact in the pursuit of organizational success and societal change.

14

Chapter 14: Crisis Management and Strategic Resilience

Understanding Organizational Crises

Navigating the Storm: The Anatomy of Organizational Crises

In the emergency command center of GlobalTech Solutions, a sense of urgency filled the air as the team gathered to explore the intricacies of crisis management and strategic resilience, recognizing the critical importance of preparing for and navigating through organizational crises with agility and resolve. Angela and Michael, the guardians of resilience, were poised to unveil the anatomy of organizational crises.

Angela's voice, charged with determination and clarity, initiated the discussion, "Good morning, everyone. Today, we confront the harsh realities of organizational crises—a test of our resilience, adaptability, and leadership in the face of adversity. In the volatile landscape of business, crises are inevitable, but our response to them can make all the difference between survival and downfall. Let us delve into the anatomy of organizational crises and uncover the strategies that empower us to anticipate, mitigate, and navigate through turbulent times."

Michael, with a nod of agreement, added, "Indeed. In the crucible of crisis, organizations are put to the test, revealing their strengths, weaknesses, and vulnerabilities. Let us explore the different types of organizational crises and understand their underlying causes, impacts, and implications for strategic resilience."

Types of Organizational Crises

Angela began by outlining the different types of organizational crises, "At the heart of crisis management lies the ability to recognize and categorize different types of crises—ranging from natural disasters and pandemics to financial downturns and reputational scandals. Each crisis presents unique challenges and requires a tailored response strategy to address its immediate and long-term impacts on the organization. By understanding the nature and characteristics of different types of crises, leaders can develop proactive measures and contingency plans to mitigate risks and minimize disruptions to business operations."

Causes and Triggers

Michael elaborated, "Organizational crises are often triggered by a combination of internal and external factors—ranging from poor management decisions and operational failures to unforeseen events and market disruptions. Understanding the root causes and triggers of crises is essential for effective crisis management, as it enables leaders to address underlying issues, anticipate potential risks, and implement preventive measures to mitigate their impact. By conducting thorough risk assessments and scenario planning exercises, leaders can identify vulnerabilities and develop strategies to enhance organizational resilience and preparedness in the face of uncertainty."

Impacts and Consequences

As the team delved deeper into the anatomy of organizational crises, they were struck by the far-reaching impacts and consequences of crises on organizations, stakeholders, and society at large.

Armed with newfound insights and determination, the team was ready to confront the challenges of crisis management and strategic resilience, embodying the qualities of foresight, adaptability, and courage as they prepared GlobalTech Solutions to navigate through turbulent times and emerge stronger and more resilient than ever before.

In the heart of Lusaka, amidst the storm of uncertainty and disruption, GlobalTech Solutions stood poised on the frontline of resilience. Armed with a comprehensive understanding of crisis management, they were prepared to weather the storm and emerge victorious, guided by the principles of anticipation, preparation, and decisive action in the pursuit of organizational resilience and longevity.

Crisis Management Planning and Preparation

Fortifying the Ramparts: The Art of Crisis Preparedness

In the war room of GlobalTech Solutions, a sense of purposeful urgency filled the air as the team gathered to delve into the strategic intricacies of crisis management planning and preparation, recognizing the imperative of fortifying their defenses and readying themselves for the inevitable storms that lay ahead. Angela and Michael, the architects of readiness, were poised to unveil the strategies for mastering crisis preparedness.

Angela's voice, infused with resolve and foresight, initiated the discussion, "Good morning, everyone. Today, we embark on a journey into the heart of crisis management planning and preparation—a journey that will illuminate the critical importance of readiness, resilience, and agility in navigating through turbulent times. In the volatile landscape of business, crises can strike without warning, but our ability to anticipate, plan, and prepare for them can make all the difference between chaos and control. Let us delve into the art of crisis preparedness and uncover the strategies that empower us to build strong defenses and weather the storms that lie ahead."

Michael, with a nod of agreement, added, "Indeed. In the crucible of crisis, preparedness is our greatest weapon—it enables us to respond swiftly, decisively, and effectively to mitigate risks, minimize disruptions, and protect our people, assets, and reputation. Let us explore the principles that guide crisis management planning and preparation and empower us to build a culture of readiness and resilience within our organization."

Risk Assessment and Scenario Planning

Angela began by emphasizing the importance of risk assessment and scenario planning in crisis preparedness, "At the heart of crisis management planning lies the ability to identify, assess, and prioritize potential risks and vulnerabilities that could threaten the stability and continuity of our organization. By conducting thorough risk assessments and scenario planning exercises, we can anticipate various crisis scenarios, evaluate their potential impacts, and develop proactive response strategies to mitigate risks and enhance our preparedness. By fostering a culture of risk awareness and resilience, we can empower our teams to identify early warning signs, adapt to changing circumstances, and respond effectively to emerging threats."

Crisis Response Team and Communication Protocols

Michael elaborated, "Crisis management is a team effort, requiring clear roles, responsibilities, and communication protocols to ensure a coordinated and effective response. Establishing a crisis response team composed of key stakeholders from across the organization enables us to mobilize resources, make timely decisions, and implement response strategies with agility and efficiency. By defining clear lines of authority and communication channels, we can facilitate rapid information sharing, decision-making, and coordination, enabling us to maintain control and manage the crisis effectively. By conducting regular training and simulation exercises, we can test our response plans, identify areas for improvement, and ensure that our teams are prepared to respond effectively to real-world crises."

Technology and Infrastructure Resilience

As the team delved deeper into the art of crisis preparedness, they were struck by the importance of leveraging technology and infrastructure resilience to enhance organizational readiness and resilience.

Armed with newfound insights and determination, the team was ready to confront the challenges of crisis management planning and preparation, embodying the qualities of foresight, collaboration, and agility as they fortified GlobalTech Solutions against the storms of uncertainty and disruption.

In the heart of Lusaka, amidst the spirit of readiness and resilience, GlobalTech Solutions stood poised on the frontline of preparedness. Armed with a comprehensive understanding of crisis management planning and preparation, they were prepared to navigate through turbulent times with confidence and resilience, guided by the principles of anticipation, collaboration, and decisive action in the pursuit of organizational stability and longevity.

Strategic Responses to Crises

CHAPTER 14: CRISIS MANAGEMENT AND STRATEGIC RESILIENCE

Triumph in Adversity: Crafting Strategic Responses to Crises

In the nerve center of GlobalTech Solutions, a palpable sense of determination filled the air as the team gathered to explore the strategic nuances of crisis response, recognizing the pivotal role of decisive action, adaptability, and leadership in navigating through tumultuous times. Angela and Michael, the architects of resilience, were poised to unveil the strategies for triumphing over adversity through strategic responses to crises.

Angela's voice, imbued with conviction and clarity, initiated the discussion, "Good morning, everyone. Today, we stand at the crossroads of crisis, where adversity meets opportunity, and our response will shape the trajectory of our organization's future. In the crucible of crisis, strategic responses are our greatest weapons—they enable us to navigate uncertainty, mitigate risks, and emerge stronger and more resilient than before. Let us delve into the art of crafting strategic responses to crises and uncover the strategies that empower us to turn adversity into advantage."

Michael, with a nod of agreement, added, "Indeed. In the face of crisis, decisive action, adaptability, and leadership are paramount. Let us explore the principles that guide strategic responses to crises and empower us to harness the power of adversity to drive organizational innovation, transformation, and growth."

Agile Decision-Making and Crisis Leadership

Angela began by emphasizing the importance of agile decision-making and crisis leadership in navigating through turbulent times, "At the heart of strategic crisis response lies the ability to make swift, informed, and decisive decisions under pressure. Crisis leadership requires clarity of vision, courage, and resilience—it requires leaders to remain calm, focused, and decisive in the face of uncertainty and adversity. By empowering leaders at all levels of the organization to act with agility and autonomy, we can accelerate decision-making, facilitate rapid response, and maintain control in the midst of chaos. By fostering a culture of accountability, transparency, and collaboration, we can mobilize our teams to work together towards common goals, adapt to changing circumstances, and overcome even the most daunting challenges."

Adaptive Strategy and Scenario Planning

Michael elaborated, "In times of crisis, strategic agility is essential for survival and success. Adaptive strategy enables organizations to pivot quickly, seize opportunities, and navigate through uncertainty with confidence and resilience. By embracing a flexible, iterative approach to strategy development, we can anticipate emerging trends, identify new opportunities, and adjust our course of action in real-time to align with changing market dynamics and customer needs. By conducting scenario planning exercises and stress testing our strategies against various crisis scenarios, we can enhance our preparedness, identify potential blind spots, and develop contingency plans to mitigate risks and seize opportunities amidst uncertainty."

Innovation and Transformation

As the team delved deeper into the art of crafting strategic responses to crises, they were struck by the transformative potential of crisis as a catalyst for innovation and growth.

Armed with newfound insights and determination, the team was ready to confront the challenges of crisis response, embodying the qualities of resilience, adaptability, and leadership as they steered GlobalTech Solutions towards a future of possibility and promise in the face of adversity.

In the heart of Lusaka, amidst the crucible of crisis, GlobalTech Solutions stood poised on the brink of transformation. Armed with a comprehensive understanding of strategic crisis response, they were prepared to navigate through turbulent times with courage and conviction, guided by the principles of agility, innovation, and decisive action in the pursuit of organizational resilience and renewal.

Building Organizational Resilience

Forge of Resilience: Strengthening the Fabric of Our Organization

In the heart of GlobalTech Solutions, a spirit of fortitude and determination permeated the atmosphere as the team gathered to explore the foundational elements of organizational resilience, recognizing the imperative of strengthening the fabric of their organization to withstand the trials of adversity and emerge stronger than before. Angela and Michael, the architects of resilience, were poised to unveil the strategies for forging an organization of unwavering strength and adaptability.

Angela's voice, infused with determination and resolve, initiated the discussion, "Good morning, everyone. Today, we stand at the threshold of resilience—a journey that will test our mettle, challenge our assumptions, and transform our organization from within. In the crucible of crisis, resilience is our greatest asset—it enables us to endure hardship, overcome obstacles, and emerge stronger and more agile than before. Let us delve into the art of building organizational resilience and uncover the strategies that empower us to fortify the foundations of our organization and navigate through uncertainty with confidence and conviction."

Michael, with a nod of agreement, added, "Indeed. In the face of adversity, resilience is not merely a trait—it is a mindset, a culture, and a way of life. Let us explore the principles that guide the building of organizational resilience and empower us to transform challenges into opportunities for growth and renewal."

Cultural Resilience and Mindset

Angela began by emphasizing the importance of cultural resilience and mindset in fostering an environment of adaptability and perseverance, "At the heart of organizational resilience lies a culture of adaptability, collaboration, and innovation—a culture that embraces change as an opportunity for growth and renewal. Resilience is not just about bouncing back from adversity—it is about embracing change, learning from experiences, and adapting to new realities with courage and conviction. By fostering a growth mindset, we can empower our teams to embrace challenges, experiment with new ideas, and overcome obstacles with resilience and determination. By cultivating a culture of trust, transparency, and accountability, we can build strong connections, foster collaboration, and unleash the collective potential of our organization to thrive in the face of adversity."

Strategic Flexibility and Adaptability

Michael elaborated, "Organizational resilience requires strategic flexibility and adaptability— the ability to anticipate emerging trends, identify new opportunities, and adjust our strategies and operations in real-time to align with changing market dynamics and customer needs. By embracing a flexible, agile approach to strategy development and execution, we can pivot quickly, seize opportunities, and navigate through uncertainty with confidence and resilience. By investing in technology, innovation, and talent development, we can build the capabilities and capacities needed to thrive in a rapidly evolving landscape, positioning our organization for long-term success and sustainability."

Learning and Continuous Improvement

As the team delved deeper into the art of building organizational resilience, they were struck by the transformative power of learning and continuous improvement as catalysts for growth and renewal.

Armed with newfound insights and determination, the team was ready to embark on the journey of resilience, embodying the qualities of adaptability, perseverance, and innovation as they forged GlobalTech Solutions into an organization of unwavering strength and adaptability in the face of adversity.

In the heart of Lusaka, amidst the forge of resilience, GlobalTech Solutions stood poised on the threshold of transformation. Armed with a comprehensive understanding of organizational resilience, they were prepared to navigate through turbulent times with courage and conviction, guided by the principles of adaptability, innovation, and continuous improvement in the pursuit of organizational excellence and longevity.

Learning from Crises: Post-Crisis Analysis

CHAPTER 14: CRISIS MANAGEMENT AND STRATEGIC RESILIENCE

Illuminating the Path: Drawing Insights from the Shadows of Crisis

In the aftermath of tumultuous events, the halls of GlobalTech Solutions resonated with a sense of introspection and determination as the team gathered to illuminate the path forward by drawing insights from the shadows of crisis. Angela and Michael, the seekers of wisdom, were poised to unveil the transformative power of post-crisis analysis in driving organizational learning and growth.

Angela's voice, filled with curiosity and resolve, initiated the discussion, "Good morning, everyone. Today, we embark on a journey of discovery—a journey that will take us into the heart of crisis, where adversity meets opportunity, and lessons are born from the ashes of adversity. In the aftermath of crisis, lies the opportunity for transformation—for learning, growth, and renewal. Let us delve into the art of post-crisis analysis and uncover the insights that empower us to navigate through uncertainty with wisdom and foresight."

Michael, with a nod of agreement, added, "Indeed. In the wake of crisis, lies a wealth of insights waiting to be discovered—insights that can illuminate the path forward, inform our decisions, and shape the future of our organization. Let us explore the principles that guide post-crisis analysis and empower us to turn adversity into advantage through the power of learning and reflection."

Root Cause Analysis and Lessons Learned

Angela began by emphasizing the importance of root cause analysis and lessons learned in uncovering the underlying factors and systemic issues that contributed to the crisis, "At the heart of post-crisis analysis lies the commitment to truth and transparency—the willingness to confront difficult truths, identify root causes, and learn from past mistakes. By conducting thorough root cause analysis and debriefing sessions, we can uncover the underlying factors and systemic issues that contributed to the crisis, enabling us to address gaps in our processes, systems, and decision-making. By capturing lessons learned and best practices, we can codify our experiences, disseminate knowledge, and empower our teams to make informed decisions and take proactive measures to prevent similar crises from occurring in the future."

Continuous Improvement and Organizational Learning

Michael elaborated, "Post-crisis analysis is not just about identifying problems—it is about finding solutions, driving continuous improvement, and fostering a culture of organizational learning and resilience. By embracing a growth mindset and a spirit of inquiry, we can challenge assumptions, experiment with new ideas, and iterate on our processes and practices to drive innovation and excellence. By institutionalizing post-crisis review mechanisms and integrating learnings into our strategic planning and decision-making processes, we can build a culture of resilience that enables us to thrive in the face of uncertainty and change."

CHAPTER 14: CRISIS MANAGEMENT AND STRATEGIC RESILIENCE

Transformation and Renewal

As the team delved deeper into the art of post-crisis analysis, they were struck by the transformative potential of crisis as a catalyst for growth and renewal.

Armed with newfound insights and determination, the team was ready to embrace the lessons of adversity, embodying the qualities of curiosity, resilience, and continuous improvement as they charted a course towards organizational excellence and longevity in the dynamic landscape of business.

In the heart of Lusaka, amidst the echoes of crisis and renewal, GlobalTech Solutions stood poised on the brink of transformation. Armed with a comprehensive understanding of post-crisis analysis, they were prepared to navigate through turbulent times with wisdom and foresight, guided by the principles of learning, adaptation, and innovation in the pursuit of organizational resilience and renewal.

Case Studies of Crisis Management

Lessons from the Trenches: Case Studies in Crisis Management

In the boardroom of GlobalTech Solutions, the air was charged with anticipation and intrigue as the team gathered to glean insights from real-world examples of crisis management, drawing inspiration from the experiences of organizations that had weathered storms and emerged stronger on the other side. Angela and Michael, the storytellers of resilience, were poised to unveil the lessons from the trenches through compelling case studies of crisis management.

Angela's voice, tinged with reverence and curiosity, initiated the discussion, "Good morning, everyone. Today, we embark on a journey into the annals of crisis management—a journey that will take us into the heart of adversity, where organizations faced extraordinary challenges and emerged victorious through the power of resilience, leadership, and innovation. Let us delve into the stories of real-world crises and uncover the lessons they hold for us as we navigate through uncertain times."

Michael, with a nod of agreement, added, "Indeed. In the crucible of crisis, lies a wealth of wisdom waiting to be discovered—wisdom that can inform our decisions, inspire our actions, and guide us on the path to resilience and renewal. Let us explore the case studies of crisis management and draw inspiration from the experiences of organizations that have faced adversity with courage and determination."

Case Study 1: Johnson & Johnson's Tylenol Crisis

Angela began by recounting the iconic case of Johnson & Johnson's handling of the Tylenol crisis in 1982, "In the fall of 1982, Johnson & Johnson faced one of the most infamous product tampering incidents in history when seven people died after consuming cyanide-laced Tylenol capsules. In a bold display of leadership and responsibility, Johnson & Johnson acted swiftly to recall 31 million bottles of Tylenol, costing the company millions of dollars. By prioritizing public safety over profits and implementing tamper-resistant packaging, Johnson & Johnson not only regained the trust of consumers but also set a new standard for crisis management and corporate responsibility."

Case Study 2: Toyota's Accelerator Pedal Recall

Michael continued with the case of Toyota's accelerator pedal recall in 2009-2010, "In 2009-2010, Toyota faced a crisis of confidence when reports surfaced of unintended acceleration in several models, leading to accidents and fatalities. Despite initially downplaying the issue, Toyota eventually issued a massive recall of millions of vehicles worldwide, resulting in significant financial losses and damage to its reputation. However, by taking responsibility for the problem, improving communication with customers, and implementing rigorous quality control measures, Toyota was able to regain consumer trust and rebound from the crisis stronger than before."

Case Study 3: British Airways' IT Failure

As the team delved deeper into the case studies of crisis management, they were struck by the resilience, adaptability, and leadership demonstrated by organizations facing adversity.

Armed with newfound insights and inspiration, the team was ready to confront the challenges of crisis management, embodying the qualities of courage, resilience, and innovation as they steered GlobalTech Solutions towards a future of possibility and promise in the face of uncertainty.

In the heart of Lusaka, amidst the stories of triumph and resilience, GlobalTech Solutions stood poised on the brink of transformation. Armed with a comprehensive understanding of crisis management, they were prepared to navigate through turbulent times with wisdom and foresight, guided by the lessons of the past and the vision of a brighter future.

15

Chapter 15: Future Trends in Strategic Management

Emerging Trends and Technologies

Navigating the Horizon: Charting the Course of Future Trends

In the innovation hub of GlobalTech Solutions, a sense of anticipation and excitement filled the air as the team gathered to explore the frontiers of future trends and technologies shaping the landscape of strategic management. Angela and Michael, the visionaries of tomorrow, were poised to unveil the transformative potential of emerging trends and technologies in driving organizational innovation and success.

Angela's voice, tinged with excitement and curiosity, initiated the discussion, "Good morning, everyone. Today, we stand at the precipice of possibility—a juncture where the horizons of innovation stretch endlessly before us, beckoning us to explore new frontiers, embrace new technologies, and envision new possibilities for the future. Let us embark on a journey into the realm of emerging trends and technologies and uncover the insights that will shape the future of strategic management."

Michael, with a gleam of anticipation in his eyes, added, "Indeed. In the ever-evolving landscape of business, staying ahead of the curve requires foresight, adaptability, and a keen awareness of emerging trends and technologies. Let us explore the transformative potential of emerging trends and technologies and harness their power to drive organizational growth, innovation, and success."

Artificial Intelligence and Machine Learning

Angela began by highlighting the transformative potential of artificial intelligence and machine learning in revolutionizing strategic decision-making and operations, "At the forefront of emerging technologies lies the transformative power of artificial intelligence and machine learning. From predictive analytics to autonomous systems, AI and ML are reshaping the way organizations analyze data, optimize processes, and make strategic decisions. By harnessing the power of AI and ML, organizations can unlock new insights, uncover hidden patterns, and drive innovation at scale, positioning themselves for competitive advantage in the digital age."

CHAPTER 15: FUTURE TRENDS IN STRATEGIC MANAGEMENT

Blockchain Technology and Decentralized Systems

Michael continued with the exploration of blockchain technology and decentralized systems, "In addition to AI and ML, blockchain technology and decentralized systems are ushering in a new era of transparency, security, and trust in business operations. By leveraging blockchain technology, organizations can streamline transactions, enhance supply chain visibility, and mitigate risks associated with fraud and data breaches. By embracing decentralized systems, organizations can empower individuals, foster collaboration, and drive innovation in a decentralized economy, unlocking new opportunities for growth and disruption in traditional industries."

Internet of Things (IoT) and Connected Ecosystems

As the team delved deeper into the realm of emerging trends and technologies, they were struck by the interconnectedness and convergence of digital ecosystems shaping the future of business.

Armed with newfound insights and excitement, the team was ready to embark on the journey of innovation, embodying the qualities of curiosity, adaptability, and foresight as they navigated the ever-changing landscape of strategic management in the digital age.

In the heart of Lusaka, amidst the dawn of a new era, GlobalTech Solutions stood poised on the cusp of innovation. Armed with a comprehensive understanding of emerging trends and technologies, they were prepared to embrace the future with confidence and conviction, guided by the vision of a brighter tomorrow and the promise of endless possibilities on the horizon.

Sustainability and Green Strategies

Sustaining the Future: Embracing Green Strategies for Tomorrow's Success

In the sustainability lab of GlobalTech Solutions, a sense of purpose and responsibility filled the room as the team gathered to explore the imperative of sustainability and green strategies in shaping the future of strategic management. Angela and Michael, the guardians of sustainability, were poised to unveil the transformative potential of green strategies in driving organizational resilience and success in the years to come.

Angela's voice, filled with conviction and passion, initiated the discussion, "Good morning, everyone. Today, we stand at a crossroads of unprecedented environmental challenges and opportunities—a juncture where sustainability is not just a choice, but a necessity for the future of our planet and our organizations. Let us embark on a journey into the realm of sustainability and green strategies and uncover the insights that will shape the future of strategic management."

Michael, with a nod of agreement, added, "Indeed. In an era of climate change and resource scarcity, organizations have a responsibility to embrace sustainable practices and green strategies that not only protect the environment but also drive innovation, efficiency, and long-term profitability. Let us explore the transformative potential of sustainability and green strategies and harness their power to create a more sustainable and prosperous future for all."

Circular Economy and Waste Reduction

Angela began by highlighting the transformative potential of the circular economy and waste reduction initiatives in driving sustainability and resource efficiency, "At the forefront of sustainable practices lies the concept of the circular economy—a regenerative system where resources are reused, recycled, and repurposed to minimize waste and maximize value. By embracing circular economy principles, organizations can design products for longevity, optimize resource use throughout the product lifecycle, and reduce their environmental footprint. By implementing waste reduction initiatives and adopting closed-loop systems, organizations can minimize waste, conserve resources, and create new revenue streams from recycled materials, positioning themselves as leaders in sustainability and innovation."

Renewable Energy and Carbon Neutrality

Michael continued with the exploration of renewable energy and carbon neutrality, "In addition to the circular economy, renewable energy and carbon neutrality are key pillars of sustainable business practices. By investing in renewable energy sources such as solar, wind, and hydroelectric power, organizations can reduce their dependence on fossil fuels, lower their carbon emissions, and contribute to a cleaner, greener future. By setting ambitious carbon neutrality targets and implementing strategies to offset remaining emissions, organizations can demonstrate their commitment to environmental stewardship, enhance their brand reputation, and attract environmentally conscious customers and investors."

Supply Chain Transparency and Ethical Sourcing

As the team delved deeper into the realm of sustainability and green strategies, they were struck by the interconnectedness of environmental, social, and economic factors shaping the future of business.

Armed with newfound insights and determination, the team was ready to embrace the challenge of sustainability, embodying the qualities of responsibility, innovation, and collaboration as they navigated the path towards a more sustainable and prosperous future.

In the heart of Lusaka, amidst the call of nature and responsibility, GlobalTech Solutions stood poised on the threshold of transformation. Armed with a comprehensive understanding of sustainability and green strategies, they were prepared to lead the charge towards a more sustainable and prosperous future, guided by the principles of environmental stewardship, social responsibility, and economic prosperity for generations to come.

The Role of AI and Automation in Strategy

CHAPTER 15: FUTURE TRENDS IN STRATEGIC MANAGEMENT

Augmenting Strategy: Unleashing the Power of AI and Automation

In the innovation hub of GlobalTech Solutions, a sense of wonder and anticipation filled the room as the team gathered to explore the transformative potential of artificial intelligence (AI) and automation in shaping the future of strategic management. Angela and Michael, the architects of innovation, were poised to unveil the profound impact of AI and automation in driving organizational efficiency, agility, and success in the years ahead.

Angela's voice, vibrant with enthusiasm and foresight, initiated the discussion, "Good morning, everyone. Today, we embark on a journey into the realm of artificial intelligence and automation—a journey that will revolutionize the way we approach strategic management, unlocking new possibilities, and redefining the boundaries of innovation. Let us delve into the transformative potential of AI and automation and uncover the insights that will shape the future of strategic decision-making."

Michael, with a nod of agreement, added, "Indeed. In an era of rapid technological advancement, AI and automation are poised to transform every aspect of business operations, from data analysis and decision-making to customer service and supply chain management. Let us explore the role of AI and automation in strategy and harness their power to drive organizational growth, efficiency, and competitiveness in the digital age."

Data Analytics and Predictive Insights

Angela began by highlighting the transformative potential of AI-driven data analytics and predictive insights in informing strategic decision-making, "At the heart of AI lies the power of data—vast oceans of information waiting to be harnessed and analyzed to uncover actionable insights and drive strategic outcomes. By leveraging advanced analytics and machine learning algorithms, organizations can sift through vast amounts of data, identify patterns, and predict future trends with unprecedented accuracy. By harnessing the power of predictive insights, organizations can make informed decisions, anticipate market shifts, and capitalize on emerging opportunities, positioning themselves for success in an increasingly competitive landscape."

Process Automation and Operational Efficiency

Michael continued with the exploration of process automation and operational efficiency, "In addition to data analytics, AI-powered automation is revolutionizing business operations, streamlining processes, and enhancing operational efficiency. From robotic process automation (RPA) to autonomous systems, organizations can automate repetitive tasks, reduce manual errors, and free up human capital to focus on higher-value activities. By embracing automation, organizations can optimize resource allocation, improve productivity, and drive cost savings, enabling them to operate with agility and resilience in a rapidly evolving business environment."

Strategic Insights and Decision Support

As the team delved deeper into the realm of AI and automation, they were struck by the transformative potential of these technologies in driving organizational innovation and competitiveness.

Armed with newfound insights and excitement, the team was ready to embrace the future of strategic management, embodying the qualities of adaptability, curiosity, and innovation as they navigated the path towards a more data-driven and agile organization.

In the heart of Lusaka, amidst the hum of innovation and possibility, GlobalTech Solutions stood poised on the brink of transformation. Armed with a comprehensive understanding of AI and automation, they were prepared to lead the charge towards a future of endless possibilities and strategic excellence, guided by the promise of technology and the vision of a brighter tomorrow.

Shifting Consumer Preferences and Market Dynamics

Navigating the Currents: Adapting to Shifting Consumer Tides

In the strategy room of GlobalTech Solutions, a sense of anticipation and curiosity filled the air as the team gathered to explore the ever-changing landscape of consumer preferences and market dynamics. Angela and Michael, the navigators of change, were poised to unveil the transformative impact of shifting consumer tides in shaping the future of strategic management.

Angela's voice, tinged with curiosity and insight, initiated the discussion, "Good morning, everyone. Today, we set sail on the turbulent waters of consumer preferences and market dynamics—a journey that will challenge our assumptions, stretch our creativity, and redefine the boundaries of innovation. Let us embark on a voyage into the realm of shifting consumer tides and uncover the insights that will shape the future of strategic decision-making."

Michael, with a nod of agreement, added, "Indeed. In an era of unprecedented connectivity and choice, understanding and adapting to shifting consumer preferences is paramount for organizational success. Let us explore the dynamic forces shaping consumer behavior and market dynamics and harness their power to drive organizational growth, relevance, and resilience in the years ahead."

Digital Transformation and Omnichannel Experiences

Angela began by highlighting the transformative impact of digital transformation and omnichannel experiences in reshaping consumer interactions and expectations, "At the heart of shifting consumer preferences lies the digital revolution—a seismic shift in how consumers discover, engage with, and purchase products and services. From online shopping to social media engagement, consumers expect seamless, personalized experiences across all touchpoints. By embracing digital transformation and adopting omnichannel strategies, organizations can create cohesive, integrated experiences that meet consumers' evolving needs and preferences, driving loyalty, and advocacy in an increasingly competitive marketplace."

Sustainability and Ethical Consumption

Michael continued with the exploration of sustainability and ethical consumption trends, "In addition to digital transformation, consumers are placing increasing importance on sustainability and ethical considerations when making purchasing decisions. From eco-friendly products to ethically sourced materials, consumers are seeking brands that align with their values and beliefs. By prioritizing sustainability, transparency, and social responsibility, organizations can differentiate themselves in the market, attract socially conscious consumers, and build long-term brand loyalty and trust."

Personalization and Customization

As the team delved deeper into the realm of shifting consumer preferences, they were struck by the importance of agility, innovation, and customer-centricity in driving organizational success.

Armed with newfound insights and determination, the team was ready to navigate the currents of change, embodying the qualities of adaptability, empathy, and creativity as they steered GlobalTech Solutions towards a future of relevance and resonance in the hearts and minds of consumers.

In the heart of Lusaka, amidst the ebb and flow of consumer preferences, GlobalTech Solutions stood poised on the precipice of opportunity. Armed with a comprehensive understanding of shifting consumer tides, they were prepared to embrace change, innovate boldly, and lead the charge towards a future of endless possibilities and strategic excellence.

The Future of Work and Strategic Implications

Embracing Evolution: Shaping the Future of Work

In the innovation hub of GlobalTech Solutions, a sense of anticipation and contemplation filled the room as the team gathered to explore the transformative impact of the future of work on strategic management. Angela and Michael, the architects of adaptation, were poised to unveil the profound implications of evolving work dynamics on organizational strategy.

Angela's voice, resonant with foresight and empathy, initiated the discussion, "Good morning, everyone. Today, we stand at the dawn of a new era—the era of the future of work—a landscape defined by flexibility, collaboration, and innovation. Let us embark on a journey into the realm of evolving work dynamics and uncover the strategic implications that will shape the future of our organizations."

Michael, with a nod of agreement, added, "Indeed. As the nature of work undergoes a profound transformation, organizations must adapt their strategies to embrace this evolution and harness its potential for growth and innovation. Let us explore the implications of the future of work on strategic management and chart a course towards a future of agility, resilience, and success."

Remote Work and Distributed Teams

Angela began by highlighting the transformative impact of remote work and distributed teams on organizational dynamics and culture, "At the heart of the future of work lies the rise of remote work and distributed teams—a seismic shift in how organizations operate and collaborate. With advances in technology and connectivity, employees are no longer bound by traditional office spaces, enabling greater flexibility and autonomy in how, when, and where work is performed. By embracing remote work and distributed teams, organizations can access global talent pools, enhance work-life balance, and drive productivity and innovation in a borderless world."

Gig Economy and Flexible Talent

Michael continued with the exploration of the gig economy and flexible talent models, "In addition to remote work, the gig economy and flexible talent models are reshaping the way organizations access and deploy talent. With the rise of freelance platforms and on-demand talent marketplaces, organizations can tap into a diverse array of skills and expertise on a project-by-project basis, enabling greater agility and scalability in workforce planning. By embracing the gig economy and flexible talent models, organizations can optimize resource allocation, access specialized skills, and drive innovation in a rapidly evolving business landscape."

Digital Skills and Lifelong Learning

As the team delved deeper into the realm of the future of work, they were struck by the importance of adaptability, learning, and continuous skill development in driving organizational agility and competitiveness.

Armed with newfound insights and determination, the

team was ready to embrace the future of work, embodying the qualities of curiosity, resilience, and collaboration as they navigated the path towards a more adaptable and innovative organization.

In the heart of Lusaka, amidst the winds of change and opportunity, GlobalTech Solutions stood poised on the precipice of transformation. Armed with a comprehensive understanding of the future of work, they were prepared to lead the charge towards a future of endless possibilities and strategic excellence, guided by the promise of innovation and the vision of a brighter tomorrow.

Preparing for Uncertainty and Strategic Agility

Thriving in Turbulence: Navigating Uncertainty with Strategic Agility

In the strategy room of GlobalTech Solutions, a sense of anticipation and resilience filled the air as the team gathered to explore the imperative of preparing for uncertainty and fostering strategic agility. Angela and Michael, the architects of adaptation, were poised to unveil the transformative power of agility in navigating turbulent waters and seizing opportunities amidst uncertainty.

Angela's voice, steady and determined, initiated the discussion, "Good morning, everyone. Today, we confront the reality of uncertainty—a reality characterized by volatility, complexity, and ambiguity. In the face of uncertainty, the ability to adapt, innovate, and pivot becomes paramount for organizational survival and success. Let us embark on a journey into the realm of strategic agility and uncover the insights that will empower us to thrive in turbulence."

Michael, with a nod of agreement, added, "Indeed. In an era of rapid change and disruption, organizations must embrace strategic agility—the ability to sense, respond, and adapt to changing circumstances with speed and precision. Let us explore the importance of preparing for uncertainty and fostering strategic agility in driving organizational resilience, innovation, and competitiveness in a dynamic and uncertain world."

Scenario Planning and Risk Management

Angela began by highlighting the importance of scenario planning and risk management in preparing for uncertainty, "At the heart of strategic agility lies the ability to anticipate and prepare for multiple future scenarios, each characterized by its own set of opportunities and challenges. Through scenario planning and risk management, organizations can identify potential disruptors, assess their impact, and develop proactive strategies to mitigate risks and capitalize on opportunities. By embracing a mindset of preparedness and foresight, organizations can navigate uncertainty with confidence and resilience, positioning themselves for success in an ever-changing environment."

Agile Methodologies and Iterative Learning

Michael continued with the exploration of agile methodologies and iterative learning, "In addition to scenario planning, agile methodologies and iterative learning are essential tools for fostering strategic agility in a fast-paced and uncertain world. By adopting agile principles such as flexibility, collaboration, and rapid iteration, organizations can respond quickly to changing market dynamics, customer preferences, and technological advancements. By embracing a culture of experimentation and continuous improvement, organizations can learn from failure, iterate on successes, and drive innovation at scale, enabling them to stay ahead of the curve in an increasingly competitive landscape."

Cross-functional Collaboration and Empowerment

As the team delved deeper into the realm of strategic agility, they were struck by the importance of collaboration, empowerment, and adaptability in driving organizational resilience and success.

Armed with newfound insights and determination, the team was ready to embrace the challenge of uncertainty, embodying the qualities of agility, innovation, and collaboration as they navigated the path towards a more adaptable and resilient organization.

In the heart of Lusaka, amidst the winds of change and uncertainty, GlobalTech Solutions stood poised on the brink of transformation. Armed with a comprehensive understanding of strategic agility, they were prepared to lead the charge towards a future of endless possibilities and strategic excellence, guided by the promise of innovation and the resilience to thrive in turbulence.

About the Author

Goodson Mumba is a multifaceted individual known for his diverse expertise and prolific contributions across various fields. As an infopreneur, thought leader, and spiritual leader, he has inspired countless individuals through his insightful teachings and impactful writings. Mumba is also an accomplished author, with several notable works to his name, including "Understanding Corporate Worship," "The Years I Spent in a Week," "Management By Harmony," "The CEO's Diary," "Change to Change" and "Creative Thinking for results" His literary works span topics ranging from business management to personal development and spirituality, reflecting his broad range of interests and insights.

With a Master of Business Leadership (MBL) and a Bachelor of Arts in Theology (BTh), Mumba brings a unique blend of business acumen and spiritual wisdom to his work. His educational background is further enriched by a Group Diploma in Management Studies, providing him with a solid foundation in organizational dynamics and leadership principles. Additionally, Mumba holds diplomas in Education

Psychology, Leadership and Management Styles, Organizational Behaviour, Financial Accounting, Economic Growth and Development, and Project Management, showcasing his commitment to continuous learning and professional development.

Mumba's expertise extends beyond traditional academic disciplines, encompassing areas such as Neuro-Linguistic Programming (NLP) and Positive Psychology. His diverse skill set is complemented by a range of certifications, including Creative Problem Solving and Decision Making, Life Coaching Fundamentals and Techniques, Professional Life Coaching, and Performance Management System Design. These certifications reflect Mumba's dedication to equipping himself with the tools and knowledge necessary to empower others and drive positive change.

As an author, Mumba's writings reflect his deep understanding of human nature, organizational dynamics, and spiritual principles. His works offer practical insights, actionable strategies, and inspirational guidance for individuals seeking personal growth, professional success, and spiritual fulfillment. Mumba's holistic approach to life and leadership resonates with readers worldwide, making him a respected figure in both the business and spiritual communities.

Overall, Goodson Mumba's diverse background, extensive knowledge, and profound insights make him a sought-after speaker, mentor, and author. His commitment to excellence, lifelong learning, and service to others continues to inspire individuals to unlock their full potential and lead lives of purpose and significance.

Goodson Mumba is renowned for initiating the concept of Management by Harmony, revolutionizing traditional management practices with a focus on balanced and holistic approaches. He has authored two influential books on this subject: "Introduction to Management by Harmony" and its sequel, "Management by Harmony."

Mumba's work has significantly impacted the field, offering innovative strategies for fostering organizational harmony and efficiency. His contributions continue to shape contemporary management theories and practices.

www.ingramcontent.com/pod-product-compliance
Lightning Source LLC
Chambersburg PA
CBHW071825210526
45479CB00001B/3